THE BIRTH OF ENERGY

ELEMENTS   *A series edited*
by Stacy Alaimo and Nicole Starosielski

THE BIRTH

OF

ENERGY

FOSSIL FUELS, THERMODYNAMICS, AND THE POLITICS OF WORK

CARA NEW DAGGETT

DUKE UNIVERSITY PRESS   Durham and London   2019

© 2019 Duke University Press
All rights reserved
Printed in the United States of America on acid-free paper ∞
Designed by Aimee C. Harrison
Typeset in Chaparral Pro and Knockout by Westchester Publishing Services

Cataloging-in-Publication is available from the Library of Congress.
ISBN 978-1-4780-0501-8 (hardcover : alk. paper)
ISBN 978-1-4780-0632-9 (pbk. : alk. paper)
ISBN 978-1-4780-0534-6 (ebook)

Cover art: *The Columbus Sphere: A Victorian New Earth.* Source: Cover of *Scientific American,*
October 25, 1890.

Publication of this open monograph was the result of Virginia Tech's participation in TOME
(Toward an Open Monograph Ecosystem), a collaboration of the Association of American
Universities, the Association of University Presses, and the Association of Research Libraries.
TOME aims to expand the reach of long-form humanities and social science scholarship
including digital scholarship. Additionally, the program looks to ensure the sustainability
of university press monograph publishing by supporting the highest quality scholarship
and promoting a new ecology of scholarly publishing in which authors' institutions bear the
publication costs. Funding from Virginia Tech made it possible to open this publication to
the world.
www.openmonographs.org

To my own bright stars, Henry and Gabriel.

And to Matt, with love for life.

This book began with research undertaken as a graduate student in the Department of Political Science at Johns Hopkins University. I owe my first, and greatest, debt to my teachers, friends, and fellow students at Johns Hopkins for supporting creative and interdisciplinary scholarship. I am immensely grateful to my committee members for their guidance. It was in a typically far-ranging conversation with Daniel Deudney that the topic of energy first arose, and I have him to thank for planting the first seed of this project. Because of the faith he invested in me, and his own encyclopedic knowledge of environmental studies, I had the liberty to roam far afield of disciplinary boundaries in my research. I was also fortunate to have the mentorship of Jane Bennett. She provided a model for how to think and write well, and with creativity, as a scholar of politics. If I entered her office feeling discouraged, I almost always left with new inspiration, and likely with some clever turns of phrase that would catapult me over the latest writer's block. Thank you also to the other members of my committee, Bentley Allen, Michael Degani, and Deborah Poole, for their helpful comments.

While at Johns Hopkins, I also gleaned inspiration from seminars and conversation with William Connolly, Siba Grovogui, Jennifer Culbert, and Richard Flathman. And I was equally fortunate to join a community of brilliant colleagues and alums, many of whom have offered suggestions, feedback, and advice, including Alexander Barder, Suzanne Gallant, Elizabeth Mendenhall, Daniel Levine, Jairus Victor Grove, Meghan Helsel, Hannah Son, Hitomi Koyama, Noora Lori, Kellan Anfinson, Anatoli Ignatov, Jacqui Ignatova, Stefanie Fishel, Benjamin Meiches, Adam Culver, Yehonatan Abramson, Derek Denman, and Kavi Abraham. I benefited from presenting early versions of this text at a graduate student colloquium organized by Bryan Brentus Carter and Stephanie Erev, where Elizabeth Mendenhall served as one of my most insightful discussants. Last but not least, I would like to thank the seventeen Johns Hopkins undergraduate students who took my course, "Energy and Global Politics," in the fall of 2015. Through teaching these concepts for the first time, I learned better ways to articulate them.

The book further took shape with the time and support I received as a provost postdoctoral scholar at the University of South Florida in the School of Interdisciplinary Global Studies from 2016 to 2017. Thank you to the entire department for the warm welcome, and particularly to Cheryl Hall, Scott Solomon, Steven Tauber, Manu Samnotra, Nicolas Thompson, and Abdelwahab Hechiche.

My friends and colleagues at the Department of Political Science at Virginia Tech, my home since 2017, were instrumental in helping this book through its final revisions, and in the drafting of two new chapters. I am especially indebted to François Debrix for his mentorship and sound publishing advice, and to Mauro Caraccioli for his friendship. Members of the department's Political Economy Working Group were early readers of the final chapter: thank you to Besnik Pula, Scott Nelson, Ryan Briggs, Timothy Luke, Deborah Milly, Edward Weisband, and Benjamin Taylor for your thoughtful feedback.

The Department of Science, Technology, and Society at Virginia Tech also offered me an opportunity to share research from this book in their seminar series; thanks to James Collier, Rebecca Hester, Daniel Breslau, Eileen Crist, Gary Downey, Saul Halfon, and all those who came to listen.

Ideas and chapters from the book benefited from feedback along the way at many panels and workshops. Anatoli Ignatov graciously invited me to share my work at the 2016 Environmental Political Theory Workshop that he organized at the Western Political Science Association meeting. I was also electrified by the 2016 Cultures of Energy 5 symposium at Rice's Center for Energy and Environmental Research in the Human Sciences. Thank you to Dominic Boyer and Cymene Howe for organizing the event, and for the invitation to share my work, both at that symposium and on their delightful *Cultures of Energy* podcast. I would also like to thank McKenzie Wark for assistance in getting this book to the right publisher.

Last but not least, thank you to my family. My parents and brother, Larry, Diane, and Ryan New, remain my most loyal and steadfast fans. They never doubted that this book would be finished, even when I did. To my children, Henry and Gabriel—loving and caring for you has been my greatest honor. And to Matt, my first and best reader, who took care of me and fueled me with coffee, ideas, meals, love, and encouragement until the final page. Now that's good energy.

A house. A car. Lights at night and heat in the winter.
A refrigerator to keep food fresh and a stove for cooking.
A better education and a good job. Modern health care.
Wireless communications. Technology and innovation.
The freedom to focus one's daily activities on something
more than mere subsistence. These are among the many
benefits of modern energy. . . . So why energy? Because
energy is vital in our everyday lives.

—EXXONMOBIL, "The Outlook for Energy:
A View to 2040" (2015)

Intensive energy consumption is necessary to the good life. At least that
is ExxonMobil's outlook for energy in their "View to 2040," quoted above.
As global warming becomes more difficult to ignore, oil and gas titans
increasingly want to brand themselves as *energy* companies that supply
much-needed power to the people, rather than as fossil fuel extractors.
Oil, gas, and coal have become the villains on a warming planet, but who
could be against energy?

Oil corporations are not alone in their devotion to energy. Energy
seems to invite grand thinking. After all, energy could be said to nourish
life itself, its production and reproduction, and all activity—"everything
in the universe may be described in terms of energy," including living organisms and human civilizations, anthropologist Leslie White proclaimed
in 1943.[1] Energy's meaning is capacious: it is provided by coal, oil, wind; it
is a scientific entity; a metaphor; an indicator of vigor, tinged with virtue.
Energy feels trans-historic and cosmic, but it is also material: it pumps
through pipelines, sloshes in gas tanks, and spins wind turbines. Most
importantly, energy has a foundational status in modern physics: it is the
quest to understand change in the cosmos.

This also makes energy the ecological concept par excellence: a unit of equivalence through which we can compare human civilizations, from the burning of coal in the nineteenth century to the horse eating a blade of grass in ancient Greece, or the early hominid foraging for berries in the Pleistocene. Forget money; "energy is the only universal currency: one of its many forms must be transformed to get anything done," observes Vaclav Smil, a leading figure in energy studies.[2] At the same time, Smil points out that energy consumption and human well-being appear to be correlated only up to a point—about 110 gigajoules (GJ) per year, per capita—and even appear to be "counterproductive" beyond about 200 GJ.[3] The United States has far surpassed both markers, with energy consumption at 316 GJ per year, per capita in 2017.[4] Nevertheless, such evidence has not pierced widespread public sentiments about energy. Humans seem to crave ever more energy, and ExxonMobil and other energy conglomerates are counting on it. The U.S. Energy Information Administration (EIA) projects a 28 percent increase in world energy use by 2040.[5] And while renewable energy use continues to accelerate, its effect has mostly been to add to the energy mix, rather than to herald a full-fledged, post-carbon transition.[6] Indeed, the EIA predicts that fossil fuel use (with the exception of coal) will continue to grow alongside renewables, and will account for three-quarters of energy consumption by 2040. Having less energy appears to be nearly incompatible with modern politics. Giving up energy sounds like sacrifice and asceticism at best, and rampant death and injustice at worst.

But having ever *more* energy is incompatible with multispecies life on Earth. Scientists warn that "a cascade of feedbacks could push the Earth System irreversibly onto a 'Hothouse Earth' pathway" that could result in a planet that is highly dangerous, even uninhabitable, for humans.[7] As dramatic as that sounds, it is hard to overstate the crisis in the midst of what biologists and ecologists are calling a sixth extinction event,[8] nothing short of a "biological annihilation" that paints "a dismal picture of the future of life, including human life."[9] Fossil fuel burning, the main driver of global warming, is not the sole cause of the massive die-off of Earth's flora and fauna. This is one reason why simply switching fuels, from fossil to renewable, is likely insufficient if we want to sustain a biodiverse planet fit for human life. Many scientists join social theorists and humanities scholars in insisting that preventing disastrous planetary change will require not only more efficient technology and renewable fuels, but also "new collectively shared values, principles, and frameworks" for what it means for humans to live well on the Earth.[10]

In terms of energy, this means that we need not just alternative fuels, but new ways of thinking about, valuing, and inhabiting energy systems. A shift in energy cultures and epistemologies, or ways of knowing energy, will entail a thorough transformation of habits of energy production and consumption. The nascent field of energy humanities analyzes energy in this way, as more than a set of fuels and their associated machines, but also as a socio-material apparatus that flows through political and cultural life.[11] Energy humanities asks how and why communities become attached to fossil fuels, not just as a practical means to operate new technologies, but also in the formation of petro-subjectivities and petro-power.[12] To date, such studies of energy have tended to focus on *fuel* assemblages and cultures—especially those of oil, coal, and gas, but also now of solar, wind, and other renewables. This book is in conversation with energy studies and humanities, but instead of focusing upon energy as fuel, I undertake a genealogy of energy itself, tracing the emergence of a dominant logic of energy that was first informed by thermodynamics. *The Birth of Energy* examines the provenance of energy—how did energy come to signify fuel as an object in need of governance? Why does energy politics refer to the acquisition and security of fuel, rather than to the politics of ensuring public vitality? A genealogy of energy helps in understanding why it is so difficult to imagine energy otherwise.

Surprisingly, energy does not have an ancient pedigree akin to scientific concepts like matter or force. Treating energy as an object of timeless human desire has obscured the historical particularity of energy as we (and ExxonMobil) know it. Energy is a thoroughly modern thing that became the linchpin of physics only after it was "discovered" in the 1840s, at the apex of the Industrial Revolution, and then proselytized by a group of mostly northern British engineers and scientists involved in the shipbuilding industry, undersea telegraph cable building, and other imperial projects. Prior to its emergence in thermodynamics, energy did not have a strong association with fuel, nor a scientific definition, especially since, as Barri Gold points out, *energy* had fallen out of usage as a result of Isaac Newton's "disdain" for the word. In the decades leading up to thermodynamics, energy is mentioned only sporadically, and was used as "a metaphor, a word to describe people, a pathetic fallacy, a word predominantly for poets."[13]

In other words, until the mid- to late nineteenth century, energy as we now know it did not exist in the English language, such that "nobody could have conceived of the study of the flow of energy in human society, . . . calculated the energy supplied by different energy sources or distinguished between the renewable and non-renewable."[14] Within the field of politics, energy has an even more recent history. It was not until the 1970s, in the wake of the so-called oil crisis, that energy (as the all-encompassing signifier of fuel) became consolidated and popularized as an object of politics. The U.S. Department of Energy was formed in 1977, and topics like "energy transitions," "energy alternatives," and "energy forecasting" proliferated for the first time, paving the way for "energy companies" and their energy outlooks.

Recognizing energy as historical is more than an etymological quibble. Long before energy became a key concept in science and politics, of course, humans were using fuels, modifying tools to harness those fuels, and experimenting with improvements to material-machinic assemblages. Prior to the science of energy, though, these various techniques and human activities were not connected by a single scientific paradigm, nor an organized political strategy. Even when, later, Newtonian mechanics advanced universal theories about the operations of machines such as levers, pulleys, and waterwheels, it still failed to explain heat machines like the steam engine. The process by which burning coal produced motion remained shrouded in mystery, even as steam engines were already well on their way to transforming European empires and economies.

Something happened to energy in the nineteenth century, when physics and fossil fuels combined to birth the energy of ExxonMobil's business-as-usual. It was more than the advent of fossil fuel systems and an uptick in energy consumption; it was also the emergence of energy as an object of modern politics. In that birth, the expansive, multidimensional figuration of preindustrial, poetic energy was captured and yoked to a mania to put the world to work. Since the nineteenth century, the human relationship to fuel has been governed by this singular ruling logic of energy, which justifies the indexing of human well-being according to the idealization of work and an unquestioned drive to put the Earth's materials to use for a profit.

Just as energy became tightly bound by the governing logic of work, so too work increasingly came to be governed through the metaphors and physics of energy. The energy–work bindings were laced tight in the nineteenth century, with the purported discovery of energy and its service to

Western, fossil-fueled imperialism. The Western epistemology of energy attached fuel systems to the gospel of labor and its veneration of productivity. The energy–work nexus was so friendly to the spread of fossil capital, so conducive to concealing its violence, and so minutely sutured as to leave little trace of its contingent pairing. The intertwining of energy and the Western ethos of dynamic, productive work was produced as cosmic truth.

The Birth of Energy follows the traces that remain, recording the rough patches and knots as evidence of what was done, and continues to be done, to produce energy as a political rationality that justifies extractivism and imperial capitalism. Making the traces visible involves narrating the history of the capture of energy—with all its aesthetic, theological, and material capaciousness—by the logic of fossil-fueled work. European-controlled fossil fuel systems did not extend smoothly across the globe; they were resisted, and they developed through ongoing attempts to extinguish lifeways and other potential energy epistemologies that challenged their projects. At the same time, work becomes increasingly understood through energetic metaphors, as a site of energy transformation that requires the maximization of efficiency and productivism. In many ways, Westerners remain locked within this energy epistemology.

ENERGY AS METAPHOR

While energy is not a transhistorical fact of nature, neither is energy purely a concept or metaphor, an invention of the human mind. Energy cannot be reduced to an artifact of Victorian culture, nor merely to a set of fuels. It is a hybrid assemblage where these things are entangled, what Donna Haraway (and others)[15] has called a *natureculture*, a term that points to the inseparability of nature and culture. To get at what natureculture means, it is helpful to consider Haraway's reading of biology, which inspires my own reading of energy physics here. In *How Like a Leaf*, Haraway describes reading biology in double, understanding it "as about the way the world works biologically, but also about the way the world works metaphorically. . . . I think of the intensely physical entities of biological phenomena, and then from them I get these large narratives, these cosmological histories if you will."[16]

A *cell*, for example, is the name we give to "an historical kind of interaction, not a name for a thing in and of itself." Again, the point is not to dismiss material reality and its cells or fuels (or energy), all of which are words that denote our engagement with things in the world. Haraway's philosophical stance relies upon staying in the world, among things, *in medias res*, resisting the impulse toward abstraction and finitude. It is therefore important to Haraway that biology has this double quality, with two aspects: first, that we do *"live intimately 'as' and 'in' a biological world,"* but second, that *"[b]iology is a discourse and not the world itself"* (italics in the original).[17] The result is that we live inside biology, which constitutes a natureculture, and this means "being inside history as well as being inside the wonder of natural complexity. I admit to finding the latter very important. But the final result, when we speak about biology, is that we are speaking about a specific way of engaging with the world."[18]

As in Haraway's reading of biology, energy is a way of telling "how the world works metaphorically," and it emerges out of "an historical kind of interaction" between people and engines. Energy science involves discourses, theories, and experiments that are material practices, but that do not simply represent nature, or life itself. Energy is materialized in part through human experiences in the world, among things, in medias res. It is a figuration, a "semiotic trope" that provides "a condensed map of contestable worlds," a map that traces "universes of knowledge, practice, and power."[19] Figurations are neither true nor false; Cynthia Weber explains that figurations "do not (mis)represent the world, for to do so implies the world as a signified preexists them. Rather, figurations . . . condense diffuse imaginaries about the world into specific form or images that bring specific worlds into being."[20] Energy is a figuration for fuel, but energy/fuel here marks more than a given concentration of molecules, poised to proffer kinetic energy, but rather "imploded atoms or dense nodes that explode into entire worlds of practice."[21] A genealogical approach to energy means treating energy as a condensed map, a set of tropes and metaphors that help to describe a "historical kind of interaction," one that is continually generated at the intersection of bodies, machines, and fuels. The dominant figuration of energy cannot be detached from the sociomaterial context in which it emerged, which was the convergence of bodies, fossil fuels, and steam engines in imperial Europe and its factories. In turn, energy "explodes into entire worlds of practice"—worlds in which thriving is indexed according to measures of productive work and indolent waste.

The figuration of energy was political; it served some interests at the expense of others. Indeed, another way to understand energy is to think about it as a *ruling idea*, a term Karl Marx used to ground a period's ideas in its material context. In *The German Ideology*, his extended critique of German idealism, Marx writes that ruling ideas "are nothing more than the ideal expression of the dominant material relationships, the dominant material relationships grasped as ideas; hence of the relationships which make the one class the ruling one, therefore, the ideas of its dominance."[22] Just as there were not "pure ideas" floating free from their historical material context, there also could not be "pure" science. Marx, who closely followed the scientific developments of evolution and energy, insisted that scientific thought, too, was rooted in the material context of its age. He opposes the notion that there are "secrets which are disclosed only to the eye of the physicist and chemist," as "where would natural science be without industry and commerce? Even this 'pure' natural science is provided with an aim, as with its material, only through trade and industry, through the sensuous activity of men."[23] To understand energy as a ruling idea is to appreciate how energy arises in the context of the power relations of fossil-fueled industrialization, with "an aim" that is oriented toward the extension of Western trade and industry.

In order to highlight the emergence of energy as a Western logic, I narrow my focus to the Anglo world of Great Britain and the United States, and to a period that ranges from the mid-nineteenth to the early twentieth centuries, from the "discovery" of energy to the peak decades of new imperialism. Rather than accept the master narrative of energy's discovery and diffusion as objective knowledge, I am interested in parochializing energy, troubling its claims to universality. Contesting the universality of energy requires putting energy into its specific, northern European context, and noticing that energy was first articulated as a modern object of politics in service to European industrial interests. Energy is bound up with the simple desire to acquire, transport, and organize the geophysical capacities of fuel for the pleasure of certain groups of humans.[24]

As part I describes, the Victorians interpreted energy as an important organizing knowledge for industrialization, one that explained the novel technologies and flows set off by fossil fuel consumption. Many of the scientists who proselytized energy treated it as an inherently political and geo-theological concept. The figure of energy could be used to address topics as grand as the meaning of work, as well as the relationship of humans to the Earth and to God. To discuss energy was to touch upon that fraught, industrial imbrication of humans, nonhumans, and machines. But although physicists claimed to have discovered energy, the resulting laws of thermodynamics ultimately raised more questions about energy and the Earth than they had answered. The stubborn paradoxes of energy—the opaque weirdness of it—has remained a driving force in the development of modern physics, and energy's meaning and dimensions only grew more complex in later investigations of quantum mechanics, relativity, cybernetics, or complexity theory.

While part I narrates the birth of energy in northern Britain, part II examines how the figure of energy reinforced the imperial governance of labor, both human and more-than-human. Energy metaphors and discourses were deployed as part of the scientific spirit of new imperialism, a momentous acceleration of European empires that began in the 1870s, with the so-called scramble for Africa, and lasted until the disintegration of European empires at the end of the Second World War. The role of thermodynamics as an imperial science, one that appeared alongside and through evolution and ecology, has been underappreciated. But while evolution might sketch an overarching narrative (the progressive ranking of civilizations) as well as the plot (a struggle for survival), it was a dominant logic of energy that supplied a script: energy knowledge had made possible the *specific activities* by which Europeans had advanced. Europeans had reached the top rung of the civilizational ladder by maximizing productive work and minimizing waste.

Categorizations of work and waste depended on energetic judgments that assumed that empires functioned as living organisms, and that energy fueled their metabolism. Energy intake allowed for work—and growth—but only if waste could be adequately processed or expelled. In offering a scientific authorization for fossil-fueled work, a dominant logic of energy thus smoothed the way for the Victorian shift "from an industrialism based on imperial slavery to industrial imperialism based on waged labor."[25] Approached as the unit that flows through organisms, energy served the "boundary project"[26] of defining the borders of living assemblages. Boundaries are inherently political. As Haraway argues, "[w]hat boundaries provisionally contain remains generative, productive of meanings and bodies. Siting (sighting) boundaries is a risky practice."[27] Moreover, boundaries also correspond to dominion, to the limits of control: that which is bounded is known, made visible, and vulnerable to governance. That which escapes the boundaries must be evacuated, policed, made invisible.

A genealogy of energy, attuned to shifting boundaries, is thus as much about energy-as-work as it is about waste, a common code applied to those bodies and activities that threaten energy governance. Waste is generated at the intersection of race, gender, class, virtue, pollution, and ecological violence. Waste is leakage, always exceeding its confinement, always lingering and threatening the bounded industrial project and markets, whether through human worker strikes, the stench of landfills, accidents, technological bugs, pollution, or, finally, global warming, species extinction, and melting glaciers. More broadly, waste also emphasizes how, with each indication that humans better understood the world, more of the world revealed itself to be in excess of human understanding. In the case of energy, the ability to more efficiently exploit fossil fuels arrived alongside the nineteenth-century awareness of the Earth as dynamic and unpredictable, as well as, at best, indifferent to the human quest for power and efficiency. Humans in the industrial age increasingly confronted the reality of, in Haraway's words, the "world as witty agent and actor."

In this sense, the Victorian era was an important prelude to the Anthropocene, the proposed geological epoch in which human actions began to have (often disastrous) planetary consequences. It is not a prelude in a geological or atmospheric sense—the Anthropocene was already up and running—but rather an ideational one. Geologists have yet to agree upon a physical signal (which must be discrete and readily observable) to mark the start of the Anthropocene, although most agree that industrialization played a central role. Candidates for the Anthropocene starting point range from the first human use of fire, to the mass death of indigenous peoples following the European arrival in the New World, the patenting of the steam engine in the eighteenth century, or the nuclear fallout of the 1960s.[28]

However, in terms of the *idea*, or dawning consciousness, of the Anthropocene, while humans have long observed their effects on the environment, it is arguably the Victorian period when humans first began to sense that these effects might be planetary and truly catastrophic for human life on Earth.[29] Victorians perceived that industrialism challenged preexisting, Enlightenment frameworks. Beginning in the eighteenth and nineteenth centuries, imperial logics of domination began to contend not just with a New World, but a new Earth, an Earth of fossils and deep time that cared nothing for human well-being. An explosion of new scientific fields and academic disciplines in this period responded with cosmologies that, in many cases, were interpreted so as to buttress anthropocentrism and Western superiority. These included neoclassical economics, evolution, and thermodynamics, all of which continue to be deployed as master tropes and metaphors precisely because they serve the interests of planetary industrialization, having helped to justify European imperialism by externalizing its ecological and social injustices. Thermodynamics mapped the new Earth through the figure of energy, a unit that retained its identity through time (energy conservation), even as its tendency to dissipate (entropy) imparted a tragic edge. In this sense, energy, too, is an Anthropocene knowledge, a response to glimpses of a new Earth made possible by fossil-fueled engines. This is an Earth that continues to resist being treated as a resource.[30]

Extending the Anthropocene into the Victorian era is useful to contemporary climate politics in that it provides evidence of the ecological culpability of a relatively small group of industrial capitalists in the Global North. That group is not the only responsible party when it comes to global warming, and the Victorian era is not the only important historical moment in terms of understanding the state of the planet today. Nevertheless, it would be difficult to overlook the centrality of that group of agents, and that period of time, to the story. Some have proposed changing the name of the Anthropocene to the *Capitalocene* to underline this point.[31] While I am sympathetic to those arguments, the term *Anthropocene* has proven to be rather sticky. If we are to continue to speak of an Anthropocene, then Victorianizing it foregrounds the political and economic fault lines in its genesis.

Moreover, to speak of a Victorian Anthropocene is to insist that we confront how historical violence persists in environmental injustices today. If we instead gesture more broadly toward the human species as the problem, with its insatiable thirst for energy and its tendency for "ecological overshoot,"[32] of which industrialization is just the latest crisis, then it becomes incredibly difficult to imagine alternative energy pathways. If humans unavoidably desire ever more energy, then what could we do short of hoping for a technological miracle, changing the human condition, or colonizing other planets? Assigning responsibility means recognizing how fossil-fuel systems work to favor certain interests, whether in Europe and North America, or in the distinct fossil-fueled visions of new industrializing states like China, India, or Brazil. Understanding the politics of fossil fuel domination is a necessary prerequisite to developing alternative energy values and institutions that are adequately just and radical.

The conclusion suggests a different vision for fuel politics, one that is opened up by a genealogy of energy. The energy–work coupling continues to inform the politics of fuel and is rarely challenged or put into context.

Indeed, the politics of energy draws heavily upon an energy logic that, in hindsight, represents an engineer's narrow application of processes of heat exchange more than it reflects the multifaceted oddities of energy physics writ large. The dominance of the work ethic in policing the boundaries of fuel governance is manifestly evident. While the work ethic itself has dramatically shifted since the Victorian era, the notion that work is central to life still reigns in the Global North, and especially in the United States, such that "the fact that at present one must work to 'earn a living' is taken as part of the natural order rather than as a social convention."[33] A concern with employment, wages, and productivity, all of which feed economic growth and are held to guarantee the continuation of the comforts and pleasures of modern life, are inextricably intertwined with debates over fuel consumption.

The work ethic appears continually as the bogeyman that stymies environmental politics. It informs the assumption that more renewable or sustainable energy systems will inevitably require sacrifice and self-denial. As a result, eco-modernists chastise environmentalists, asking how the Global North can justly deny the path of development and industrial growth to the Global South.[34] One implication of this argument is that the denial of intensive fuel consumption means the denial of the higher planes of civilization and life, predicated on the availability of productive work for all citizens.

A genealogy of energy suggests that there are other ways of knowing and living energy, and that energy and work can be decoupled. The maps that organize human–fuel practices do not need to be arranged along work-based coordinates. Not only can energy and work be decoupled— they *should* be. Without challenging dominant practices of work and leisure, and the high valuation of waged, productive work in a neoliberal economy, it will remain difficult to dislodge fossil fuel cultures. Creating space between energy and work could take a number of paths. The conclusion highlights one potential partnership: an alliance between post-carbon and feminist post-work politics. Putting these two movements— one against fossil fuels and the other against work—into a more enduring conversation can benefit both, especially when inflected with feminist epistemologies and an appreciation of (re)productivity. A post-work energy politics suggests one more route by which environmentalists can escape the neoliberal resonance machine,[35] which obliges fossil fuels to be contested from within a work-and-waste paradigm. Meanwhile, by allying more explicitly with environmentalists, post-work movements can expand their relevance beyond anthropocentric critiques of capitalism, showing how not just human life, but Earthly life, are at stake in the contestation of work.

FREE ENERGY

That which is bound can be picked apart, untied, set free. In studying the bindings between work and energy, we discover the weak points, sites ripe for struggle. We begin to appreciate the possibility of decolonizing energy, of noticing other energy epistemologies, ways of knowing and living with fuel. The liberation of energy has never been more urgently required, and not just for the sake of human life, but for the sake of many other living bodies on Earth. *The Birth of Energy* joins a multitude who are thrashing at the tethers, struggling to free energy from the bindings of exploitative work.

Even if energy does not name a universal knowledge, or stand for the only possible epistemology of fuel, perhaps the commonsense understanding of energy is correct in one way: energy is "vital in our everyday lives," as ExxonMobil suggests at the opening of this book. Energy signifies that which flows through systems, through ecologies, through bodies and organisms. What we do with our energy, how we know it, count it, govern it, and use it (or not!) shapes the possibilities for life on Earth. The project of putting the world to work has led to biological annihilation; we need new energy figures and metaphors, and new ways of valuing energetic activity.

PART I THE BIRTH OF ENERGY

THE NOVELTY OF ENERGY

It was thermodynamics that shook
the traditional world and shaped
the one in which we now work.
—MICHEL SERRES, *Hermes:*
Literature, Science, Philosophy (1982)

Energy was born in plumes of coal smoke, wafting from Glaswegian ship-building factories and the British steamships that corralled its Victorian empire. With the so-called discovery of energy in the 1840s, scientists finally had an explanation for how coal was remaking the world. Energy was not out there in the world waiting to be found, a fact of nature finally revealed to human consciousness. Energy was an ungainly bricolage of new engines and old parts, animated by very old fossil fuels.

Because energy drew upon ancient pedigrees, it was easy to think of it as timeless and cosmic, just as thermodynamics claimed it was. For one, the word *energy* itself is old, much older than the Victorians. Like most illustrious terms in Western thought, *energy* claims an ancient Greek heritage. Second, there were multiple intuitions of energy science, or thermodynamics, prior to the nineteenth century. Many religions and philosophies devised conservation laws and attempted to understand heat, the two puzzles that energy addressed (but did not completely resolve). Third, humans have always used fuel to do work, and have studied the capacities of different fuels and machines, even if they did not refer to fuel as energy. Finally, fossil fuel has its own deep history that predates human animals by millions of years.

Most histories of energy treat these streams—etymology, cosmology, materiality—as the early chapters of a continuous story of human energy systems. However, histories of energy have been curated only retroactively by humans already immersed in fossil-fueled systems. Energy does not travel across history, a unit free of context, but rather arose at the moment when a handful of deep historical things collided: fossil fuels, steam engines, global capitalism, human terraforming, the slave trade, climate systems, empires. From the perspective of deep history, the industrial assemblage that coalesced in the nineteenth century was not the beginning of the Anthropocene, but it was an inflection point; it was the moment in which some humans became increasingly aware of their planetary agency, and did so through the lens of their fuel consumption. The birth of energy science captured the spirit of that moment, and its mixture of hope and dread. The curation of a deep energy history by modern, usually Western, humans represents an effort to make sense of *Homo pyric*, humans as a species both blessed and cursed with the Promethean gift of combustible fuel.[1] Energy was the new language that made heat-work commensurate regardless of fuel source, while at the same time relating hearth fires, plowing, windmills, and steam engines to the unfolding of life in the universe.

This chapter reexamines the deeper history of energy-things prior to the nineteenth century in order to disrupt the seeming continuity, or timelessness, of energy. Disrupting energy involves two claims: First, energy as we know it in the social sciences, as a sign for fuel, is a modern invention. And second, energy has a long-standing moral and etymological connection to work, which gets imported into thermodynamics, with significant political effects (the subject of the remainder of the book).

Who, and what, is served by treating energy as a cosmic unit? As a Victorian science, thermodynamics lent natural, and even cosmological, validation to the industrial project and its celebration of work. Additionally, work, exemplified in the Victorian era by the steam engine, came to be governed as a site of energy transformation. Now that energy was no longer a philosophical abstraction, but (also) a measurable unit, problems with work could be treated as technocratic energy problems, amenable to better energy governance. The energetic model of work thus helped to obscure the political contestability of modern work, and became a technoscientific means for governing workers, both human and more-than-human.

The word *energy* originated with Aristotle (384–322 BC). His ἐνέργεια (*energeia*) laid the foundations for the Latin *energia*, the French *énergie* (first used in the sixteenth century), and the English *energy* (also originating in the late sixteenth century). Prior to the nineteenth century, references to energy bore little resemblance to its future incarnation as a unit of thermodynamics, with one exception: work. Energy appears to have been frequently connected to work and its relationship to human virtue, a link that also became central to the ethos of the science of energy.

Energeia is a combination of the Greek *en-*, meaning "in" or "within" and *-ergon*, meaning "work." It is often roughly translated into English as activity or actuality, though classicist Joe Sachs proposes "being-at-work" as the best sense of what Aristotle meant. Sachs writes that *energeia* should be a jarring and thought-provoking word for the reader of Aristotle, as it is "a special word, dear to Aristotle, at the heart of his theoretical works and giving depth to everything he writes."[2] Aristotle uses energeia as a way to talk about happiness and goodness; for Aristotle, goodness is an ongoing, dynamic project (being-at-work, energeia), rather than a static achievement. Importantly, energeia was used almost synonymously with ἐντελέχεια (*entelékheia*, or entelechy), another term coined by Aristotle and one that would later be adopted into nineteenth-century vitalist debates.[3] If energeia is being-at-work, Sachs translates entelecheia as "being-at-work-staying-the-same" or "being-at-an-end."

The terms are related in a circular fashion. They describe life as constant motion: things achieve their actuality through being-at-work, and this work is striving toward, or maintaining, the completion or actuality of each thing. But even if a thing reaches its completion, it has to continue to work to maintain it (thus, entelecheia, or "being-at-work-staying-the-same"). A more pessimistic way to say this is that life entails struggle; even to stay alive requires ongoing effort. Aristotle, then, invests energy from the start with a sense of dynamism and vitality. Because these terms are at the center of his philosophy, they also carry a metaphysical weight that connects activity (being-at-work) and goodness. While energeia and entelecheia, as well as the concept of work itself, are quite specific to Aristotelian philosophy and do not touch upon later principles of thermodynamics, these associations remain significant when they are adopted into the science of energy.

Following Aristotle, energy continued to be advanced with its "honorable Greco-Roman pedigree," such that "the term entered its modern scientific usages carrying a large freight of classical associations."[4] The *Oxford English Dictionary* lists five different inflections of the word, all of which retain Aristotelian connotations of vigor, actuality, motion, and change: "force or vigour of expression"; "exercise of power, actual working, operation, activity"; "vigor or intensity of action, utterance, etc."; "power actively and efficiently displayed or exerted"; and "ability or capacity to produce an effect." The central role of energeia in Aristotle's metaphysics also remains influential, both in premodern usage and in the science of energy, wherein "the possible equivocations, the multivalent expressions, of such power have wired into Western languages a proverbial connection between physics and metaphysics, material effect and divine cause."[5]

As a Western concept, energy combines a materialism, in the description of activity, with moralism, expressing a bias toward dynamism over stasis. The bias toward dynamism accords with what Arjun Appadurai has described as "trajectorism," a "narrative trap" of the West that serves as the central faith of modernity. Trajectorism assumes "that there is a cumulative journey from here to there, or more exactly from now to then, in human affairs, as natural as a river and as all-encompassing as the sky."[6] Importantly, for Appadurai, trajectorism is about more than temporality, more than an awareness of time's arrow and irreversibility. Trajectorism has political effects. As a Western imperial project and a "bad habit" of thought, trajectorism became an ideology of expansion in which time's arrow must lead to a single destination, "the world written in the image of Europe."[7] The West, then, is unthinkable except as a trajectory, as an act of expansion from here (a region, a piecemeal dominion) to there (world as Europe). Such an expansion could be synonymous with faith in progress, but its possibilities are broader.

By the nineteenth century, not only progress, but unlimited progress, had become an almost universal faith in the modern West. What is important, above all, is the preference for constant motion, action, dynamism, growth—with the progressive effects assumed to follow post hoc. Europe, or the West, then, cannot be conceived of as a steady-state project, an entelechy whose efforts are directed at maintenance; such a notion remains difficult, if not impossible, to think. Hannah Arendt quotes Proudhon from the 1850s (just after energy has been "discovered"): "motion is *'le fait primitif'* and 'the laws of movement alone are eternal.' This movement has neither beginning nor end: *'Le movement est; voilà tout!'*"[8] Motion is otherwise understood as kinetic energy; the laws of motion are inscribed in energy.

All this is to show that energy, even before it became a scientific thing, was always about more than fuel or the material potential for action. Energy provided the grammar for a preference for the transformation of fuel, for putting it to use to do work and make change, and for stamping teleological activity as a virtuous achievement. Even after thermodynamics adopted the term *energy* as a concept for physics, these older meanings of energy continued to be used alongside, or interchanged with, energy as a scientific term, such that the metaphysical and scientific connotations inflected and supported each other. Indeed, Bruce Clarke points out that, following the advent of the science of energy, "its prior layers of meaning did not vanish. The already overdetermined term *energy* became even more charged with powerful semantic currents. Emotional and spiritual meanings were mingled with the letter and interpretation of physical concepts."[9] *Energy* continues to be a slippery word, traveling easily between vigor, virtue, and fossil fuels, and implicitly disparaging its opposites: rest, stasis, stillness, lassitude.

A COSMOLOGY OF CHANGE

While *energy* is a Western word that derives etymologically from Aristotle, there were parallel inquiries across human civilizations that aspired to understand change in the world. The wish to locate a universal concept, or force-flow, that underlies natural transformations appears to have been widely shared across human civilizations. The Chinese had the concept of *qi*, which Dainian Zhang defines as "both what really exists and what has the ability to become. . . . As a philosophical category qi originally referred to the existence of whatever is of a nature to change."[10] Tellingly, Zhang also argues that a succinct way to understand qi would be through Albert Einstein's matter–energy equivalence equation, $E = mc^2$, as "in places the material element may be to the fore, in others, what we term energy. Qi embraces both."[11] Hinduism has *prana*, which associated the breath with a life force that permeated the cosmos. In Stoic physics, *pneuma* was central; it was a mixture of fire and air, "an all-pervading medium which intelligently directs the cosmic cycle" and was at the basis of all life.[12] Unlike Aristotle, who separated the heavens from the Earth, pneuma as a universal medium meant that the Stoics viewed the stars, planets, and cosmos as continuous with the Earth, and as involved in cyclical flows and exchanges of pneuma over time. Pneuma even anticipates some facets of the science of energy, which views the cosmos as constituted by flows of energy, and the Earth as depending upon energetic flows from the Sun.

The philosophies of energeia, pneuma, qi, or prana advanced different visions of the cosmos. However, they all reflected an interest in understanding change and stasis experienced by living things over time, and in connecting these universal experiences to moral frameworks. The morality attached to these earlier presentiments of energy did not necessarily share the West's bias toward dynamism and trajectorism. For example, goodness might involve understanding and sometimes governing the flows of qi or prana, while evil involved their blockage or misapplication. Good governance of qi or prana might entail balance and harmony rather than constant change.

These multiple histories of energy remain relevant today. From oil and gas corporations to yoga studios, from Buddhism to interior design, from Burning Man festivals to biological and ecological sciences, from computing to quantum physics, energy has many valences, and these are determined by the context of its articulation. However, this book narrows its focus to energy's appearance as an object of politics, where it almost always operates as a sign for fuel. In its manifestation as energy/fuel, energy imports the physical and cultural meanings of one particularly dominant figuration of energy: that of the science of energy, or thermodynamics.

It is through thermodynamics that energy became a newly soluble problem for the state, as a unit of work that was amenable to technical governance. It is also through thermodynamics that energy became a problem for the Earth, and a crisis—global warming—that also seems to demand new human governmentalities. What distinguishes thermodynamic energy from its other cultural dimensions is its emphasis on heat-work, on the transformations made possible by burning fuel. The thermodynamic rendering of energy—as the measurement of productive, valuable work—has arguably become so dominant in the modern West as to crowd out other possible ways of imagining energy.

FIRE AND FLUX

The science of energy that emerged in the nineteenth century drew indirectly upon these multiple philosophical histories, but it was not just an extension of centuries-old theories about a universal life force. What made thermodynamics so unique and successful was that it managed to marry the life-force tradition, which tended toward ideals of balance, to an understanding of heat transformations. Heat transformations propelled the new steam engines, and these were inherently machines of change, rather than symbols of harmony.

Moreover, heat transformations challenged the concept of conservation.[13] For alongside those long-standing intuitions of a universal life force were equally ancient theories about its conservation: in other words, if there were a life force, most philosophical traditions surmised that it was ontologically stable across time and space. But what happened to the universal life force during a fire? To the human eye, all the ingredients of a fire appeared to be radically changed, if not entirely destroyed, but if there were a universal life force, then *something* must be conserved across all transformations, no matter how violent. Just what that something was, however, remained mostly a mystery. The insistence upon conservation was for the most part metaphysical and tightly bound to religious and philosophical precepts. Belief in the conservation of something in nature is evident in the Greek aphorism that "nothing comes from nothing," attributed to the thought of Parmenides ("for things that are not can never be forced to be").[14] Nothing can be created out of nothing, and once created nothing can be destroyed—ergo the basic forces of the universe must be conserved.[15]

Conservation theories stretch back to at least the ancient Greeks, and Philip Mirowski observes that "the concept of a conservation principle is practically inseparable from the meaning of 'energy.'"[16] Heraclitus (535–475 BC), often understood as a founding inspiration for later Stoic thought, was a philosopher of "fire-and-flux," and foreshadowed thermodynamics by over two thousand years. He argued that fire was central to all things; that the cosmos "always was, is, and will be, an ever-living fire, being kindled in measures and being quenched in measures," and therefore that change was the central phenomenon of the natural world (later Greeks cited him as offering the famous aphorism that "you cannot step into the same river twice").[17] Amid this change, there are equivalences between oppositions (up and down, alive and dead, goods and gold), and in this sense Heraclitus suggested an early version of the conservation of matter across radically different forms.

"Nothing comes from nothing" was also a totemic starting point for Lucretius, another early prophet of energy, though he added a tragic twist to the notion of conservation.[18] Lucretius insisted on the senescence of the Earth, asserting that the planet, like any living thing, would inevitably decay toward death.[19] Conservation might just mean the conservation

of ruin and wreckage. In his gleefully blunt style, Lucretius reminds his
readers that

> There is never lack
> Of outer space, available to take
> The exploded rampart-rubble of the world.
> The doors of death are always open wide:
> For sky, for sun, for Earth, for ocean's deeps
> The vast and gaping emptiness lies in wait.[20]

His *De Rerum Natura* is full of declarations that the Earth is always changing, and headed toward death, as "all that might, / All that machinery of
the universe, / Upheld so proudly through so many years, / Will tumble
down, crumble to ruin, die."[21]

Lucretius intends his brusque handling of death to have an ethical effect on his readers. If death is universal and inevitable, and far beyond
human control, then we should accept it, rather than fear it. It is death,
along with a host of other anxieties, that leads people to worship false
gods, Lucretius insists, and to toil after possessions and luxuries, for "the
brief / Capacity of pleasure for increase," which delivers humans over and
over "to the great tidal depths of storm and war."[22] Clearly, Lucretius, unlike so many of his peers, does not subscribe to the virtue of dynamism
for the sake of dynamism, or to the pleasures of growth. He spends many
lines rehearsing the pointlessness of human striving to improve agriculture, law, art, and war. Instead, Lucretius's knowledge of the universe
leads him to embrace a more restful disposition, wherein "wealth, / The
greatest wealth, is living modestly, / Serene, content with little."[23]

Lucretius anticipated modern physics, including the science of energy,
with his description of atoms moving in a void. His manuscript, lost for
hundreds of years until its rediscovery in a fifteenth-century monas-
tery, would later inspire a minoritarian tradition of political ecologists
and philosophers in modern Europe, from Michel de Montaigne to Henri
Bergson and Alfred North Whitehead.[24] Readers from the late industrial
world might shiver with recognition at the "great tidal depths of storm
and war" that *De Rerum Natura* prophesied over two thousand years prior
to climate change. Nevertheless, Lucretius to this day remains almost too
avant-garde for Western cultures. Although his physics was strikingly
modern for its time, his ethical interpretations of the cosmos are in direct
opposition to the energy ethics that have come to prevail in the industrial
West. Lucretius's vision of the cosmos suggested the wisdom of serenity,

modesty, and caution, which are all at odds with the dominant Western narrative of trajectorism and dynamic change. Weirder and more disconcerting still for modern readers are his tragic ethos and unflinching rejection of religion. Lucretius's Earth was not a harmonious planet, divinely planned for human purposes, but rather a random collection of atoms sliding toward death and completely beyond the control of humans.[25]

Enlightenment science embraced a variation of the former and more comforting planet. Even if the world was not divinely ordained, the hope was that human knowledge could eventually triumph over earthly complexity. This meant that scientists could not rest at asserting conservation laws; they wanted to devise mathematical equations that proved them.[26] René Descartes, for instance, argued that motion was conserved in the universe; he believed that "motion, like matter, once created cannot be destroyed, because the same amount of motion has remained in the universe since creation."[27] Descartes defined the conserved quantity as mass times velocity (mv). Later, Gottfried Leibniz initiated a vigorous debate with Descartes by arguing that it was not motion (mv) that was conserved, but rather what Leibniz called *vis viva*, or "living force," defined as mass times velocity squared (mv^2).[28]

The debate over vis viva, which raged through the eighteenth century, is often read as a simple misunderstanding corrected by later knowledge: without an agreement as to the meaning of terms like *force* or an understanding of the science of energy, Descartes was actually positing the conservation of momentum, while Leibniz was arguing for a conservation of what is now known as kinetic energy. Both were to be proved correct in a sense, as both conservation rules are now understood to be valid and not mutually exclusive. However, historians of science have pointed out that the controversy was more complex than this implies.[29] Leibniz was proposing an entirely different philosophical perspective than was Descartes, one in which both time and space, and thus motion across time and space, were relative.

The idea that space was relative was an eccentric view at the time, more than two hundred years before Einstein. But if motion were relative, Leibniz concluded, then it could not serve as an absolute entity that was conserved in the universe. Instead, Leibniz proposed that there was a vital, living force that was absolute (vis viva), and this force meant that "what is real in the universe is activity; the essence of substance is action, not extension as Descartes had insisted."[30] Leibniz's vis viva, which calculated kinetic energy, came closer to the modern notion of energy, and thus Leibniz was adopted post hoc in the building of a pedigree for the science of energy.

Here again, there is an evident preference for activity in both the philosophical and physical precursors for the science of energy. Existence, for Leibniz, is best captured by activity, in motion and change across time, rather than by extension, the mere fact of taking up space. Energy over matter, time over space. Vis viva can be understood as a scientific descendant of Aristotelian energeia, where goodness is not a state of being (extension), but rather an ongoing effort of becoming (activity). Thermodynamics, too, continues the emphasis on dynamism rather than stasis.

By the time of Leibniz, then, almost two hundred years before the science of energy, many of the pieces were already in place to cobble together something like a conservation law, if not a fully articulated concept of energy as a universal unit of exchange. However, despite the energy pedigree claiming Leibniz's vis viva as a forebear, there was "no simple line of descent from Leibniz's principle of conservation of vis viva to nineteenth century energy conservation."[31] The problem was that, as much as vis viva was useful as a conservation law, it still could not explain how steam engines worked. And the science of energy did not emerge as a result of mathematically abstract debates about conservation. Rather, energy science arose among those with more practically minded goals: scientist-engineers whose chief interest was in solving the puzzle of steam engines. Steam engines were heat machines, and the transformative power of heat remained little understood. Ultimately, it was the merging of Leibniz-like intuitions about universal conservation with a study of steam engines that produced the modern concept of energy.

The resulting science of energy differed from the historical tradition of conservation laws. It was technological in its basis, as it was inextricably wound up with the proliferation of the steam engine, and thus with the upheavals of global industrialization. While natural change had always been of interest to humans, the changes wrought by steam engines were exponentially magnified. As the philosopher of science Bruce Clarke notes, energy was "a discipline for the production of the sort of knowledge that enables persons to seize powers previously reserved to the agency of the divine," and so "science has often taken on the allegorical attributes of the Luciferian enterprise."[32] If divinity was displayed in the acts of creation, in the appearance of novelty on the Earth with each dawning day of the first week of Genesis, then steam engines brought humans closer than ever to the glory of God.

Steam engines are little creative divinities, but like many creative endeavors, they feed on death, running on the detritus of a long-lost world. As
with fire, which had always seemed magical to humans, engines convert
matter that is usually described in terms of spatial extension—cords of
wood, seams of coal, and reservoirs of oil—into motion that is best described in time—acceleration, intensity, and work. Like the host of other
fossils dug up by humans in the nineteenth century, fossil fuels illuminated the Earth as a hive of constant activity, even in zones that appeared
inert or lifeless. The Earth, formerly understood as an extension in space,
gained a new dimension: Earth as historical, as a duration in time, and
thus as a potential reservoir for work.

Up to this point, I have elided any distinction between energy-as-
knowledge and energy-as-fuel. Rather than hew to a material–ideational
division, the aim is to recognize their mutual entanglement, as well as
the multiple lifetimes and histories that were assembled into fossil-fueled
systems and interpreted through the science of energy. Steam engines are
modern, the word *energy* and its philosophies are ancient, but the fossil
fuels are more palpably older still—exploding time capsules that originated in a world without humans. Rather than approach these histories
linearly, it is more helpful to imagine time in loops and spirals, as in the
U.S. Geological Survey's depiction of Earth's history (figure 1.1) or, more
poetically, in the "widening gyre" of falcons' flight and things falling apart
in William Butler Yeats's "Second Coming."

Life on Earth relies almost entirely upon the nuclear reactions of the
Sun (with the notable exception of geothermal energy and human-derived
nuclear reactions on Earth), including the forces of wind and water as well
as so-called fossil fuels. In the words of global environmental historian
Rolf Peter Sieferle, "the Earth's biosphere is a powerful solar energy system."[33] Fossil fuels are part of this solar energy system, as they are the
remains of once-living plants and/or animals.

Coal is often made up of fossilized swamp plants, while oil and natural
gas derive from mostly marine plants and animals. Coal formations began
when plant life accelerated around 350 to 400 million years ago. Except
for a relatively short gap at the end of the Permian (fifteen million years is
short when we are talking about coal), when there was a mass extinction
and 90 percent of life on Earth died out, coal formation has continued
and is ongoing today. Today's peat bogs will one day become coal, albeit

FIGURE 1.1. "The Geologic Time Spiral." Source: Designed by Joseph Graham, William Newman, and John Stacy. Digital preparation by Will Stettner for the U.S. Geological Survey.

millions of years from now. Coal needs special conditions to form, and these conditions were ideal during the so-called Carboniferous period of the Late Paleozoic, from about 359 to 300 million years ago, when much of the coal mined today originated (note the term *Carboniferous*: even our periodization of Earth history stems from our interest in fossil fuels). Oil and natural gas are not necessarily as old as coal, although it likely takes at least several hundred thousand years for these fossil fuels to form. About 60 to 70 percent of the world's known oil—including the oil in the Middle East—is thought to come from the Mesozoic Era, about 100 million years ago.[34]

For hundreds of millions of years, the bulk of this carbon energy remained buried beneath the Earth's surface, while life on Earth existed on more immediate circulations of solar energy. For human animals, this meant technologies that harnessed wind, water, and muscle, as well as an underlying dependence on plants. Fire offered another important source of energy, rapidly releasing the concentrated energy stored in plants as heat, a kind of fossil-fuel burning in miniature. The emergence of fire use remains unknown, but evidence has recently been found of *Homo erectus* using fire one million years ago.[35] The control of fire was "a crucial turning point in human evolution,"[36] playing "a decisive role not only in human prehistory but in the very process of humanization itself."[37] (Although even the assumption that fire manipulation is specific to human evolution is under pressure, given research documenting raptors using fire to catch prey in Australia, a phenomenon that was already well known to indigenous peoples.)[38] Much later, burning wood and charcoal was instrumental to the slow emergence of agricultural civilization, as it helped to clear forests as well as to make certain crops more digestible. The relationship between humans, domesticated animals, food, climate, and terrain—all of which could later be charted under the rubric of energy exchange—is important to understanding the rise of hierarchical human societies.[39]

While early agricultural civilizations mainly tapped into immediate circulations of solar energy, there were varied attempts to take advantage of fossil fuels. The use of oil dates back at least five thousand years: asphalt was used in building in ancient Sumeria and Babylon, Ancient Egyptians and Native Americans each used oil for medicinal purposes, and Native Americans also made tar for tool construction. Ancient China developed deep drilling for natural gas, bringing it through bamboo pipes as heat to make salt, or "brine."[40] There is evidence of coal being burned as fuel as early as 1000 BCE in China, and it is also mentioned in ancient Greek texts and later during the Roman Empire. However, coal was unpopular due to its impurities and the dirty, black smoke it emitted. Wood was preferable for heating and cooking purposes, and people only grudgingly turned to charcoal or coal for home use, often when forced to by deforestation.[41]

England's own coal consumption began as early as the thirteenth century and rose in slow fits and starts. There were important geographic influences: England had easily accessible coal mines in combination with a river and forest system that made it comparatively more difficult to transport wood than it was to ship coal by sea.[42] The substitution of coal for wood freed up land for other commercial purposes, such as raising sheep for textiles. Those goods could then be traded to import more food than the land could have produced. The density of coal, whose power was determined by duration rather than extension, thus helped to increase the ecological footprint of Great Britain, which was now effectively importing food energy to feed its growing population.[43] By the sixteenth century, Britain experienced an "Elizabethan leap" in its coal consumption, which has been widely chalked up to a timber shortage alongside increased fuel demand by a rising urban population. Andreas Malm, however, also points to the human forces at work that made coal production profitable, and thus desirable, in the first place: a royal edict in 1566 transformed mineral resources from Crown property to private property, leading to an acceleration in elite land appropriations and tenant evictions. Coal became increasingly good business. A self-reinforcing cycle of mineral privatization and land enclosure, which pushed more people into swelling cities where fuel demands outstripped the nearby organic material, set the stage for the eventual intensification of fossil fuel economies.[44]

Britain's early flirtation with fossil fuels was further accelerated by a technological innovation. Coal and oil had not yet been used to power what Vaclav Smil, an energy historian, calls a prime mover technology.[45] The eventual marriage of coal to an increasingly effective prime mover—the steam engine—played a decisive role in industrialization by tying together many areas of the economy that had already been moving toward increasing mechanization, including textiles, agriculture, and chemical industries.[46] Global coal use catapulted exponentially in a short period of time, from just under ten million tons at the start of the nineteenth century to almost 100 million tons in the middle of the century, and then to 1,000 million tons by the first decades of the twentieth century.[47] The rise of coal also amplified the global circulation of metals like aluminum, nickel, pig iron, and lead. Sieferle, an environmental historian, reflects that "with the utilization of coal the bottleneck that had until then slowed down all technical economic innovations was overcome."[48]

Despite the centrality of coal to the story,[49] the coal–steam engine apparatus should not be overstated as a determining factor in the Industrial Revolution. The dramatic rise in coal consumption occurred only toward the last half of the nineteenth century, at the tail end of industrialization. It was through the convergence of a number of processes—technologies, scientific cultures, forestry practices, river flows, the geology of coal deposits, slavery, and the global circulations of resources and money—that coal "gained its strategic importance."[50] Nevertheless, "the central importance of coal as the energy basis of the Industrial Revolution" is undeniable, even if Sieferle argues that "it has been almost completely ignored by economic history."[51] Emphasizing coal also helps to downplay the Western miracle narrative of industrialization. For instance, historian Kenneth Pomeranz has convincingly shown how a host of material and imperial vectors, rather than the presumed superiority of Western culture and science, were important in understanding the "great divergence," and why Europe and not, for instance, China, industrialized when it did.[52]

But as with the Elizabethan leap, supply, demand, and technological innovation are insufficient to explain the rise of coal. Malm goes further than Pomeranz in overturning the consensus explanation of the fossil-fuel transition, which generally holds that humans naturally hunger for more and more energy, that their hunger was stymied by fuel shortages, and that coal offered a breakthrough technological advantage. Instead, Malm points out that coal-fired machines were neither cheaper nor obviously superior in this period. Nor were other possible energy sources absent at the time. In fact, water power was a viable, and often more affordable, alternative for the new factories of the nineteenth century.[53]

So why did capitalists end up preferring steam to water? While coal may not have been cheaper, Malm argues that it was more conducive to the relations of power that sustained capitalism. More specifically, steam power opened up better opportunities for capitalist owners to dodge the growing demands of laborers for shorter work hours, higher pay, and other social protections—in Malm's pithy phrasing, "steam won because it augmented the power of some over others."[54] Water power, with its seasonal variability, required cooperation among factory owners and public institutions, and it also rooted industries to specific sites alongside waterways.[55] If those sites were rural, as many were, mill owners might be responsible for managing labor colonies, and would also be reliant upon a relatively static pool of workers.[56] In contrast, steam power was certainly cheapest near coal pits, but it could be consumed anywhere, and did not need to be coordinated with others. It satisfied a competitive, individualist style of profit making.[57] Coal's mobility meant it could also feed urban factories located near large pools of expendable labor. Urban laborers did not need to be fed or housed by their bosses, and it was much easier to replace resistant or unruly workers in a city teeming with people who had been uprooted from land and family.[58] If the "logic of water" was more communistic, the logic of fossil fuels was conducive to predatory and violent economic relations.[59]

By reading fossil fuels through the lens of human power, Malm reverses Marx's famous dictum—that the hand mill gives us the feudal lord, while the steam mill gives us the industrial capitalist.[60] Instead, Malm contends, the industrial capitalist led to the dominance of steam power. Capitalism was ill-matched to water power—so much so that "the anarchy of capital had to become fossil,"[61] given that "the more capital tries to extract itself from the absolute, concrete qualities of space and time, the *deeper must be its exploitation of the stock of energy* located in their exterior."[62] The demand for profit by some at the expense of others drove capitalists toward a fuel that could be mobile, privatized, highly controlled, and burned all night in tireless prime movers. In other words, the advantages of coal had more to do with human power than with mechanical power.

While coal girded the explosion of industrialization and remains a significant source of fuel for electricity needs worldwide, oil emerged in the latter half of the nineteenth century and quickly rose to prominence by the early twentieth century. As with coal, humans had used oil for centuries, but it was not until the mid-nineteenth century that kerosene was distilled from petroleum and proposed as an attractive fuel for lamps. When Edwin Drake found oil in Pennsylvania in 1859, the petroleum business was still perceived as a risky venture, but within a couple of decades, the U.S. oil industry took shape and oil consumption expanded.[63] Here, too, the transition from coal to oil had as much to do with human power as it did mechanical power. Timothy Mitchell has shown how the urge to escape the demands of labor—in this case the demands of organized coal miners—became a significant factor in the turn toward oil.[64] By the late 1800s, the oil industry was truly global, with European companies drilling for oil abroad, including Royal Dutch Shell in the Caucasus and British Petroleum in Persia. By the early twentieth century, with the advent of diesel engines that ran on petroleum, oil began to overtake coal in fueling transportation technologies. The rise of crude oil production was even more sudden and dramatic than the rise of coal, building as it did upon the socio-energetic demands already inculcated by coal systems: oil grew from only one million tons globally in 1870 to over ten million tons in 1900 and over 100 million tons in the 1930s.

The consequent spike in industrial expansion and consumption following the spread of fossil-fuel systems is hardly surprising if one considers that some humans suddenly had a superabundance of fuel at their disposal, far beyond the transitory flows that could be captured from the Sun's daily allowance. John Tyndall, an early scientist of energy, marveled at the power of coal, "vast truly in relation to the life and wants of an individual, but exceedingly minute in comparison with the Earth's primitive store."[65] Sieferle notes that human societies might have been confronted with similar energy abundances in the past, as when pioneers clear-cut ancient forests. However, these moments provided only temporary spikes when compared with fossil fuels, which might supply abundant energy for a few centuries.

Unlike solar regimes, though, fossil fuel society is necessarily "transitional,"[66] given that fossil fuels are both practically nonrenewable and ecologically disastrous. In effect, burning fossil fuels is somewhat like sparking the spontaneous decomposition of a large number of long-dead plants and animals all at once, thus garnering an exponentially denser amount of energy than if these plants and animals had decayed over a shorter period of time and were in less compact form. William Stanley Jevons, who famously warned of the exhaustion of Great Britain's coal in 1865, described coal as "like a spring, wound up during geological ages for us to let down,"[67] a metaphor that conceives of the Earth as a grand apparatus waiting for human operators to release its potential animation. As such, fossil fuels are also, technically, *renewable energy*—the spring can be wound back up again, so long as plants and animals keep living and dying—but only over the course of hundreds of millions of years. Whether energy is renewable, then, is less a material description of fuels than it is a human judgment about time. The fossil fuel interlude in human life will likely prove to be extremely short-lived when compared to solar agricultural regimes, which prevailed for over 10,000 years, and certainly when compared to the hybrid subsistence methods of hunter-gatherers, which determined human life for about 95 percent of its existence, for nearly 190,000 of the 200,000-year history of *Homo sapiens*.[68]

Having teased out some of energy's historical forebears, from Carboniferous swamps to ancient human philosophers, we are better situated
to understand why the energy/fuel/machine assemblage swerves in the
nineteenth century, generating energy as we now know it, as a sign for
fuel. There are no clean edges in history, nothing born *de novo* without pre-
cedent, but in an important way our world was shaped in the nineteenth
century, where industrial assemblages crossed a *threshold of perception*,
a term adopted from Gilles Deleuze and Félix Guattari's topographical,
rather than linear, approach to history.[69] Some economic historians have
pointed out that industrialization was slow to take root, and that the "Industrial Revolution" was less a sudden big bang and more a multivalent,
complex, and slowly unfolding set of processes.[70] Nevertheless, by the
mid-nineteenth century, the European public perceived the "dawning of a
new age" that provoked as much anticipation as trepidation.[71]

2

A STEAMPUNK PRODUCTION

By the time energy arrived on the scene in the 1840s, coal-fed steam engines were multiplying, remaking landscapes, labor, cities, and imperial
processes. The pace of change felt relentless and almost inexorable. Michel
Serres says of this period that "the entire world becomes a steam engine
between Carnot's two sources: the cold and the hot."[1] To be sure, trends of
globalization, capitalism, empire, democratization, global trade, and the
beginnings of industrialization were evident and even significant before
this era, but the consolidation of a fossil-fueled economy in the nineteenth
century helped to accelerate these patterns. Global historians William
H. McNeill and J. R. McNeill argue that, with the exploitation of fossil
fuels, "the Industrial Revolution helped extend, tighten, and quicken the
[worldwide] web" that had been unified in prior centuries, as "humankind
broke loose from long-standing constraints on human numbers, food supply,
mobility, and economic output."[2] In their view, fossil fuels, in combination with improving steam engine technology, were no less transformative for human civilization than the agricultural revolution had been.[3] By

the nineteenth century, fossil fuel use had "locked us into a high-energy society, in which we must continue to mobilize, transport, and use vast quantities of basic items."[4]

These disruptions were widely felt across academic fields and popular culture, both as hopeful and as frightening. With the steam engine and the Industrial Revolution, Serres reflects, the old world of geometry and lines of force were overturned, and "a sudden change is imposed on the raw elements: fire replaces air and water in order to transform the Earth."[5] Across Britain, the populations of cities were exploding, as the growing industries of coal, cotton, or shipbuilding, all increasingly using the new steam engines, required more labor. Glasgow, for instance, the site of many of the scientists of energy, tripled from a population of 84,000 in 1801 to over 270,000 in 1840.[6] In the newly teeming industrial cities, the poor lived in squalor. There were constant fears on the part of the wealthy industrialists of popular revolution or unrest, as the economy was an "unstable explosive, verging simultaneously on incomparable wealth and unspeakable poverty."[7]

But just as the steam engine–run factories were taking advantage of laborers exposed to an urbanized hell of soot and rampant fevers, the steam engine was also believed to be capable of offering improvement and progress. Indeed, the problem of the urban poor was met by a never-ending series of reform bills, "always with the optimistic belief, from the side of scientific culture, that industrial progress would produce a greater store of happiness for the laboring classes and not only for the elites of property and profession."[8] As an ideology of natural balance was replaced by one of change, the expected role of science turned from explaining nature's harmony to "harnessing the energies of change to man's purpose."[9] More cynically, autonomist philosopher George Caffentzis notes that the problem was no longer centered upon inspiring an inert laboring class to work, but rather controlling their volatile chaos so that "their energy and revolutionary heat could be transferred into work. Not surprisingly, thermodynamics, 'the study of energy, primarily with regard to heat and work,' becomes *the* science after 1848."[10]

As should be clear by now, energy does not have a simple birth story. Even if the frame is narrowed to the scientists themselves, the emergence of thermodynamics was not a tidy process. The dozen, and likely many more, scientists who are purported to be the forebears of energy knowledge ranged across Europe and were for the most part working alone in their stabs at a theory of energy conservation, with the exception of the circle of British and Scottish scientists who would eventually consolidate the laws of thermodynamics.[11] For instance, Sadi Carnot was unacknowledged during his life and died young of cholera, only to be resurrected later by the Glaswegian crew as a grandfather of energy science. Like Carnot, much of the work that has been knit together post hoc was little recognized at the time as anything momentous. There was no single moment when energy was "discovered," and once discovered, the figure of energy remained confusing and difficult to synthesize.

The discovery, instead, was a social process. Economic historian Philip Mirowski writes that there were "literally dozens of people in the nineteenth century who insisted in one form or another that the world was really One, that there was no free lunch, that life and force were identical, and that protean interchangeable and interconvertible natural forces governed the world."[12] And it was Glasgow—the heart of British shipping and "Second City of the Empire"—that proved especially ripe for developing these wide-ranging musings into a science of energy. In Glasgow, engineers, the university, the shipbuilding factories, the wharves, and the river Clyde congealed to help produce energy. Scottish scientists such as William Thomson (later Lord Kelvin), the ringleader of the science of energy, and William John Macquorn Rankine were directly connected to the Clydeside industries, where the steam engine was becoming ubiquitous. Carnot, who had attempted to depict an "ideal" engine and intuited that the engine required a difference in temperature, was not alone in recognizing that engines were "destined to produce a great revolution in the civilized world."[13]

The obsession with the work of steam engines led to a preoccupation with one theme: waste. Importantly, this was not the waste produced *by* the operation of engines, but rather the waste *of* the engines in converting coal into motion. It was waste from the perspective of work, as that which detracted from it. As Andreas Malm argues, steam engines were not necessarily adopted because they were cheaper or provided superior power, especially given the advantages of water power in the early nineteenth century. Instead, as chapter 1 detailed, steam power was attractive because it better accorded with the needs of industrial capitalists in making a profit while simultaneously dodging the rising demands of laborers.[14] The demand for steam engines, despite their inefficiency and expense, made it all the more urgent for capitalist industry that the engines be improved.

The Glaswegian scientists, working alongside new industries, perceived that much potential work was getting lost when engines, and other machines, were running. Engines did not work with perfect efficiency, and perhaps never could. Thomson and his associates also came to believe, with the support of the recently excavated Carnot, that these machines operated by taking advantage of some kind of fall—whether the fall of water from a height, or the fall from hot to cold. For instance, what happened when there was a fall but no machine to harness it into work? What happened to the work that was potentially available during that fall, but was never brought forth by human hands? The two concerns—waste and the dissipation of energy into unusable forms—resonated not only with the capitalist drive for profit, but also with long-standing theological obsessions in Protestantism with sin and sloth.

These questions began to be cobbled together into a more comprehensive set of ideas once Thomson came across the work of James Prescott Joule at a British Association for the Advancement of Science (BAAS) meeting in 1847. As befell so many of energy's early proponents, Joule's work had been met with much skepticism up to this point—so much so that he was not even allowed to present a full paper at the 1847 meeting. Joule's experiment claimed to prove that heat could be produced from motion. Ironically, though, given Joule's obsession with measurement (as well as the centrality of measurement and precision to the future science of energy), his experimental data were wholly unconvincing. Thomson remembers one scientist griping after the meeting that "he did not believe in Joule because he had nothing but hundredths of a degree to prove his case by."[15]

Joule blamed his experimental apparatuses for the data discrepancies, and obsessively tinkered to improve them, but was never able to observe consistent results. In large part, this was because there were losses to things like friction, conduction, and so on that Joule did not guess at or measure at the time. However, the difficulty remains, and Carolyn Merchant Iltis reflects that "the general conservation law which states that the total energy of the universe is conserved is a theoretical statement which cannot be verified empirically except in isolated closed systems."[16] We should pause here to marvel once again at the underlying irony: energy, which would come to serve as a unit of labor accounting and fuel supply, traceable and governable down to the nth degree as a sign for quantifiable, brute matter, is at its heart theoretical, and tends to escape, exceed, and stymie empirical measurement. Instead of discovering energy through experiment, then, it seems likely that Joule was motivated by a belief that something in nature was conserved, rather than by empirical proof; Joule "harbored a cacodemon that said 'heat is motion'" and that drove him forward as a prophet of energy conservation.[17]

Drawing on what he learned from Joule, it was Thomson who had the insight to put Carnot and Joule together. After the fateful 1847 meeting, Thomson reflected that "Joule is, I am sure, wrong in many of his ideas, but he seems to have discovered some facts of extreme importance."[18] Drawing on Joule's notions, Thomson combined Carnot's insight that a "fall" from hot to cold is necessary with a mechanical view that heat and motion are interchangeable. Out of this synthesis came the two principles of a new science of energy.

Up to this point, I have delayed talking about how physics textbooks actually define energy in order to follow along a circuitous historical path that situates energy as a specific concatenation of human–machine experiences in nineteenth-century industrial Europe, as well as to unsettle any notion that energy was a natural fact that was discovered by European men, revealed to adorn a growing pile of human knowledge about the world. Sandra Harding contests such "discovery narratives," in which science is presented "as the discovery and testing of hypotheses, implying that the laws of nature had been there all along, untouched by human hands or thought, until some clever or lucky scientist managed to detect them."[19] The discovery narrative remains a seductive and popular account of science, especially as it conforms to the European optic of trajectorism. Even Thomas Kuhn, who is celebrated as one of the first historians of science to explore the wider social context of scientific transitions, veers into these objective terms when writing about the discovery of energy. In his groundbreaking 1959 essay, "Energy Conservation as an Example of Simultaneous Discovery," Kuhn confidently writes that "we know why [the early concepts of energy conservation that heralded its discovery] were there: Energy *is* conserved; nature behaves that way."[20] The result is the wholehearted acceptance of energy as a natural fact that elides the politics and history of its production. As Harding explains, "valuable insights" can be wrought from a discovery narrative, but by instead attending to how science is manufactured, we begin to see that "distinctive concerns of particular nations, of imperial and colonial projects, and class, racial, and gender concerns all have left their marks on work in the history of science."[21]

By understanding energy science as manufactured, *The Birth of Energy* emphasizes its entanglement with the grand Western imperial project of the period—putting the world to work for the profit of some—and in the governance of laboring bodies and nonhuman assemblages toward that goal. Indeed, given the industrial climate of optimistic progress and vast profit, it is hardly surprising that many of the scientists of northern Britain, steeped in the burgeoning shipbuilding and engineering industries, would be captivated by the desire to improve upon and understand steam engines, both to expand the nation's economy and to earn accolades and prestige for their own theories, and also with the idea that such improvements would benefit European society. For while tinkerers like James Watt had been able to design engine components that improved the steam engine's capabilities, there remained a great deal of mystery as to how exactly an input (such as coal, which produced heat) became an output (motion), and therefore how to assemble a machine that could eke the most out of this transformation. Moreover, steam engines and fossil fuel systems would force a rethinking of how humans, the Earth, and God were interrelated.

Energy was imagined as an answer to this challenge and, in many ways, it was successful. Just not as successful as most imagine. The history of thermodynamics belies the notion that energy is the name for a universal, natural entity. Energy is contested within physics itself. Even among the first scientists of energy there were complications and confusions. Ambivalence was rooted in the science, as the first two laws of thermodynamics were contradictory, and ultimately unsatisfactory, in some ways to this day. Through the two laws, humans combined a desire for stability (the first law, the conservation of energy) with a new recognition of disruption and inevitable decay (the second law, entropy).

THE FIRST LAW: CONTINUITY

Early energy scientists were strategic in proselytizing energy as the keystone to understanding the universe. In order to build a new science, one needs some fundamental laws, and in short order, Thomson and co-conspirators like Rankine and Peter Guthrie Tait, went about refining these. Historian Crosbie Smith notes that the science of energy was a valuable property, and that the northern British crew led by Rankine, Thomson, and Tait used an intentionally dry and legalistic tone in laying down the first and second laws. Rankine offered one of the earliest versions of the "law of the conservation of energy," which he explained as the law that "the sum of the actual and potential energies in the universe is unchangeable," where "the term energy is used to comprehend every affection of substances which constitutes or is commensurable with a power of producing change in opposition to resistance, and includes ordinary motion and mechanical power, chemical action, heat, light, electricity, magnetism, and all other powers, known or unknown, which are convertible or commensurable with these."[22] Many of Rankine's close friends and family members were lawyers and businessmen, and Rankine, along with Thomson, was "quick to apply the language of patents to scientific property which could then be marketed to a scientific public in return for increased credibility."[23]

Besides revealing a desire to claim ownership and authority over the science of energy, Rankine's fastidious tone also points to the difficulties involved in pinning down the purported laws in the first place. Energy was not obvious, even in its early days, and debates over its precise definition ensued. Energy as a scientific principle had to be defined and redefined. Hence Rankine's lengthy list, which attempts to include every possible manifestation of motion and power in its definition of energy. The first scientists of energy did not always even agree with each other and continued to squabble among themselves over phrasing. This uncertainty has haunted energy ever since, and physics in the decades after the science of energy emerged has "transmuted [energy] beyond all recognition and coherence," to the point that "energy was turned on its head."[24]

These definitional struggles are apparent in the musings of physicist and Nobel laureate Percy Bridgman, who observes that "the laws of thermodynamics have a different feel from most of the other laws of physics. There is something more palpably verbal about them—they smell more of their human origin. . . . Why should we expect nature to be interested either positively or negatively in the purposes of human beings, particularly purposes of such unblushingly economic tinge?"[25] Similarly, physicist Walter T. Grandy Jr. asserts that "entropy and the Second Law are essentially epistemological concepts, whereas the fundamental dynamical laws that presumably drive the latter are on an ontological level. We should be well advised to avoid confusing reality with our perception of reality."[26] These may be somewhat remarkable observations, especially to nonphysicists who assume that the laws of physics believe themselves to be objective and neutral reflections of the natural world, because it reflects a "feeling" that energy is more epistemological than other laws of physics, something "more palpably verbal" and of "human origin." In other words, it points to a unique awareness among physicists themselves of energy and entropy as human constructs.

The murkiness in defining energy is evident even in the seemingly straightforward first law of thermodynamics. This is the law of the conservation of energy and it becomes mysterious and contradictory the more it is queried, despite its ubiquity in modern science. In today's physics textbook, the law states that energy in a closed system cannot be created or destroyed—it is always constant. This feels commonsensical in its reflection of an ordered and balanced universe, but it is in fact a very strange notion.[27]

To understand the strangeness of this idea, it is worth quoting physicist Richard Feynman at length here, as his approach to teaching energy, as documented in his famous physics lectures at Caltech in the early 1960s, remains foundational for the field. In the textbook based on these lectures, Feynman explains that "there is a certain quantity, which we call energy, that does not change in the manifold changes which nature undergoes. That is a most abstract idea, because it is a mathematical principle; it says that there is a numerical quantity which does not change when something happens. It is not a description of a mechanism, or anything concrete; it is just a strange fact that we can calculate some number and when we finish watching nature go through her tricks and calculate the number again, it is the same."[28]

Feynman uses Dennis the Menace and his toy blocks as a metaphor for what we know about energy. Dennis's mom (presumably the scientist seeking to bring order and discipline to the world) knows that Dennis (presumably the mischievous and unruly nature) has twenty-eight blocks. After Dennis scatters them throughout the house, she may not find all the blocks, as some may be under the rug, out the window, or even in places where she is not allowed or able to look (Dennis's secret toy box, for instance, or the bubble-obscured bathtub). However, using the blocks' weight, or their volume in the case of the blocks in the bathtub, she can still use mathematics to find them all, and she discovers a "phenomenal" law: "no matter what he does with the blocks, there are always twenty-eight remaining!" Even as her world grows more complex, and the blocks become increasingly difficult to find, mathematical equations help her to infer the presence of the missing blocks.

Dennis the Menace is a playful pedagogical tool, but it can also be recognized as a significant metaphor that describes the modern physicist's relationship to nature. Carolyn Merchant reminds us that "it is important to recognize the normative import of descriptive statements about nature . . . Descriptive statements about the world can presuppose the normative; they are then ethic-laden."[29] Merchant charts the shift from older nature-as-mother philosophies, which employed organicist frameworks, to more mechanical descriptions of nature, where humans dominate or manage the world. In Dennis the Menace, the mechanical view is given an interesting twist befitting the mysteries of entropy and energy. The scientist is not the rational manager of nature-as-machine, nor the child of nature-as-mother, but instead the mother of nature-as-naughty-child. The metaphor acknowledges nature's unruliness, and its tendency to escape supervision and household rules, but in figuring nature as a child, the metaphor retains the spirit of mechanistic models in which the world can be improved by human guidance and discipline. Besides the characters in Feynman's energy drama, the setting is also significant: we are in a middle-class American home, implying that scientists who tend after nature-as-trickster contribute to an orderly and secure suburbia for a modern public. The image of the mother is deployed in order to domesticate energy and nature, although women themselves remain rare in mid-twentieth century physics, industry, and engineering.

Meanwhile, what Feynman famously takes as the key lesson from this story, wherein we use math to measure energy where we cannot see it, is the "remarkable" realization that "*there are no blocks*" and "we find ourselves calculating more or less abstract things." Thanks to the equations, all we know is that no matter what transformations Dennis causes, we will do the math and end up with twenty-eight. Feynman goes on to famously claim that energy does not actually exist as a tangible thing. It is only a relational aspect of things. We can calculate energy's many transformations, measure some of its effects, as it turns from chemical to heat, or from potential to kinetic. Nevertheless, Feynman concludes that "we have no knowledge of what energy *is*. We do not have a picture that energy comes in little blobs of a definite amount."[30]

This has led some historians to conclude that energy reflected the desires and beliefs of its discoverers rather than a thing of nature—that "the energy concept was not at all a descriptive entity, but rather an assertion of the very ideal of natural law: the mathematical expression of invariance through time, the reification of a stable external world independent of our activity or inquiry. This ideal, at first so very plausible and reassuring in its form and appearance, was turning out to be a ticket to Bedlam if followed to its logical consequences."[31]

In other words, the conservation of energy reflects the scientists' desire to know and understand the world, which requires that the world is know-*able*. Energy points to the enduring faith in nature as divinely designed to be accessible to human perception.[32] In order to be know-able, the world must have some constancy through time—pure, random chaos would mean prediction and calculation are impossible. However, as scientists studied energy it became almost immediately obvious that the energetic world was not constant, and that even if the math of the first law was successful in limited contexts, something was still getting lost to human use in the transformations. The first law, in other words, contained the seeds of its own contradiction, which necessitated a second law that would attempt to neutralize the problem.

THE SECOND LAW: DISSIPATION

If the first law of thermodynamics provided some comfort in its balance and stability, the second law, which eventually introduced the concept of entropy, did the opposite. The second law was all about dissipation and decay, and it presaged twentieth-century physics—quantum physics, relativity, complexity theory. Entropy, like energy, is as abstract as it is baffling. Like energy, entropy was the result of the human desire to un-lock the secrets of steam engines. While the traditional story has it that these experiments led scientists toward the discovery of energy, in fact, as mentioned earlier, the experiments were largely unsuccessful. Indeed, as early scientists of energy began to intuit, and then to try to prove, the conservation of energy, they were dogged by the sense that something was getting lost in their experiments—something that they could not yet account for. Something about the engines exceeded their command, and this was frustrating mainly because it meant that humans were losing precious power and work. Thomson bemoaned this unaccounted-for loss as a "difficulty which weighed principally with me," given that it was a misfortune for human industry.[33]

Even those scientists who are said in hindsight to have empirically shown energy conservation through experimentation, such as Joule, were not actually able to prove anything with statistical certainty. We think we know now that something was getting lost in the experiments because there were a great many facets, or proposed types, of energy that were not known at the time; "hence, in that era, there were just too many ways energy could get lost."[34] In other words, scientists did not yet know how to look for Dennis's blocks in the bathtub or out the window. It is not as though physicists in the twenty-first century have yet mastered the measurements; in his 2008 study of entropy, Grandy points out that not only do we know almost nothing about the entropy of the universe but, "on a more prosaic level, we have no idea how to envision, let alone calculate, the entropy of a worm!"[35]

Even more confusing to nineteenth-century experimenters, there also seemed to be losses of useful, or available, energy, which was evident in the fact that the heat engine could not run in reverse. This led Thomson and others to perceive that the transformations they were studying were *irreversible*. Heat engines, unlike mechanical machines such as waterwheels, necessarily entail transformation. Waterwheels enact a simple exchange of motion for motion: the motion of water begets the motion of the waterwheel's blades. But with steam engines, motion leaps out of fire, and "thus the heat engine is not merely a passive device; strictly speaking, it *produces* motion."[36] Because the heat engine transforms fire into motion, it is irreversible. Waterwheels can run in reverse: blade moves water, water moves blade. With steam engines, a change in form has occurred. Burning coal moves a piston, but no amount of pumping pistons can reconstitute ash into a lump of coal. Running some events, or engines, backward—from dispersed to concentrated energy, or from cold to hot—is, strictly speaking, impossible. In other words, it will not happen spontaneously, and in many cases may not happen at all no matter how much energy is applied.

If energy is conserved across all transformations, then science still could not explain why heat engines—or life itself—could not run in reverse. As a result, the first law of thermodynamics, tidy and comforting as it was, struggled to make sense of heat engines. Conservation was predicated on an understanding of time as reversible, and if energy was conserved, there was no reason why these exchanges could not happen both backward and forward. Furthermore, if heat *was* mechanical and molecular, as Joule and Thomson were coming to suspect, then why did it not obey Newtonian mechanics, which are also reversible? This proved a thorn in the side of the new science of energy. It was not enough to enunciate a conservation law, even if the new term, energy, differentiated itself from force or vis viva. Descartes and Leibniz had not had steam engines roaring in their cities, undermining their principles. The conservation law would not be a truly universal paradigm if it could not explain steam engines as well.

The second law of thermodynamics, the law of entropy increase, was a necessary qualification. *Entropy* is, roughly, a measure of how diffuse energy is, where concentrated energy is able to do more work. The second law describes a world of energy running down beyond forms that could do work. The world of the second law unfolds toward a destination of maximum entropy, until the sun eventually burns out, the universe slows to a cold equilibrium, and life becomes impossible.

Although entropy was trumpeted as part and parcel of the science of energy, it provoked problems from the start, and would eventually contribute to the unraveling of linear, deterministic physics.[37] Nevertheless, the first scientists of energy dealt with entropy handily, so that rather than undermining the science of energy, entropy was made to buttress it. Thomson and his colleagues simply made another law out of it. Irreversibility could be a conceptual partner to energy conservation rather than a challenge to it. After all, Thomson, who was famously critical of metaphysics (and Hegel in particular), was convinced that "paradoxes have no place in science. Their removal is the substitution of true for false statements and thoughts."[38] For Thomson, the two laws of thermodynamics resolved the paradox of energy, although for later physicists, they only underlined it. In 1910, a biographer observed that, despite Thomson's disdain for paradox, "his own conclusions are intensely paradoxical."[39]

If the first principle was that energy was conserved, the second principle said, in its early manifestations, that heat flowed only from hot to cold. Since (relatively) cold matter is not useful in doing work, which was the essence of energy, then Thomson also posited that all energy runs down to less useful forms. By *useful*, Thomson and the other scientists of energy often meant *useful to humans*. In effect, the second law meant that any loss is not actually a loss of energy per se, but instead a loss of a *useful* type of energy from the perspective of work. The energy still existed—after all, the first law maintains that energy cannot be created or destroyed—but it was now in a diffuse state relative to its surroundings. In order to do work, more energy would need to be applied to reconcentrate or relocate it.

In 1865, shortly after Thomson's insight about energy's tendency to dissipate, a German scientist named Rudolf Clausius first coined the term *entropy* and offered a mathematical equation describing it. For Clausius, entropy describes how heat tends to spontaneously disperse. Entropy, which stands for how widely heat is dispersed, is thus always increasing (e.g., hot goes to cold) in a closed system. Riffing off of energy's Greek origins, Clausius adopted entropy from the Greek *en + tropein*, or in-turning. Clausius translates it as transformation. Just as Thomson related irreversibility to energy, so Clausius also considers entropy and energy as partnered observations about the universe. He notes that "I have intentionally formed the word *entropy* to be as similar as possible to the word *energy*; for the two magnitudes so denoted by these words are so nearly allied in their physical meanings, that a certain similarity in designation appears to be desirable."[40]

According to Clausius, there are now two "fundamental laws of the universe" and he lists these as:

1 The energy of the universe is constant.
2 The entropy of the universe tends to a maximum.[41]

While entropy helped boost the science of energy by adding another universal law to scientific knowledge, things were not so smooth under the surface.

For starters, entropy was just as abstract as energy, and even more difficult to measure. Moreover, entropy and energy, even if paired as two universal laws, remained dissonant, in that they painted contradictory pictures of temporality and change on Earth. Because energy conservation was timeless, it resonated with classical, Newtonian science, whose laws treat change as reversible. This view of time, or better yet, this elision of time, opens up the possibility of control. As Nobel physicist Ilya Prigogine puts it, "reversible transformations belong to classical science in the sense that they define the possibility of acting on a system, of controlling it." This control can happen by manipulating the initial conditions or the "boundary conditions" of a transformation, such as changing the temperature or pressure at a desired rate.[42]

However, entropy dismantled any promise of certainty and control by revealing that certain changes were *not* reversible. Prigogine observes that "there exist in nature systems that behave reversibly and that may be fully described by the laws of classical or quantum mechanics. But most systems of interest to us, including all chemical systems and therefore all biological systems, are time-oriented on the macroscopic level."[43] While billiard balls can be knocked forward or backward without changing the calculations of their trajectories (in other words, it does not matter to the math whether they are running forward or backward), the same cannot be said of heat. The dissipation of heat through, for instance, friction, runs in one direction, and one direction only.

With cases of irreversibility—cases that were more interesting to humans, as they involved engines as well as life itself—entropy showed that time has a direction. This has been called the arrow of time, meaning that time, like an arrow, has directionality. Entropy also showed that the Newtonian promise of control was an illusion. Prigogine argues that irreversibility means the "end of certainty,"[44] and "this feeling of confidence in the 'reason' of nature has been shattered. . . . We were seeking general, all-embracing schemes that could be expressed in terms of eternal laws, but we have found time, events, evolving particles."[45] Prigogine seems to be directly negating Rankine's grandiose claims about the first law. Our only guide to the future becomes the study of probabilities. Irreversibility, spawned by entropy, "shows that, unlike dynamic objects, thermodynamic objects can only be *partially* controlled. Occasionally they 'break loose' into spontaneous change."[46]

Here lies much of the stuff that was getting lost in nineteenth-century experiments on heat engines. And it was lost not just in the sense that it could not be measured; it was also lost in the sense that, once used, it could not be used again. Dennis the Menace's blocks are an imperfect analogy, as, even if the mom finds them all, some of them cannot be played with again. Perhaps they were eaten by a dog in the yard, or smashed in the toy box, or waterlogged and distorted in the bathtub. This is entropy's other crucial teaching, and one that was deeply felt by the engineers who advanced the science of energy in the heady days of nineteenth-century industrialism—that the spontaneous increase in entropy simply means that energy will tend to be more dispersed and more disorderly over time. In other words, it means that there will be more and more energy in forms that *cannot be used to do work*, which is why the Earth relies upon the Sun for a continual supply of more energy to do work for living things.

A NEW ENERGY COSMOLOGY

The two laws concerning energy seem to combine well to describe the reality we observe. And yet the marriage of energy and entropy creates an awkward tautology: "given that every freshman physics student is told that energy is the ability to do work, the notion of energy that cannot do work does seem a contradiction in terms."[47] One might say that energy is always conserved because we merely expand the definition of energy to include what is lost. The laws of energy are semantic entities as well as responses to natural forces.

But while energy is a historically specific concept-thing, rife with contradiction, it relies upon the elision of its history. Energy claims to be *life itself across cosmic space-time*, and it almost immediately achieved this status. Most popular and scientific discussions of energy in the nineteenth century included a paean to its universality and cosmic significance, often in breathless, almost religious tones. By 1903, historian and industrialist John Theodore Merz reflected back on *A History of European Scientific Thought in the Nineteenth Century* and called energy the "greatest of all exact generalisations," and "the term under which we now comprise, and by which we measure, all natural agencies."[48] Such assertions are just as commonplace today: energy is a unit of equivalence through which distinct fuels (oil, solar, nuclear) can be compared regardless of space and time, even as what counts as energy changes dramatically.

But why did it matter so much that energy was cosmic? In short, the claim is an expression of an underlying provocation that drove the science of energy in the first place. Steam engines were changing everyday human life and cities, but they were also perturbing older cosmologies that had perceived nature as harmonious and static. The goal for scientists was to naturalize engines, to bring them under control by charting the planetary regularities that explained their operations. Steam engines could be new and exciting, but they also must fit within a narrative of continuous linear progress. The need for two contradictory laws therefore reflected the confusion that industrialization had sowed in the nineteenth century. Europeans had come to feel like strangers in their own home, and they ricocheted between a worldview that assumed a balanced Earth, uniquely fit for human pursuits, and one that recognized the Earth as indifferent, and possibly antagonistic, toward the survival of the human species. Again, we might reflect on the significance of Feynman's Dennis the Menace metaphor and its suburban home setting, in which the tricks of energy and entropy are converted into the exasperating, but ultimately lovable and controllable, antics of a middle-class kid.

The desire for conservation laws, which would show the identity of things in time, accorded with an older, balanced Earth that allowed for causal explanations. It is a desire that remains widespread in both physics and economics, and Philip Mirowski observes "how susceptible scientists have been to belief in conservation principles, even in the absence of any compelling evidence; and conversely, how loath scientists have been to relinquish a conservation principle once accepted."[49] In order to understand the attraction of conservation principles, Mirowski suggests turning to the musings of Émile Meyerson, an early twentieth-century philosopher of science. Meyerson explains that the ability to trace cause and effect was all the more desirable in a world that appeared to be "infinitely changing, becoming incessantly modified in time. Yet the principle of causality postulates the contrary: we must needs understand, and yet we cannot do so except by supposing identity in time."[50] The first law of thermodynamics helpfully locates energy as identical through time, enabling observers to chart the inputs and outputs of heat engines (whether metallic or fleshy). Energy provided a unit of equivalence that was legible to human accounting and surveillance techniques.

However, while identity in time may be useful in some contexts, Meyerson warns that it is only ever an illusion that "makes us accept as substance what in the beginning is but a relation between two limited terms, such as velocity, or a concept impossible to clearly define in its entirety, such as energy."[51] Meyerson concludes that the desire to mark an identity in time reflects an urge to excise time altogether from mathematical equations.[52] Excising time from the operations of reversible waterwheels is one thing; studying irreversible steam engines while ignoring time is another. Steam engines required the qualification of the second law and its mood of decay.

Once extended beyond the workings of a steam engine, entropy made a difference to how the Earth itself was conceived: older, decaying, and less comforting to humans. Scientists of energy inferred that, even while the new knowledge about energy promised awesome capabilities for humans, the second law of thermodynamics threatened death for the Earth itself, which would indeed "wax old like a garment," just as the Bible promised. Especially for northern British scientists of energy, the so-called heat death of the universe was the logical conclusion to the ongoing dissipation of energy. Once equilibrium in temperature occurred, life would be impossible.

The heat death hypothesis remains valid as one possible fate of the universe—now colloquially referred to as the "Big Chill"—though it has been qualified thanks to the caveat for both laws of thermodynamics: that they are only true in a *closed* system. A closed system is a system in which energy does not enter or leave. While closed systems could be theorized and sometimes assumed without consequence to the math (as in the case of machines like the steam engine), in reality there are no known closed systems. The Earth and its life, including human bodies, societies, and states, are obviously open systems, as they all ultimately rely upon energy from the Sun. No one knows whether the multiverse has some kind of closure, whether there is ultimately a vast container that holds all energy in existence. Grandy, a physicist who specializes in entropy, scoffs at attempts to extend the second law to the ends of the universe, noting that "it is rather presumptuous to speak of the entropy of a universe about which we still understand so little."[53]

Despite this caveat concerning the heat death hypothesis, a tragic edge remains to the second law of thermodynamics. Life, which is a negentropic situation, means sustaining a low entropy state, but this is only ever temporary and requires unceasing effort. Entropy speaks of limits, of the march of time, and of lost opportunities; it is a reminder that the Sun itself, the fuel for the Earth, will indeed run down. Entropy underlined the promise of technological progress with a certain pessimism, a darker sensibility. In this way, entropy harkens back to ancient views of the Earth as senescent (evident in Lucretius, most famously),[54] but reinterprets this tragic Earth in light of the industrial era. Indeed, energy, as well as other scientific fields that emerged in this period, heralded the return of a minority tradition of tragic philosophy, launched by Lucretius, but newly adapted for industrial machines.

The return of Lucretius was a return with a difference. The fears that exercised Lucretius and his peers now wore the mien of fossil fuels, hulking machinery, sooty air, crowded cities, and polluted waters. Energy was among the first modern sciences to directly confront the return of fears about the unpredictability of the cosmos, now bathed in the grimy light of industrial technology. The tragic view accepted that, no matter how useful the first law and careful accounting could be in improving engines and societies, these endeavors were situated within the overarching promise of decay enshrined in the second law. In this sense, energy reflects an early Anthropocene consciousness, and some energy scientists interpreted it as a strategy for responding to the threats posed by a new, senescent Earth. This emergent logic of energy reinforced Western industrialization by doubling down on the first law, on the dream of mastery, and perceiving the new Earth as an object to be governed to the best of human knowledge. This was, in effect, the response of the majority who deployed the science of energy: put the planet to work. Engineering successes fed the desire to industrialize the Earth, to better manage its lurching transformations.

At the same time as energy inspired a technocratic politics, thermodynamics also launched an array of more radical approaches to the physical world. Figurations of energy multiplied, engaging with the new Earth of modern industrialism in different ways, including the physics of probability, relativity, ecology, and complexity, all of which would enable the twentieth-century recognition of global warming and other planetary crises.

CONCLUSION

The two laws of thermodynamics reveal the paradox at the heart of the concept of energy, between balance and change, or stability and progress. Almost as soon as the conservation of energy was posited and nature appeared in harmonious balance, the specter of entropy appeared, spawning a great deal of doubt and reflection among nineteenth-century scientists of energy, even after it had been tamed by explaining it with a law. Its impact did not stop there: the concept of entropy, like energy, was to have a long-lasting significance for Western philosophy and politics, as, unlike the "ordered and monotonous world of deterministic change," Prigogine argues that irreversibility "marks the beginning of a new science that describes the birth, proliferation, and death of natural beings."[55]

Entropy and its tragic perspective "laid the foundation for a new cosmological synthesis" between science and Christianity, a synthesis that remains relevant to energy politics today.[56] As the next chapter shows, figuring out steam engines in the nineteenth century was both a practical and a spiritual concern whose solutions touched upon the larger relationship between Christianity, industrialism, and the Earth. Some of the leading early energy scientists of the northern British camp, as devoted Scottish Presbyterians, made sense of the laws of thermodynamics by putting them into conversation with the existing Protestant work ethic and its enemy, waste. Energy scientists were thus engaged in a double reading of energy from the start. They always had in mind the cosmological, the metaphorical, the theological. Energy laws could be deployed to endorse an ethos—the ethos of the engine, the maximization of work, and the minimization of waste—that reconciled the spatiotemporal registers of Earth time and human time, God's beneficence and cosmic indifference.

3   A GEO-THEOLOGY OF ENERGY

> Man has been here 32,000 years. That it
> took a hundred million years to prepare the
> world for him is proof that that is what it was
> done for. I suppose it is. I dunno. If the Eiffel
> tower were now representing the world's age,
> the skin of paint on the pinnacle-knob at
> its summit would represent man's share of
> that age; and anybody would perceive that
> that skin was what the tower was built for.
> I reckon they would, I dunno.
>
> —MARK TWAIN, "Was the World
> Made for Man?" (1903)

Industrialization has had ambivalent effects. In the late nineteenth century, many Westerners benefited from new commodities; improvements in medicine, nutrition, and education; the acceleration in global communication and travel; and the slow expansion of political rights to working-class white men. At the same time, critics pointed to slavery, long and dangerous hours of labor, urban poverty and disease, smog, poisoned rivers, denuded forests, and industrial modes of mass violence. Working conditions throughout the nineteenth century were grim; historian Bernard Semmel reports that recorded testimony in "blue books" are full of "stories of eighteen hours a day of work for women, of little children being dragged, still half-asleep, to draughty, damp, dark, factories after only four hours of sleep, of children who were strapped if they could not maintain the rapid pace of the shop."[1]

Paeans to British industrial glory were countered by elegies that mourned environmental and cultural degradation, penned by early Anthropocene luminaries like George Marsh, one of the founders of modern ecological science, who titled his 1864 treatise *Man and Nature; or, Physical Geography as Modified by Human Action.* John Ruskin's famous 1884 lecture, "The Storm Cloud of the Nineteenth Century," linked the historically unprecedented weather of Britain ("the plague-wind and the plague-cloud") to its proliferating chimneys and engines,[2] while in 1865 William Stanley Jevons had already posed his gloomy "Coal Question" concerning "the probable exhaustion of our coal mines."[3] The "fluttering and dancing" daffodils of William Wordsworth's "I Wandered Lonely as a Cloud" (1807) and the Romantic poets had given way to the more pessimistic, uncertain Victorian nature poetry of Matthew Arnold's "Dover Beach" (1851):

. . . for the world, which seems
To lie before us like a land of dreams,
So various, so beautiful, so new,
Hath really neither joy, nor love, nor light,
Nor certitude, nor peace, nor help for pain;
And we are here as on a darkling plain
Swept with confused alarms of struggle and flight,
Where ignorant armies clash by night.

By 1912, Thomas Hardy's description of the sunken *Titanic* ("The Convergence of the Twain") could just as easily be a description of the aftermath of human civilization, presaging the twenty-first-century thought experiment of *The World Without Us*, of Earth after the extinction of the human species.[4] Hardy imagines the *Titanic* lost "In a solitude of the sea," where "Over the mirrors meant / To glass the opulent / The sea-worm crawls—grotesque, slimed, dumb, indifferent." It is not difficult to imagine Hardy's "Dim moon-eyed fishes," who casually peruse the sunken, "black and blind" *Titanic*, swimming about the inundated lower Manhattan of the future, asking, "'What does this vaingloriousness down here?'"

Likewise, Mark Twain's extended joke, from 1903, quoted in the epigraph above, reflects the misgivings of the period. In light of the deep time of the planet, Twain pokes fun at the Christian notion that the world was made for "man" and his vainglorious Eiffel Tower. The Earth had been revealed as far older, and more unpredictably dynamic, than the Bible had suggested. If the Earth predated humankind, and might not always be habitable for humans, did it really make sense to assume that God made it for humans? Twain's feigned tone of befuddlement mocks such logic. How could the unpredictable complexity of industrial capitalism be harmonized with an abiding faith in God's omnipotence?

Faced with such challenges to traditional Christianity, as well as to Enlightenment ethics, energy science suggested one mode through which to make sense of the human project of industrialization. Among the most prominent proselytizers of energy science were a group of Scottish scientists, led by William Thomson, many of whom were engineers as well as devoted Scottish Presbyterians. For them, energy formed the basis of a geo-theology[5] that offered a response to a frightening specter: *a planet that cared nothing for human happiness.* As Crosbie Smith shows in his cultural history of energy, the science of energy could be interpreted as a way to reconcile the new Earth, indifferent to human pursuits, to Scottish Presbyterianism.[6] Entropy, and the metaphor of energy dissipation, was key to the synthesis. If Earth's energy was running down—a tragic vision—then the planet could not be a reflection of God's perfection, nor a stable backdrop for human dramas. Rather, the Earth was a flawed system to be worked upon and improved by humans. God alone was exempt from the vagaries of entropy.

Of course, this geo-theology of energy was not the only possible interpretation of thermodynamics. Thermodynamics was also not the only nineteenth-century science that challenged traditional Christianity and Enlightenment values. The most well known and influential of the new sciences, at least in the realm of popular culture and politics, was evolution, which rose to prominence just two decades after the birth of energy. Energy and evolution are often mentioned together as having remade modern science: one in physical conceptions of the world and the other in biological understandings of life; one remaking what historian John Theodore Merz calls the "abstract" science of universals (energy), and the other remaking the "descriptive" science of the richness of nature's particular entities (evolution).[7] In a period where science and its positivist methods became the preeminent intellectual pursuit, and scientists wrote with confidence of having discovered natural laws that drove the progressive unfolding of history, these two sciences had great popular appeal. Much of this scientific knowledge was also accessible to the educated layperson; Eric Hobsbawm notes that "never again was it to be so easy for blunt common sense, which knew in any case that the triumphant world of liberal capitalist progress was the best of all possible worlds, to mobilize the universe on behalf of its prejudices."[8]

This chapter analyzes the geo-theology of energy by comparing and contrasting it to the political adoption of evolution. Doing so situates energy within the larger scientific trends of the nineteenth century, while at the same time clarifying what was distinctive about thermodynamics: its closer relationship to Christianity. While evolution had an ambivalent, and often antagonistic, relationship with Christian doctrine, some of the most prominent scientists of energy were devoted Scottish Presbyterians who reconciled industrialization with Protestantism through the laws of thermodynamics. In other words, Scottish Presbyterians appreciated energy as a scientific validation of the Protestant ethic of maximizing work and minimizing waste, a geo-theology that reverberates in energy politics today.[9] The northern British crew imprinted energy and its politics with a more palpably religious flavor than its Victorian counterpart, evolution.

Given the status of its leading figures, the Presbyterian interpretation of energy became a dominant one, but it was not without its detractors; attempts to inject religious tones into thermodynamics were challenged from the start by energy scientists with a more secular bent, like John Tyndall, or by those from a German materialist tradition, such as Rudolf Clausius.[10] But I am less interested here in naming a victor in the cosmological debates over energy. Rather, through a genealogical approach to the history of energy, I want to notice how the early engagement with Presbyterianism and Scottish shipbuilding cultures left an indelible trace on energy politics. This trace is evident in the industrious ethos that continues to sustain modern petrocultures. Moreover, from this perspective, it is precisely the parochial specificity of this early Glaswegian culture of energy that is important. The very particularity of this early energy culture, which infused energy as it became a global logic of domination, challenges energy's claim to universality, which has helped to naturalize dominant Western narratives about how humans should relate to energy.

There is a multidisciplinary literature examining how evolution has interwoven with political practice and the social sciences. In contrast, there is comparatively little discussion of whether and how the science of energy may have been deployed politically,[11] despite the fact that, for historians of the nineteenth century, as well as historians of modern science, the science of energy is of paramount importance. As an example, at the turn of the twentieth century, Merz reflected that, alongside evolution, "no scientific ideas have reacted so powerfully on general thought as the new ideas of energy. A new vocabulary had to be created; . . . and problems which had lain dormant for ages to be attacked by newly invented methods."[12] Over a hundred years later, historians still roundly acknowledge the importance of energy to nineteenth-century thought; Jürgen Osterhammel, in his comprehensive history of the century, calls energy nothing less than "a *leitmotif* of the whole century."[13]

One reason for the discrepancy may lie in the aesthetics, epistemologies, and concerns of the sciences themselves. The biological subfields are often easier to access and more applicable to political areas of concern than are the fields of chemistry or physics, which became increasingly mathematized and abstract. Evolution also more directly addresses living organisms and human life. Indeed, one of the major implications of evolution was that the history of humans and the history of the Earth were not separate but conjoined, paving the way for the partnering of biological, geological, and social sciences. The proposed mechanisms of evolution—natural selection, the desire for survival—were also more amenable to common sense and everyday empirical evidence. The science of energy, meanwhile, concerned intangible mathematical relations at a molecular level, evidenced only spottily through technical experiments with engines and, later, by the mathematics of statistics and probability. The laws of thermodynamics and their popularizers did try to appeal to common sense, but these laws ultimately contradict each other and can seem illogical, as discussed in chapter 2. Moreover, their application to human life was abstract and often technologically mediated.

Energy and evolution also constituted two sides of a growing rift between the biological and physical sciences. During the nineteenth century, the philosophical pursuit of natural history, once the province of gentleman-scholars, was replaced by the novel discipline of science and its multiplying subfields, which was to be practiced by experts, with physics often the furthest removed from popular understanding. While Darwin's terms and imagery could be transplanted wholesale, albeit clumsily for the most part, into the popular imagination, the concepts and images of energy worked in more subtle, partial, and often implicit ways.

Admittedly, thermodynamics is a tributary in relation to the oceanic political and cultural effects of evolution. Nevertheless, energy, as a political rationality or ruling logic, played a noteworthy role in the constitution of industrial, global modernity. It did so not as an opponent of evolution, as one side of a biophysical division, but rather in the mutual entanglement of evolutionary and energetic thinking. In many cases, it is only by recognizing the sites where thermodynamics imbued evolutionary thinking, which were not always explicitly avowed, that we can discern how thermodynamics played out in political and cultural life. In other words, thermodynamics was often smuggled into cultural and political life via evolutionary metaphors and narratives. In this chapter, energy and evolution are first read against each other in order to contrast the geo-theology of energy, which was more triumphal about industrialization, with the moral ambivalence of evolution. Evolution is agnostic about work and industrial capitalism; it does not dictate in advance which adaptations will result in the best fit to an ecological niche. It is thermodynamics that induces an eschatological anxiety about entropy among its Protestant readers, and that better serves to lend capitalism and its work a certain moral urgency, one that gets couched in the language of efficiency and productivism.

A PRELUDE TO THE ANTHROPOCENE

It was no accident that the two most influential bodies of scientific knowledge that emerged in the nineteenth century both involved fossils, in the form of animal bones, Neanderthal skulls, and coal. Rock strata and their fossils, which were increasingly hunted and studied in the late eighteenth and early nineteenth centuries, were an empirical testament to the dynamism of the Earth. Meanwhile, the emerging fossil fuel regimes connected the dizzying pace of industrial time to the deep time of planetary change. The reigning notion of the Earth as balanced and harmonious was undermined as the Earth was increasingly perceived as historical and without a driving teleology, echoing the tragic physics of Lucretius and his fellow atomists.[14] Indeed, Timothy Morton argues that it was precisely in the Victorian era that humans began to confront what he calls hyperobjects, or "entities that are massively distributed in time and space." Hyperobjects like climate change, species extinction, and the other calamities of the Anthropocene have proliferated in the twenty-first century, but in the nineteenth century there was already a growing awareness of other, Anthropocenic hyperobjects, including "geological time, capital, industry, evolution, cities, the unconscious, electromagnetism, climate phenomena such as El Niño, and so on." When we think about hyperobjects today, Morton argues that "we are still inside the Victorian period, in psychic, philosophical, and social space."[15]

The spirit of the Victorian Anthropocene is captured, for instance, in a "colossal monument" to Christopher Columbus dreamed up by a Spanish architect named Alberto Palacio, who hoped to upstage the Eiffel Tower's pomposity at the 1893 Chicago World Fair (figure 3.1 and the cover image). Palacio dreamed up an iron Earth approximately one thousand feet in diameter (the height of the Eiffel Tower).

Visitors could mount the Earth via a tram that would ascend a spiral path nearly four miles long, leading to a North Pole "crowned . . . by the caravel which carried Columbus to the New World," while "at night the sphere will be illuminated by the lines of light which will form the outlines of the continents and islands, thus casting over the city torrents of refulgent brilliancy."[16] In Palacio's vision, which was never built, the Earth is a hyperobject glimpsed, but then transformed into a size amenable to human consumption; it becomes a symbol not of human limitation but of "the geographical completion of the earth which was realized by Christopher Columbus' discovery of the New World."[17] A new Earth, now "completed" by Western colonialism, is born again in iron and coal-powered twinkle lights. While the monstrosity of such a design signals human arrogance, at the same time, it reflects an uneasy recognition of the Earth-as-hyperobject: only the boldest and most extravagant human schemes could ever hope to capture it, and even then, they had better involve an iron cage.

This extends the history of Anthropocene-tinged thinking deeper than typically understood. The call to name the industrial period as a new *geological* epoch—the Anthropocene—was popularized in the twenty-first century to account for human-caused climate change.[18] It has provoked an urgent desire on the part of the social sciences to relate the deep history of the Earth, of humans as a species, and of humans as geological actors on the planet. In other words, it has flagged the difficult task of reconciling anthropocentric constructions of history, politics, and economics with the cosmic time of geology, evolution, and planetary change.

Most assume that these two chronological registers have only very recently been put into conversation by ecological thinking; for instance, Dipesh Chakrabarty asserts that "geological time and the chronology of human histories remained unrelated" prior to the rise of modern climate science.[19] On the one hand, there is some truth to the notion that Anthropocene thinking is relatively novel. It is uniquely distinct from prior ecological thought in the recognition that human actions can have disastrous planetary effects. Nineteenth-century thinkers might have bemoaned the local or regional environmental effects of industrialism, but they did not

SCIENTIFIC AMERICAN

[Entered at the Post Office of New York, N. Y., as Second Class Matter. Copyrighted, 1890, by Munn & Co.]

A WEEKLY JOURNAL OF PRACTICAL INFORMATION, ART, SCIENCE, MECHANICS, CHEMISTRY, AND MANUFACTURES.

Vol. LXIII.—No. 17.
Established 1845.

NEW YORK, OCTOBER 25, 1890.

[$3.00 A YEAR.
Weekly.

M. PALACIO'S DESIGN FOR A COLOSSAL MONUMENT IN MEMORY OF CHRISTOPHER COLUMBUS.—[See page 260.]

imagine these effects to be planetary. On the other hand, the Anthropocene claim—that humans are planetary agents—is related to the longer-standing need to figure out how industrial processes were ethically and practically related to the Earth that emerged in the industrial era.

In the nineteenth century, change was construed as occurring along two very distinct chronological and spatial registers: Earth time and human time, Earth scale and the scale of human cities, states, and regions. What did the geological layers of rock strata, which pointed to Earth changes over thousands (and perhaps millions) of years, have to do with Christianity or industrialism? Some conservatives hoped nothing, but these artifacts that spoke of a historical Earth that had not always housed humans as we know them—including the digging up of the first Neanderthal fossil in 1856—were increasingly difficult to ignore. The problem lay in how they should be (or whether they could be) reconciled. The new Earth time involved complex change processes that spanned an unfathomable number of human generations (and beyond). But alongside the deep and slow Earth time, there was also a new sense of industrial time, where awe-inspiring change could disrupt human life in a handful of decades, or even months. Fossil fuels rested at the crux of the puzzle, as they connected industrial power to Earth power, and the long compression of fossils to the explosive propulsion of steam engines.

The deep time of geological, energetic, and fossil processes openly challenged a literal reading of the Bible, which placed human life at the center of the creation story. The Earth of the Bible was old, but still comprehensible in the context of human life and generations. In contrast, the time scales of Earth processes were difficult for humans to imagine. Charles Darwin reflected that the human mind could only "feebly" "comprehend the lapse of time" that he found exhibited in the geological record.[20] Even more humbling for humans, the fossil record showed that Earth had not always housed humans, and that at some point in the future it would no longer be habitable for humans. The new perception of the Earth was thus no less than the beginning of the thorough decentering of the human with, as Stephen Jay Gould put it, the "notion of an almost incomprehensible immensity, with human habitation restricted to a millimicrosecond at the very end!"[21]

FIGURE 3.1. (*opposite*). The Columbus Sphere: A Victorian New Earth.
Source: Cover of *Scientific American*, October 25, 1890.

The new Earth glimpsed by industrial Victorians was bewildering. As historian Greg Myers dryly reflects of the science of energy, the Victorian public "may have wondered what exactly they were supposed to do about the continuing dissipation of the energy of the solar system."[22] While we can infer only so much without having lived in that era, primary sources are rife with a disorientation similar in intensity to that provoked by the later energy crises of nuclear holocaust or climate change. If nature was now constituted by change instead of by balance, what did this mean for Christianity and its omnipotent God? How did human ethics and agency relate to the immensity of planetary actions? These tensions in space and time, between Earth time and human time, and between Earth power and industrial power, were at the heart of the sciences of evolution and energy.[23] Each science offered a different conception of Earth time and Earth power that then played into conceptions of human power and ethics in the age of industrial technology.

Energy science, as well as evolution, should be appreciated as preludes to Anthropocene thinking; they predate climate and Earth systems science by at least a century. The following sections explore these two fossil knowledges of the nineteenth century, with an emphasis on the science of energy. I begin with evolution, even though it gained prominence just *after* the science of energy, as it is a more familiar narrative in global political theory, and as such it is a fitting reminder of how knowledge about the changing material world infused nineteenth-century politics.

THE EARTH OF EVOLUTION

In the course of centuries the naïve self-love of men has
had to submit to two major blows at the hands of science.
The first was when they learnt that our Earth was not
the centre of the universe but only a tiny fragment of
a cosmic system of scarcely imaginable vastness. This is
associated in our minds with the name of Copernicus. . . .
The second blow fell when biological research destroyed man's
supposedly privileged place in creation and proved his descent
from the animal kingdom and his ineradicable animal nature.
This revaluation has been accomplished in our own days
by Darwin, Wallace and their predecessors, though not
without the most violent contemporary opposition.
—SIGMUND FREUD, *Introductory Lectures on Psychoanalysis*[24]

Charles Darwin was not the first to advance a theory of evolution, although he would become the most influential. Evolutionary ideas were circulating in the decades before Darwin's publications, alongside the rising interest in studying fossils and geological strata. Scientists who had proposed various versions of evolution to explain the geological record had been met with strong opposition from the church and from traditionalists. According to Hobsbawm, the theory of evolution could only begin to gain ground in the mid-nineteenth century, with Darwin's theory, in part because of the "happy conjuncture of two facts, the rapid advance of a liberal and 'progressive' bourgeoisie and absence of revolution." In other words, in the wake of the failure of the 1848 revolutions, there was some reassurance that challenges to traditional knowledge, such as the science of evolution, would not necessarily result in massive "social upheaval."[25]

What Darwin, as well as naturalist Alfred Russel Wallace, contributed to the general trend in evolutionary thinking, most notably with Darwin's *On the Origin of Species* in 1859, was a theory about the mechanics of evolution—*how* and *why* species changed, emerged, and disappeared over time. The theory was premised on an understanding of nature as a competitive struggle for the means of procreation, a vision that was inspired by Darwin's reading of Thomas Malthus. The mechanism for evolution was the theory of natural selection, which held that organisms that were better adapted to their environments would survive and procreate more successfully. The better-adapted traits would then more likely pass down to future generations—such "modification by descent" occurred through an unknown mechanism, as there was not yet a genetic explanation for how variations arose or were transmitted from parent to offspring.[26] Over vast but ultimately unknown periods of time, natural selection had resulted in a diversity of species.

Theorizing about evolution was hugely controversial, in many ways more so than the science of energy had been, as evolution more directly addressed the position of the human species. Darwin's theory contradicted a literal reading of the Bible's creation narrative and also challenged the supremacy of humans by positing a familial link between humans and other animals, adopting the metaphor of a great tree of life, a Romantic concept that was "intended to illustrate that the whole of nature is an organic unity, developing from a single set of roots and diversifying in interconnected branches with no more conflict or competition than that exhibited by the organs of one body."[27] Moreover, like the science of energy, evolution asserted that "henceforth the whole cosmos or at least the whole solar system must be conceived as a process of constant or historical change."[28]

According to evolutionary theories, though, these changes did not necessarily have a guiding telos, other than representing the piecemeal survival strategies of different species. The Earth and its many creatures lurched along, branching here and there as a result of a "web of complex relations" that were all but incalculable for humans.[29] The agentic forces of the Earth, expressed as an emergent phenomenon from this web of relations, and sensed through environmental changes to which living organisms adapted, was far grander in scale than human agency, taking place over millions of years and operating on both microscopic and cosmic levels. Darwin's famous closing lines of *On the Origin of Species* (from the first edition) marvel that "there is grandeur in this view of life, with its several powers, having been originally breathed into a few forms or into one; and that, whilst this planet has gone cycling on according to the fixed law of gravity, from so simple a beginning endless forms most beautiful and most wonderful have been, and are being, evolved."

Controversially, both God and humans are absent from Darwin's narrative of the unfolding of the planet over deep time. He had extended only a subtle nod to religion by mentioning, in the passive voice, powers "having been originally breathed into" life, a biblical metaphor (God breathed life into Adam) that gently implied that there could still be room for God as the "first cause" that set evolution going. In later editions, Darwin capitulated by further clarifying this role, specifying that "the Creator" had been the one to first breathe powers into life.[30]

Darwin's nod to God did not stop evolution from coming under considerable attack by theologians. Even in Darwin's later editions, humans were no different than any other living organism in being completely at the whim of a chaotic, and in many senses adversarial, Earth, as "every single organic being may be said to be striving to the utmost to increase in numbers; that each lives by a struggle at some period of its life; that heavy destruction inevitably falls either on the young or old during each generation or at recurrent intervals."[31] Darwin had said little about humans in *On the Origin of Species*, but in his 1871 *The Descent of Man, and Selection in Relation to Sex*, he makes clear that humans share common ancestors with other animals and organisms, and that all human "races" likely belong to the same species and are kin. Despite this later work, which attempted to relate the deep time of evolution to the more immediate time of human development, many questions remained for Darwin and his interlocutors:

How did life begin, how did variations arise, how did human morality emerge and was it special in any way?

Evolution did not offer any consistent ethical program to answer these questions. Darwin remained ambivalent about the connections between the Earth time of evolution and human time, including the role of God as well as the notion of progress. He did not subscribe to any teleology in the evolution of species, and he refers to progress with some inconsistencies, both of which continue to incite debate.[32] On the one hand, Robert Richards argues that the "deeply ingrained sense that [Darwin's] theory explained progress in organisms permeates his text,"[33] which refers to higher and lower forms of organisms, and which also notes that "natural selection will tend to render the organization of each being more specialized and perfect" in the sense of "beings better fitted for their new walks of life."[34] On the other hand, the only standard for organic perfection is, as Darwin often repeats, not a moral ideal but rather an organism's fitness for a particular environment, such that "natural selection, or the survival of the fittest, does not necessarily include progressive development—it only takes advantage of such variations as arise and are beneficial to each creature under its complex relations of life."[35]

Darwin is also somewhat ambivalent about the Earth of evolution. While he famously adored the English countryside around his home, Down House in Kent, which was the site of many of his observations and experiments, his theory of evolution also carried a tragic undertone. The Earth of evolution was not a happy place, even for the fittest. Darwin repeatedly urges us to remember this, perhaps because he himself was so tempted to forget it. Organisms will strive to multiply endlessly, Darwin reasons, and the Earth obviously cannot support infinite numbers of organisms. Applying Malthus and his "struggle for existence" broadly, Darwin concludes that a complex web of interactions with climate, terrain, food supply, predators, and other organisms will create multiple checks on the well-being and numbers of each species, requiring an ongoing struggle for survival on the part of each organism.

Importantly, and this is often ignored by overly simplistic political readings of Darwin, Darwin uses the struggle for existence in "a large and metaphorical sense" in which direct violence plays only a small, and sometimes nonexistent, part. Struggle also might mean surviving drought, relying on birds to spread your seeds, or competing with other plants whose seeds might also entice birds, much of which involves indirect and passive interactions.[36] All the same, the results are frequently death and devastation.

Darwin reflects with melancholy that "we behold the face of nature bright with gladness, we often see superabundance of food; we do not see or we forget that the birds which are idly singing round us mostly live on insects or seeds, and are thus constantly destroying life; or we forget how largely these songsters, or their eggs, or their nestlings, are destroyed by birds and beasts of prey."[37]

There is never a moment when an organism is not struggling; there is no Edenic endpoint when the fittest can exempt themselves from struggle. Any progress that evolution might support is limned with a sense of anxious necessity.

EVOLUTION, INDUSTRIALISM, IMPERIALISM

The ambivalence of evolution on matters of God, progress, and humans' relationship to nature helps to explain why evolution could be interpreted in such a wide array of religious and political directions. In the late nineteenth century, "virtually every political position was advanced as consistent with Darwin's ideas," spanning both the left and right of the political spectrum.[38] It would be impossible here to catalogue every aspect of evolution's influence on nineteenth-century politics. Rather, I want to focus more narrowly on how evolution was applied to the problems, and promise, of industrialization.

To start with, it is well known that evolutionary theories proved amenable to progressive views, and both the liberal left and the socialist left readily adopted them. Evolution resonated with socialists because they had already embraced evolutionary ideas into their theory, as well as the importance of human interactions with the changing technomaterial environment in shaping historical developments. Evolution resonated with liberal economic theories because it could be used to support the ideology of progress through competition in human civilizations; it did not hurt that Darwin drew directly upon Malthus and "the model of capitalist competition."[39] Evolution also helped to launch the many threads of social Darwinism, which applied often simplistic caricatures of the survival of the fittest to human societies, emphasizing struggle and violent power politics. Evolution would also be deployed in racist eugenics theories, despite evidence that Darwin was a committed abolitionist who was arguably more motivated to prove commonalities among human races rather than distinctions.[40] However, such crudely reductionist theories were not the only way to translate Darwin. David Paul Crook describes how an emergent "peace biology" drew upon the cooperative aspects of evolution. The connection between humans and animals could be figured not as a lowering of humanity but as an elevation of animals, contributing to "a holistic ecology that postulated a web of coexistence linking organisms" and that influenced "reform-collectivist and 'new liberal' directions."[41]

Evolution also did not offer a unified, ethical position on industrialization. Unlike some of the leading scientists of energy, who lived in bustling shipbuilding cities like Glasgow, and who interacted early and often with steam engines, Darwin spent most of his life at his rural Down House in Kent, where he lived off a gentleman's income and was not centrally concerned with industrial technologies. This did not stop others from finding evolution relevant to the industrial predicament. Pro-industrialists could read optimism about industrialization into evolution, viewing the use of fossil fuels as evidence of a higher form of civilization that allowed for population and resource increases. It was not difficult to infer this from Darwin's own writing. In *The Descent of Man*, Darwin outlines the rise of "civilized" humans as owing to improvements in intellectual capacity and therefore in arts and tools that aid humans in survival, a combination that had bestowed upon humans "the preeminent position in the world."[42] He also mentions the importance of a cool climate in "leading to industry and the various arts," a development by which "civilized races have extended, and are now everywhere extending, their range, so as to take the place of the lower races."[43] In this vein, a geographical deterministic thread in the science of evolution was deployed to buttress the European claims of superiority across its imperial projects.[44] Technology was the mark of higher races, as it represented the ability to manage nature, and to exempt humans from the limitations still faced by the "lower" races. Alfred Wallace, who had developed the theory of evolution independently of Darwin, was a key proponent of this type of argument, which gained popularity among anthropologists at the time in Europe and the United States (including C. S. Wake, Lewis Henry Morgan, and Gustave Le Bon).[45]

However, at the same time, Darwin reminds us that "development of all kinds depends on many concurrent favourable circumstances," and that "progress is no invariable rule." Sometimes, a "nation will retrograde" as its "inferior" members begin to outnumber the superior ones.[46] Change could produce multiple trajectories and dead ends.[47] While the superior "energy" of England referred to by Darwin—and here he uses the more vague, metaphysical sense of energy—might improve the entire European race, the complexity of environmental interactions also points to the possibility that unforeseen disadvantages could lead to disaster. Darwin concludes that it is difficult to explain the collapse of the ancient Greeks or the Spanish, as well as the rise of England and western Europe, as "individuals and races may have acquired certain indisputable advantages, and yet have perished from failing in other characters."[48] This single line could encapsulate ecological thinking on the risks posed by the Anthropocene today.

Indeed, Darwin, often considered a grandfather of ecology, developed techniques that could be deployed against fossil fuel assemblages. Evolution was itself a robust ecological treatise, charting the multiple interrelationships between life and its environs, although it never referred to itself as ecological. Ernst Haeckel, a Darwin enthusiast, was the first to invent the term *ecology* in 1866, just seven years following the publication of *On the Origin of Species*. Ecology was not new. The study of human–environment interactions was as old as any lineage of human thought, and Haeckel was only giving a name to a tradition that has been traced—in the West at least—from the ancient Greeks to Carl Linnaeus, Jean-Baptiste Lamarck, and Alexander von Humboldt, many of whom influenced Darwin. Darwin also read and cited Haeckel's work, teasing in a letter that Haeckel had a passion for "coining new words,"[49] though Darwin never used the word *ecology* himself.[50] Nevertheless, Haeckel had invented ecology as a term precisely to describe the consequences of Darwin's work on thinking about the human–Earth relationship.

By ecology, Haeckel was playing on the Greek οἶκος (*oikos*, or house, also the root of *economy*), and he defined it as "the body of knowledge concerning the economy of nature—the investigation of the total relations of the animal both to its inorganic and to its organic environment; . . . in a word, ecology is the study of all those complex interrelations referred to by Darwin as the conditions of the struggle for existence."[51]

Ecology, in other words, studied the connection between animals and environment, man and nature. In this sense, ecological thinking, whether ancient or contemporary, has always offered what Eugene Odum calls "a bridge between science and society,"[52] a drive to relate humans to the Earth. The shift that sets the late nineteenth century apart from this longer tradition, besides the naming of ecology as a self-conscious and organized discipline, was the novel challenge of relating a changing Earth to a dynamic, industrial human civilization. In the concept of natural selection, Darwin had proposed a powerful explanatory mechanism for change that could integrate these time spans. Moreover, the struggle for existence could be interpreted as an ethical program that took the new

Earth into account, in which progress was defined simply as one's ability to survive amid the congeries of environmental interactions. Even the emergence of human morality and rational thinking could be explained by evolutionary theory as an adaptive advantage for species survival.[53]

Another distinction that sets nineteenth-century political-ecological thinking apart is the consequences of the new Earth for human and non-human agency. Natural selection practices its "tentative,"[54] but pervasive, agency through a multiplicity of struggling interactions and favors only those chance combinations that are best adapted to a given context. While evolution can (and has) been interpreted as a thoroughly materialist explanation of the world, it is not a world of simple determinism, or linear cause-and-effect.[55] Later biologists and political theorists have pointed out that it is the complexity of those interactions that leaves room for creativity, indeterminacy, and, ultimately, an ecologically inspired caution about human life on planet Earth.[56] Even great civilizations have "degraded" due to unknown circumstances, and so while industrialization could well offer some advantages to particular nations, evolution could also be used to raise concerns about the unforeseen effects of industrialization.

This was a different approach to the new Earth, and to human ethics, from the one offered by the science of energy, although both inspired a variety of positions on industrialization, including pro-industrial, progressive views as well as more ecological thinking. However, while evolution provided an ecological model that tended to be rather cautious and tentative, with the role of human agency nuanced and constrained, the discourse of the science of energy, and especially its strident, apocalyptic readings of the death of the Sun, would feed into a more urgent, and triumphalist, narrative about human life on Earth.

A GEO-THEOLOGY OF ENERGY

The political influence of the science of energy may be less well known than that of evolution, but this was not due to any circumspection on the part of the early scientists of energy. The northern British proselytizers of energy, in particular, were much more willing than Darwin to insert energy into political and religious debates, and they embraced an energy logic that was friendly to industrial capitalism and that came to inform the dominant, Western relationship to fuels. This is not to say that their early energetic thinking has remained intact across the intervening decades.

But while the dominant logics of energy have morphed over time, this early geo-theology of energy continues to haunt how Westerners engage with fuel, especially when it comes to the governance of work as a site of energy transformation.

Three themes were prominent in this early energy logic:

1. Earth conceived as an engine
2. Universal aspirations
3. Work

First, the new Earth, composed of energetic flows, suggested ambivalent possibilities to those intent on industrialization, reflecting the Janus-faced nature of the two laws of thermodynamics. Like the science of evolution, energy science treated the Earth as an ever-changing entity. With the first law of thermodynamics, industrial processes could be understood as merely local currents within the surrounding oceans of energetic transformations, whose energy was fundamentally stable in overall quantity. On the other hand, the Earth of the second law of thermodynamics was one of energy dissipation—energy was never lost, per se, but it could become less useful to humans—and this resonated with more pronounced fears about technology and its consequences, as well as about the limits of the Earth in the face of industrialization.

The words *dissipation* and *decay*, which recur in energetic studies, happened to be satisfactorily "loaded with moral connotations."[57] As N. Katherine Hayles notes, the language of dissipation in the second law "places entropic heat loss in the same semantic category as deplorable personal habits. The reversal of this tendency requires a 'restoration' to be wrought by humans and their newfound knowledge of the Earth."[58] Dissipation also enabled the northern British energy scientists to downplay the deep Earth time that evolution seemed to necessitate. Again, energy functioned as middle way. The Earth was certainly older and more dynamic than once believed, Thomson hypothesized, but the inevitable dissipation of the Sun's energy meant that the planet could not be old enough for the gradual evolutionary changes that Darwin proposed.[59]

Second, the science of energy satisfactorily resonated with the universalizing aspirations of industrial capitalism. Evolution speculates on the general mechanism for how organisms change over time, but the science of energy purports to explain change, in sometimes atomic detail, *everywhere and across time*, from geological actions to human labor and planetary motion. If energy was to be the linchpin to understanding change in the cosmos, then it made sense that it was also the crucial element fueling human civilization and the power of the British Empire, and that the laws of thermodynamics could potentially have practical applications in all aspects of human life.

Energy suggested that the Earth, riven by newly glimpsed hyperobjects (fossilized swamps, species extinction, and evolution), could be managed as an engine, which was energy's preeminent metaphor for explaining natural change. This was partly metaphor, but also literal, in that an engine could be understood as an energy transformer converting inputs (solar rays, carbon, glucose, oxygen) into outputs (work) that could be measured, mapped, and governed. However, engines have a touch of magic. They are machines of difference, relying on temperature or potential energy gradients, which they promptly flatten in the service of "the creation of another difference," that is, the movement of matter.[60] Industrial heat engines, fed by fossil fuels, dealt with enormous gradients, converting planetary deep time into industrial quick time, as the lives of hundreds of plants and animals become a thrust of pistons.

Armed with the fertile metaphor of the engine and its manifold inputs, outputs, and components, it seemed that anything and everything could be connected to energy expenditures, efficiencies, and waste. The universality of energy contributed to the difficulty in defining it, even among physicists, but especially when it was employed as a logic of governance. What was to be counted as energy, and therefore governed by the laws of thermodynamics, was a shifting, and usually expanding, terrain. This is evident, for example, in Jevons's *The Coal Question*, which points to coal as the foundation of the British nation, such that "even things that at first glance seemed to have little to do with coal, such as the city's water supply, were revealed to be part of an interlocking fossil-fuel system."[61] From the earliest consolidation of the science of energy, then, the process of making something count as part of an energy assemblage was a political one, given that counting as energy meant becoming visible to increasingly centralized, scientific schemes of governance.

Moreover, recall from chapter 2 that energy and entropy are epistemological constructs. Thermodynamics describes how we can organize or understand change over time through mathematical equations, but things called energy and entropy do not actually exist. The claim that energy is universal, then, can also be understood as a Western claim that a certain epistemology of change is universal. Energy therefore helped to advance what Walter Mignolo has called the "Western code," a "belief in one sustainable system of knowledge," and one superior epistemology that trumpets itself as the best epistemology for the planet.[62]

Third, the science of energy translated the human relationship to deep Earth time, and to immense Earth powers, through the lens of work, and this formed the basis of the northern British ethics of the science of energy, as well as its approach to human agency. The handful of prominent scientists of energy in northern Britain, many of whom were devoted Scottish Presbyterians, had an interest in charting a middle road between evangelicals, who read the Bible literally, and the threat of materialist atheism that seemed to lie beneath evolution. Evolution suggested a modicum of human impotence, as survival would simply be granted to organisms that were fortunate enough to be the fittest. Recall Freud's judgment that evolution dealt a "major blow" to the "naïve self-love of men" (the first being Copernicus, and another being Freud's own efforts "to prove to the ego that it is not even master in its own house").[63]

Thermodynamics also deals humans a major blow: humans were impotent in the face of the laws of thermodynamics. Entropy *would* increase regardless—"Things fall apart; the centre cannot hold; / Mere anarchy is loosed upon the world"—and some amount of waste was inevitable in engines and in life.[64] The science of energy advanced particular techniques by which human ingenuity could make the best of the situation, codified in the new discipline of engineering. But for Scottish Presbyterians, the practical pleasures of engineering were limned with moral import. Given that energy was constantly running down beyond the grasp of humans, humans had a moral imperative to milk the most out of whatever energy they could by maximizing work and minimizing waste, what historians of science M. Norton Wise and Crosbie Smith call an ethos of "work and waste."[65] This geo-theology of energy helped to inject the work ethic, which already appealed to Protestant discipline, with new scientific rigor and systematicity that was appropriate to the Second Industrial Revolution. Perhaps the most telling and politically consequential definition of energy is the engineer's: energy is the ability to do work.

WORK AND WASTE

Scottish scientists of energy were among the key proselytizers of thermodynamics, and they advanced their own ethical program for relating the energetic Earth to industrial life. They combined an engineering concern for efficiency with the pragmatic spirit of Scottish Presbyterianism to ultimately make sense of the vastness of the energetic Earth from the perspective of the limited domain of human life spans. My analysis of the geo-theology of energy is indebted to Smith and Wise and their study of Thomson's commitment to an ethos of "work and waste." However, I deploy their biographical and historical studies of Thomson and other energy scientists in order to more fully appreciate energy in a global political context. The moral framework of this group of scientists, on the one hand, emerged from the specific material practices of a Scottish shipbuilding context. On the other hand, elements of this geo-theology helped to constitute a broader, Western energy logic that would have planetary repercussions. Exploring energy as a "ruling idea," to adopt Marx's term,[66] involves analyzing work and waste alongside evolutionary ethics, and also investigating its political application as a strategy for governing work and workers (the subject of part II).

Not all of the early energy scientists were Scottish Presbyterians (or even Scottish). Nevertheless, the northern British group of scientists, which included Thomson, Rankine, Tait, and Maxwell, contributed to imparting a Protestant grammar into energy that traveled easily in Anglo-European contexts, and that mapped onto more generic Christian theologies that privileged asceticism and thrift. The Protestant geo-theology of energy proved sticky, especially when it accorded with the dominant religion of another rising industrial power, the United States.

The logic behind work and waste stemmed from struggles with the consequences of the second law of thermodynamics, which stated that entropy would tend to increase in a closed system. One way of interpreting this was that the energy of the Earth, and perhaps the solar system and even the wider cosmos, was running down, and this meant that time was running down too. Even if one quibbled with the so-called heat death hypothesis, which envisioned the eventual exhaustion of cosmic energy and, thus, the cold, dark death of the universe, the irreversibility of time and the incontrovertible aging of the Earth remained pressing metaphysical problems. Lucretius could resign himself to a dying Earth, and find respite in peaceful gardens, and others in the nineteenth century could carve out their own philosophical retreats (Darwin, Thoreau), but for energy's proponents, as well as the many less privileged inhabitants of the world, most of whom were increasingly entwined with engines and industry, such a retreat was untenable.

According to the science of energy, humans were thus limited in two ways. First, humans could only take advantage of energy inside a rather small window of space-time, when it was manifested in forms that were available to human technologies. Even still, much of it was inevitably destined to be lost as waste. Jevons, who warned of the exhaustibility of coal, argued that "material nature presents to us the aspect of one continuous waste of energy and matter beyond our control. The power we employ in the greatest engine is but an infinitesimal portion withdrawn from the immeasurable expense of natural forces."[67] The second, and more daunting, limitation for humans is that the entropic decay of energy points toward the limitations of the Earth and its resources, at least from an industrial perspective. At the same time, it suggests that humans are only marginally important, as temporary occupants of the Earth, rather than as the central feature of the planet's life span. While this second realization helped to buttress early environmental thinking, it also made room for faith in a God who could rescue humans from entropic dissipation. In the words of Thomson, "As for the future, we may say, with equal certainty, that inhabitants of the earth can not continue to enjoy the light and heat essential to their life for many million years longer unless sources now unknown to us are prepared in the great storehouse of creation."[68]

Although energy emerged at a time in which the ideology of progress reigned, Thomson and the other scientists of energy were rather ambivalent about it. They sounded a distinctly tragic note when they wrote about the moral consequences implied by entropy. Prigogine contrasts Thomson's tone to the attitude of evolutionary thinking, noting that Thomson "reminds us more of ancient mythological and religious archetypes than of the progressive complexification and diversification described by biology."[69] In this way, energy reflected the resurgence of ancient motifs that, through the lens of Scottish Presbyterianism, motivated thermodynamic ethics. Smith emphasizes that, like many Christian denominations in this period, the Presbyterian Church was in upheaval over how to respond to the new scientific doctrines of change. In 1843, just before the science of energy emerged, the Presbyterian Church suffered a great "Disruption" that reflected a growing dissatisfaction among some more evangelical members, who resented the aristocratic, moderate culture that had prevailed in the eighteenth century during the Scottish Enlightenment.[70] Thomas Chalmers, the leader of an evangelical movement called the Free Church, attempted a synthesis of evolution and theology that retained a theistic role for God as the original cause that set the natural laws into motion, alongside a political program that "was essentially static and cyclical" rather than progressive.[71] Meanwhile, the moderate wing of the Church struggled to respond to the challenges from Chalmers and the Free Church on one side, and to the most recent scientific knowledge on the other, at least in a way that left room for God.

For the northern British wing of energy science, energy appeared to herald a way through this morass. Smith outlines how energy was aligned with a "new 'moderate' presbyterianism" that aimed to adapt the Church to the industrial era by serving as "a counter to the seductions of enthusiast biblical revivals on the one hand and evolutionary materialism on the other."[72] The middle way found a place for God in a dynamic and changing world, accommodating religion to physics. Entropy was a cornerstone concept, as it was something that could be identified by science and math, and even measured, while also resonating with the tragic views of evangelicals. From the perspective of Christianity, entropy was more appealing than evolution because it implied that natural laws still had unfathomable dimensions. Entropy kept the thoroughly mechanistic universe of the first law of thermodynamics from having the final word.[73]

The religious overtones of entropy were not lost on scientists and scholars with more secular leanings. Friedrich Engels, for example, vociferously objected to the heat death hypothesis as contradictory and "stupid," and warned that the heat death narrative could become a doorway through which religion entered physics.[74] Similarly, entropy is absent in Tyndall's writings, and historian Elizabeth Neswald surmises that its absence is due to "his uneasiness about its cosmological consequences," and his preference for a secular model "of a balanced world of cycles." Entropy also proved uncomfortable for German materialists, who had much in common with Tyndall, and "who viewed the dissipation hypothesis as an attempt to smuggle the Biblical creation-to-apocalypse narrative back into science."[75]

So on the one hand, entropy was deeply seated within science, where it seemed that despite the decay and dissipation, there were also some law-like behaviors that could help humans along. On the other hand, the evident limitations that humans faced—the fragility of the world, and the mortality of all living bodies—left room for God the eternal and ever-energetic, just as the book of Isaiah promised in its view of the planet: "Lift up your eyes to the heavens, and look upon the earth beneath: for the heavens shall vanish away like smoke, and the earth shall wax old like a garment, and they that dwell therein shall die in like manner: but my salvation shall be for ever, and my righteousness shall not be abolished."[76]

This very passage inspired Thomson, a central figure in the science of energy, as he came to terms with the directional flow of energy. In a draft of Thomson's famous "Dynamical Theory of Heat," he delivers his energy cosmology in terms that echo the poetic chant of the Nicene Creed ("We believe in one God, the Father Almighty, maker of heaven and Earth"). Thomson's creed goes, "I believe the tendency in the material world is for motion to become diffused, . . . I believe that no physical action can ever restore the heat emitted from the sun. . . . 'The Earth shall wax old &c.' The permanence of the present forms & circumstances of the physical world is limited."[77] For Thomson, God was the ultimate source for all energy in the universe, which meant that God alone was exempt from the laws of thermodynamics. Only He could create and destroy energy. Only He could reverse its dissipating flow in an act of creation.

Humans were left with these constraints, that "the Earth shall wax old &c," and, as the book of Isaiah continues, that "the moth shall eat them like a garment, and the worm shall eat them like wool."[78] The only choice while on Earth was to make the best use of energy as it appears.[79] Thomson muses about this "difficulty" posed by entropy:

> it is not known that [the lost energy] is available to mankind. The fact is, it may I believe be demonstrated that the work is *lost to man* irrecoverably; but not lost in the material world. Although no destruction of energy can take place in the material world without an act of power possessed only by the supreme ruler, yet transformations take place which remove irrecoverably from the control of man sources of power which, if the opportunity of turning them to his own account had been made use of, might have been rendered available.[80]

The urgent, moral dimensions of thermodynamics are clear in this passage. Thomson sets up the problem with dramatic language and italicized emphasis ("*lost to man* irrecoverably") and then concludes with judgmental regret—"if the opportunity of turning [energy transformations] to his own account had been made use of."

Thermodynamics thus pointed to an opening that rescued God from the thoroughly mechanistic universe by reasserting the separation between God and the world. Wise and Smith observe that, because God was outside processes of decay, then decay was associated with evil. As a result, goodness was realized by wresting progress from decay, by using human knowledge of the first law to fight back the second, which was perceived as ultimately "choosing whether to turn nature's decay to the benefit of humanity or to lose it entirely."[81] According to this geo-theology of energy, the waste of an imperfect engine was not only an engineer's loss of work, and therefore a loss of money; it was also a kind of evil, a local manifestation of a much larger truth, a glimpse into the frightening abyss beyond the human-made world, a world that "resonated with traditional, harsh Calvinist views on the fallen nature of a world now inhabited by a 'drunken and dissipated crew.'"[82] Waste exercised an existential fear that was "not simply the failure to turn available resources into salable commodities, or the waste of an individual's time on Earth; it is the waste of TIME absolutely, for all humanity and for all time."[83] For if time is an arrow and not a cycle, then waste means an *absolute* loss to the past, with no possibility of restoration.

Energy's "fall" from work to irrecoverable waste, and from hot to cold in a piston's thrust, is mirrored in the doubled laws of thermodynamics, in the newly complicated figuration of nature, and in the fall from good to evil. As with many mythologies of nature, the laws of thermodynamics, and the doubled threat/opportunity implied by the fall from work to waste, also has gendered aspects. In his study of allegories of thermodynamics, Bruce Clarke reflects that the first law of energy conservation is "classical patriarchal ideology" that reifies energy as virile, as opposed to dull, feminine matter, such that "the first law infinitely conserves God's divine energies and patriarchal prerogatives. The Devil is in the material and temporal details—entropy, friction, and waste, the demons of the second law."[84] Because the second law and evil are inevitable and tragic, humans' only recourse is to wrest what goodness (masculine order) they can from the potential of the hot/chaotic feminized matter available.

Read through Scottish Presbyterianism, energy resources like coal or water were "freely provided" gifts from God, such that waste—or at least the failure to work toward reducing waste—became the failure to properly accept these gifts. If coal was a gift of grace, then it was also imperative upon humans to *use* it, as "once the gift of grace had been accepted, man had a moral duty to direct, and not waste, the natural gifts."[85] It was nothing short of "the duty of humanity to make use of the limited sources of disequilibrium available for industry and improvement, sources continually going to waste in the course of time."[86] The alternative—leaving the coal, oil, or gas in the ground, where its slower dissipation over many millions of years serves no human purpose—would be to abandon nature to dissipation, a term that, through energy, rang with both physical and moral (and gendered) connotations.

The geo-theology of the northern British scientists, detailed in Wise and Smith's work, was only one wing of thermodynamics—albeit a popular one—but it had the advantage of being conducive to imperial politics and industrial interests, while at the same time appeasing Protestantism. This early culture of energy was soon outmoded and reworked, while other aspects, like Thomson's Earth age calculations, were publicly disproven. Nevertheless, the Scottish Presbyterian synthesis, and its geo-theological justifications for work and waste, are important in that they represent a foundational model for how thermodynamics could be folded into imperial, Christian, and industrial projects. The religious undertone made possible by this version of energy, even if stripped of the particularities of Scottish Presbyterianism, would prove eminently useful to mine managers, colonial administrators, and social reformers.

A PRO-INDUSTRIAL ENERGY LOGIC

The tactics of work and waste could be inserted into many aspects of industrial and imperial life. The engineering discourse of energy "became a ubiquitous feature of the programs and controversies of progressive and conservative reformers alike."[87] On an energetic Earth, everything under the Sun was connected by energy and the fundamental law of its stability in quantity (if not in quality) through time. Tyndall is worth quoting at length here to get a sense of the breathlessness of much of the discourse about the energetic Earth: "Waves may change to ripples, and ripples to waves,—magnitude may be substituted for number, and number for magnitude,—asteroids may aggregate to suns, suns may resolve themselves into florae and faunae, and florae and faunae melt in air,—the flux of power is eternally the same. It rolls in music through the ages, and all terrestrial energy,—the manifestations of life as well as the display of phenomena are, but the modulations of its rhythm."[88]

Tyndall's Earth or "Nature"—to which "nothing can be added; from Nature nothing can be taken away"[89]—was on this reading "a cosmic abstraction . . . rather than a limited terrestrial environment, or material ecosystem" as in Darwin's theory of evolution.[90] The grandiosity of energetic thinking, which connected humans to a "cosmic abstraction," also blurred "the distinction between industry and nature, mechanism and organism."[91] In breaking down such boundaries, energy became the basis for ecological thinking, alerting humans to the ways in which industrial systems were nested within other nonhuman flows (discussed in chapter 5). Energetic worldviews might also be used to challenge anthropocentrism, as all bodies could be depicted as composed of energy, with "vegetable and animal bodies as machines within a matrix of energy relations."[92]

In practice, though, many of the early scientists of energy, including the northern British group, drew pro-industrial conclusions. For one, by naturalizing fossil fuel regimes, elites could elide the radical difference between fossil fuel and solar regimes, as well as paper over the novel problems of pollution, consumption, and waste presented by the industrial era.[93] Industrialization might be nested within Earth flows, such that it was depicted as a tiny, "infinitesimal" process within the vastness of Earth time. The naturalization of industry was used to effectively neuter its ramifications, as the fundamental stability of the Earth of energy conservation would drown out any untoward impact.

Likewise, if industry was naturalized, then the challenging mismatch between human, industrial, and Earth temporalities was also smoothed over. Through the geo-theology of energy, the public could be reassured that there was a theological and philosophical stability beneath the otherwise frightening newness of industrialization. In his study of the Victorian "ecological imagination," Allen MacDuffie explores this paradox: Europeans could marvel over industrial innovations, but because fossil fuels were only tapping into the tiniest portion of Earth's majesty, they could find solace in the belief "that such a world was merely the latest expression of forces and laws already known, or anticipated, by preceding generations."[94] After all, while nature was constantly changing, it was also marked by a conservative stability at its deepest levels, as depicted in the first law of thermodynamics.

Moreover, if energy was supposed to be the keystone to explaining the world and all of its transformations (not to mention a gift from God), then its possession and exploitation was an obvious good. The future prosperity of nations could be directly connected to the quality of their energy and their energy-driven machines through a geopolitical judgment that hinged upon energetic accounts. William Gourlie, a Glaswegian botanist with an interest in fossils, sums up this sentiment, directly linking Glasgow's "valuable deposits of coal, ironstone, limestone, and sandstone" to its global prosperity, as "this almost unlimited supply of coal and iron has enabled [Glasgow] to stretch a hundred arms to the most distant corners of the Earth."[95] The relationship between supplies of energy and national prosperity was manifestly evident to the scientists of energy and their early followers, who saw in energy a knowledge that could govern imperial flows of goods and power. As historian Anson Rabinbach observes, "the nation that most efficiently used and conserved the existing supply of the world's energy—including both labor power and technology—would also win the race for industrial supremacy."[96]

Energy, however, was not a stable descriptor, and "because energy was perceived to be elusive, the means of measuring and representing it became a matter of concern and debate throughout the nineteenth century."[97] As a result, the politics of energy began with the question of which things were to be counted as energy and governed by its techniques. From the human body to the universe, the metaphor of the engine as a closed system, with energy as its foundational unit, provided guidance for administrators. As Scottish physicist Balfour Stewart proclaimed in 1875 in *The Conservation of Energy*, "We may regard the Universe in the light of a vast physical machine," and thus regard "the laws of energy as the laws of working of this machine."[98] From an initial desire to improve steam engines, scientists and administrators could now apply energetic metaphors to such problems as the design of factories, the nutrition of laborers, the laying of underwater telegraph cables, the freshwater needs of imperial trade and military ships, the availability of healthy and vigorous workers for steam engines, or disease outbreaks in burgeoning, polluted, and filthy industrial cities.[99] Energy was a unit through which all of these problems could be connected, measured, charted, and managed.

EFFICIENCY

Efficiency was a key organizing strategy for the energetic "improvement" of human laborers, "wastelands," and engines, the means by which to "[turn] unproductive waste into productive work."[100] The desire to measure inputs and outputs, and to compute the "effectiveness" of machines has a long history, but with the laws of thermodynamics, the concern for efficiency intensified into a broader scientific fascination.[101] The scientific knowledge of energy and efficiency were born together, both emerging out of the polluted miasma of nineteenth-century industrial northern Britain. This is more than temporal coincidence; energy and efficiency appear to have been so intimately intertwined in their emergence as to be almost inseparable. While the science of energy emerged through the desire to improve steam engines—that is, to make them more efficient— likewise, efficiency only "reach[ed] its mature technical form" through the science of energy and the techniques of measurement and technologies it engendered.[102]

Like energy, efficiency started out as a "technical invention, created by engineers and physicists" in an industrial context, but quickly "became promiscuous, describing activities of all sorts, including marriage, fuel consumption, use of leisure time, and political and moral behavior."[103] Also like energy, efficiency can be understood as having dual, and sometimes contradictory, implications. In her history of efficiency, Jennifer Karns Alexander notes that efficiency has both a conservative meaning and a dynamic one. The conservative meaning posits efficiency as static, suggesting balance and conservation through minimization of waste (akin to the first law of thermodynamics). Meanwhile, the dynamic meaning "brought as its reward not merely conservation but growth" through careful management.[104] Similarly, the second law of thermodynamics gives energy the dynamic quality of decay, the careful surveillance of which is necessary for industrial progress. The drive for efficiency in the use of energy, as both the improved operation of bodies and machines, but also as the progressive ability to do ever more work, was implemented at the level of individual bodies and machines and also at the level of populations, cities, and imperial flows of resources and goods.

Improving efficiency requires the ability to measure things as precisely as possible. The ability to quantify work and waste in particular "had become the foundation of progress, industrial and scientific, theoretical and practical."[105] Advances in measurement had also been crucial to the science of energy. Joule had relied upon improved thermometers to record the "mechanical equivalent of heat," and his efforts were echoed by experiments to improve chlorimeters, which measured chlorine and were used in cotton mills; pyrometers, which measured the melting points of metals and were used in iron smelting; and dynamometers, which aimed to measure the work done by machines, so as to compare steam engines as well as "carriages, ploughs, canal boats, machinery, and tools of every description."[106] The nutrition and health of human bodies could also be better quantified and improved, as "the value of mechanical effect [of a machine] was the value of physical labour, which in Glasgow's oversaturated labour market was the value of bread, or the cost of subsistence."[107]

Anson Rabinbach refers to this nineteenth-century figuration as the "human motor," a metaphor inspired by thermodynamics that claims that "the protean force of nature, the productive power of industrial machines, and the body in motion were all instances of the same dynamic laws, subject to measurement."[108] Humans, nature, and machines were interconnected through the nexus of energy, but they became legible only to the extent that they were dynamic, or productive. The resulting rise of "productivism" as a leading political goal asserted "the primacy and identity of all productive activity."[109] This was evident in the concept of labor power, which viewed human bodies as sites of energy exchange, but which also applied the concept of work to all social activities, becoming "a totalizing framework that subordinated all social activities to production, raising the human project of labor to a universal attribute of nature."[110]

STATISTICS AND STANDARDS

If governing energy meant inserting one's measuring tools into incredibly complex cosmic flows, then new mathematic techniques were required in order to make sense of them. The science of energy faced this problem on a molecular level. Heat was now understood as molecular, but it was practically impossible to know the positions, speeds, and vectors of each and every molecule, which would be necessary in order to accurately predict molecular behavior. In answer, scientists like James Clerk Maxwell, Ludwig Boltzmann, and Josiah Willard Gibbs devised a statistical mechanics that examined the properties of gases and other substances at the population level through statistics and probability.

Just as probability contributed a better understanding of heat, so, too, did it propose a new explanation for entropy, or the second law of thermodynamics. The general statement—entropy will increase spontaneously in a closed system—could be more accurately rephrased through the language of probability: it is *extremely likely* (though not absolutely preordained) that entropy will increase in a closed system. In other words, energy tends toward a more dissipated organization (higher entropy) because there are many more ways, or microstates, for molecules to be distributed randomly throughout a substance than there are for it to be concentrated, and thus a sustained concentration of energy is highly unlikely, but not impossible.

The probabilistic explanation of entropy made the phenomenon more quantifiable, but still not completely transparent to humans. It is impossible to know everything about a group of molecules at once, an obstacle later underlined by the Heisenberg uncertainty principle (1927), which states that you cannot simultaneously know the position and velocity of a molecule. Dennis the Menace (nature the trickster) still has his secrets.

The difficulty of knowing the position, vector, and speed of every molecule in a substance is in many ways analogous to the difficulty of charting energy flows in factories, cities, nations, and on Earth as a whole, when multiple sites of energy transformation (i.e., bodies, machines, or organisms) are interacting. Statistics proposes to make sense of this enormous data set by finding trends that can then be acted upon. In effect, statistical math was a tool that could hope to connect the enormity of Earth time and powers to the practical needs of human life in maximizing work.

If measuring tools were to be helpful in governing work and workers across imperial sites, then measuring units must be both standardized and globalized. In *The Mechanics of Internationalism*, Martin Geyer traces standardization movements for the metric system, coinage, and the gold standard between 1850 and 1900 as an important dimension of the "rise of internationalism."[111] We should not be surprised to find that the scientists of energy, specifically Joule, Thomson, and James Clerk Maxwell, were key figures in pushing for global standards for units to measure length, mass, and time. The inventors of new measurement gadgets would profit from standardization, as "the value of that property [e.g., the pyrometer] depended on its transferability throughout Europe, its universality."[112] While the global diffusion of measuring tools was profitable, it was also necessary to a civilizing mission that aimed at improving wasteful peoples and lands. The activities of peoples and lands around the world needed to be made comparable to each other in order to be integrated into global markets and global systems of governance. It is not for nothing that Britain's global measuring standard was called the *imperial* system.

Of course, the rising popularity of precise measurement, along with the techniques of probability and statistics to understand population-level data, did not appear de novo with the science of energy. Rather, what was novel was the way in which a dominant energy logic could connect these techniques to the work that made up fossil fuel systems. Energetic governmentality emerges at the moment when it becomes possible to perceive energy as the standard unit that produces data for fossil capital and its desire to put the world to work.

CONCLUSION

At this point, it should be clear that energy cannot be reduced to purely scientific knowledge, nor to fossil fuels and machines. Fossil fuels, by virtue of being fossils, connected humans to gargantuan assemblages that escaped human understanding and its schemes of industrial governance. Victorians may not yet have realized the planetary changes set in motion by fossil fuels, and yet the mood of terror, even horror, that is so pronounced in climate politics today was not lost on those who lived in the nineteenth century. In part II, I show how Victorian empires responded to the frightening new Earth by doubling down on efforts to capture and govern forces coded as chaotic or wasteful, and extending a veneer of ecological control globally as part of "a long ascent from chaos and disorder to perfect managerial control."[113] Thermodynamics, when captured by a logic of energy that emphasized the value of efficient and productive work, contributed to the dream of perfect managerial control. Through a geo-theological rendering of energy, industrial imperialism could be justified as a moral project in line with the maxim of work and waste.

Energy did not invent work, nor the drive to put the world to work. The geo-theology of energy was simply another method for tackling the much older problem of labor governance. Nevertheless, in the domain of fuel, the energy–work connection would become momentous. While this chapter showed how work seeped into energy science, the next chapter traces how energetic metaphors began to inflect the ethos and management of work in the Victorian era.

4   WORK BECOMES ENERGETIC

> We now employ the term Energy to signify the
> power of doing work.
> —PETER GUTHRIE TAIT, "Recent Advances
> in Physical Science" (1876)

Like energy, work does not have a stable ontology. The very notion that
it does—that work is somehow foundational to human life—is itself a
modern phenomenon. Amy Wendling asserts that labor is a ruling idea, a
"bourgeois political construct" on which capitalist modernity is erected.[1]
Laboring, the human-inflected activity of work, is the foundation of the
modern subject,[2] and it has expanded into a "black hole, collapsing other
modes of conceptualizing human activity under its hegemonic purview."[3]
All human activity is under pressure to relate itself to laboring. Because
labor is a ruling idea, even those who resist capitalism learn to frame their
demands accordingly. Movements for the working class, women, immi-
grants, or the unemployed ask to join the ranks of waged workers and
to be treated equitably at work, or to have their unpaid or invisible labor
remunerated as work. Work remains necessary to becoming a worthy
citizen.

The ruling idea of labor is intertwined with energy in that, following
the birth of thermodynamics, work was increasingly understood through
energetic metaphors, and valued and measured as a site of energy transformation. The term *labor* is often intended to refer to human work. In
this book, I am less interested in making those distinctions, and so use

the terms somewhat interchangeably, although my emphasis is on the concept of work. This is because one of the hallmarks of energetic thinking, and of industrialization, is the universalization of energy as the unit that underlies all activity. The machine, the horse, and the human were all energy transformers when they worked, and their power (rate of work done) and efficiency (minimization of energy wasted) could be compared, as in the evaluation of engines according to horsepower. Watt's standardization of the unit of horsepower is an exemplary precursor to the logic of energy. Work captures this larger sense of the planet conceived energetically and dynamically through the new sciences of energy and evolution.

Like energy, work integrates manifold streams of ancient wisdom into a purportedly novel, modern construct. It is a move shared by all ideologies of progress: in order to show improvement, it is necessary to assemble a history of connected practices that demonstrate a linear progression, against which the current moment is to be compared favorably. Only after the invention of energy could we conceive of histories of energy stretching back to Neolithic foragers. Curated histories of energy are, at the same time, wrapped up with histories of work. For example, in order to make the claim that fossil capitalism improved society by putting the world to work, a history must be curated in which work is fundamental to becoming human but, prior to industrialization, had been somehow inadequate to liberal democratic notions of self-development. The very same history of work/energy might also be interpreted otherwise: that the unfolding of energy, or work, has not been one of progress but of decay, and that industrialization has augured sorrow not only for workers, but for life on Earth.

Regardless of the prognosis, such histories agree on one thing: like energy, work underwent fundamental alterations in the modern era. From Max Weber's *The Protestant Ethic and the Spirit of Capitalism*, to E. P. Thompson's "Time, Work-Discipline, and Industrial Capitalism," to Hannah Arendt's ruminations on work, labor, and action as constituting *The Human Condition*, and most influentially in Karl Marx's insights about labor, social theorists have sought to understand the complete reversal in the Western valuation and social organization of work, from the ancient Greeks' disdain for it, to its revered status in the modern era. How did we get from Aristotle, who was repelled by the vulgarity of work, and insisted that freedom required leisure, to Locke or Hegel, who located the possibility of property (Locke) and self-actualization (Hegel) in the activity of labor?

The shift in the value of work, from a task that got in the way of citizenship, to an activity that was at the very foundation of it, began well before energy science and the proliferation of fossil-fueled machines in the nineteenth century. Locke and Hegel were still mostly pastoral (and thereby solar) in their understanding of labor, and yet both were advancing a modern, and positive, valuation of work as central to human identity. The capacity for work was what vaulted humans above the natural world, and what differentiated human activity from horse activity—as well as men's activities from women's. Human labor transformed the common Earth into private property, Locke famously asserted, and politics arises mainly to ensure the security of that property.[4] Hegel, meanwhile, referred to work as a "formative" activity for achieving selfhood. In his master–slave dialectic, it is only the slave who has the ability to become truly self-conscious by laboring upon objects: "Through work, however, the bondsman becomes conscious of what he truly is."[5]

Perhaps most famously, Weber dated the emergence of a capitalist-friendly work ethic to the Calvinist offshoots of the Reformation in the sixteenth and seventeenth centuries. By the time thermodynamics arrived in the mid-nineteenth century, the work ethic, at least as Weber describes it, was fully entrenched as the "spirit" of capitalism—so much so that work no longer had need of its religious justifications. For example, by the eighteenth century, when a young Benjamin Franklin was advocating the virtue of thrift, and James Watt was keeping a careful Waste Book of his expenditures, the work ethic had already become a kind of secularized Protestant attitude, self-replicating beyond the reach of the church. The thriftiness of Franklin and Watt was limned by Protestantism, but was advocated as an end in itself, rather than as a doctrinal creed. Franklin's famous thirteen virtues included temperance, order, frugality, and industry: "Lose no time. Be always employed in something useful. Cut off all unnecessary actions." However, in this list, crafted by the son of devout Boston Calvinists, there was no mention of God. The single reference to divinity comes only at the end, in virtue thirteen, which places Jesus on the same plane as a pagan philosopher: "Humility: Imitate Jesus and Socrates."[6]

If energy was not responsible for the transvaluation of work, what *did* energy contribute to its practice and governance? In short, energy was key to yet another, albeit more minor, shift in the work ethic, one that better adapted it to the working rhythms and demands of industrial capitalism in the nineteenth century.[7] The science of energy contributed to the further development of the governing logics surrounding work. Through the dominant logic of energy, which was infused with its own Protestant inclinations, work appeared as both a Western virtue associated with Protestantism, and as a physical activity that could be perfected through natural law. This is not to say that older, religious commitments to work disappeared. Biblical references to diligence remained popular in reformers' tracts. Rather, energy helped to adapt the work ethic to a technoscientific era. The energetic model of work buttressed work's cultural value in the West—already high—with a new scientific justification and language. Daniel Rodgers describes how, in this transitory period for work, "the result was not to shatter the presumptive tie between work and morality but to reinforce it, pitched at a new level of abstraction."[8] Energy science was interpreted as a validation of Christian imperialism, demonstrating that the spread of industrial lifestyles was not only mandated by the particular faith of Protestantism, but also happened to be in service to a truth of nature.

But energy did more than aid in the scientific valorization of work. It also democratized the activity of work by demoting human labor from its revered status in Locke or Hegel to just one force among others.[9] If human activity could be conceived of energetically, and energy was a universal unit, then there was nothing fundamentally distinct about human efforts. When work is defined energetically, the only distinction to be made between the efforts of a horse, a human, or a steam engine would be in their relative energy efficiency. According to what Amy Wendling calls the "energeticist model of labor," the effect of thermodynamics is that "labor now confers no particular dignity, political or otherwise, on the agent who undertakes it."[10] Demotion is not quite the right word, though, for Westerners still retained a belief in human superiority. Human activity may be judged by the same energy equations as those applied to machines, but human-directed power had dramatically increased thanks to new human–energy–machine complexes. Becoming machinic was not such a bad thing, provided humans were the operators. After all, these were not the dull machines of the Enlightenment, but awesome fossil-fueled motors; Tamara Ketabgian argues that Victorians had a "capacious vision of engines as living instinctive organisms, of animal bodies fueled by industrial forces, and of allied natural, mechanical, and psychic energy driving these systems."[11] Moreover, humans retained a special status by virtue of their knowledge of what fueled these machines: energy and its laws. As a result, Wendling observes that intellectual ability—especially that of engineers and scientists—becomes increasingly heralded as the marker of human distinction, even if it, too, "can be quantified energetically."[12]

Indeed, the energetic model of work was above all useful to industrial managers and engineers, which will be further explored in part II of this book. Iwan Rhys Morus, a historian of physics, records how scientific culture became industrial culture, and how the experts in "the new physics of work" became the trusted overseers of industrial operations, as they understood that "the universe operated on the same principles as those that governed, or at the very least ought to govern, the well-regulated Victorian factory."[13] Engineers (a relatively new profession) became positioned as the ideal industrial-capitalist managers, the subject of chapter 7. And despite significant differences in twenty-first-century work, most notably in the emergence of digital and information commodity cultures,[14] a hollowed-out Protestant asceticism, joined to thermodynamic assumptions about energy, persists in attaching citizens to the fictional necessity of waged work.

This chapter locates energy in the more familiar story of the industrial shift in the governance of work. Conceiving work as energy expanded its scope and, from a political point of view, helped to make the governance of work insidious. If work meant energy transformation, then almost everything, organic and nonorganic, human and animal, could be perceived as potentially engaged in work and legible to thermodynamic accounting. In the late nineteenth century, there was an expansion in the political domain of work: a multiplication of the sites of work in which the state could intervene, an intensification of the techniques for intervention, and a louder insistence that work was fundamental to citizenship. The special place accorded certain kinds of work, or certain working bodies and technologies, was open to reevaluation according to energy-infused metrics such as efficiency and productivity. The hierarchy of work and workers was augmented by energy, encompassing not just human workers, but all things on the Earth involved in activities deemed potentially useful to humans.

Humans could distinguish themselves in this hierarchy, rising above nonhumans, through disciplined labor: efficient work reflected superior scientific knowledge, itself a purported marker of civilization. However, some workers—certain humans and nearly all nonhumans—were deemed to require a disciplinary regime in order to ensure their efficient participation. As with older hierarchies of work, these judgments mobilized racial and gendered tropes, as well as anthropocentric assumptions of human superiority. The novelty lay in the energetic underpinnings of these hierarchies, which traversed the atomic and the cosmic. Machines, people, animals, forests, or rivers that were resistant to capitalist systems of work, often because they were deemed to be unruly, turbulent, or lazy, were understood to require the management of white men in order to better organize their energetic accounts. Energy provided a universal unit by which to understand all activity on Earth as related to work, and therefore as governable according to standards of efficiency and productivity.

ENERGY: A UNIVERSAL UNIT FOR WORK

During the nineteenth century, the governance of work changed, becoming less moralistic and more scientific in its aims.[15] The effort to establish work as a necessary activity for the social good became intensely systematized at the level of the state, and a matter for governmental control through the scientific reform of institutions such as prisons, schools, workhouses, and asylums. Alongside the more familiar political deployments of biological and medical sciences, a dominant energy logic was also at work in reinforcing liberal governance. The dominant, Western logic of energy was centered on a general aim—to put energy to effective use—that was translated into governance schemes for putting the planet to work in the service of fossil-fueled empires.

Energy made possible new tactics for labor governance, all of them focused on the maximization of efficiency and productivity. In order to be governable, work had to be measurable in terms of both its quantity and its quality. Measuring work had always proven difficult for industrial capitalists, keen to systematize and synchronize laborers. Starting in the seventeenth century, time emerged as a preferred method to ensure labor discipline, and by the nineteenth century, wage labor, paid by time worked, had eclipsed the tradition of "taken-work," which was paid by the task or piece.

Waged workers were enjoined to match the regularity of machines, and to leave behind older rhythms of work and leisure. Nonindustrial work rhythms do not separate leisure and labor as strictly; labor historian E. P. Thompson describes "alternate bouts of intense labour and of idleness, wherever men were in control of their own working lives."[16] Such fitful, irregular rhythms of work and leisure persist among those with more autonomy in performing their tasks, whether they involve writing or childcare. The wage and its corresponding system of time discipline cordoned off leisure time and regularized work time, but it had a major shortcoming. Wages paid by the clock could synchronize workers and keep them working longer hours, but the clock could not tell managers about the *quality* or intensity of work completed in any given block of time. Employers were well aware of this limitation. They complained frequently that, without constant surveillance, workers were prone to be idle and careless; workers might show up on time and stay for the designated work period, but they would slack off as much as possible.

In the older tradition of paying by the piece, work quality had been ensured by paying for each task completed. Shoddy work could simply be rejected; slacking off would result in fewer pieces to sell. But the system of piecework could not easily be adapted to the more complex, continuous work activities required by industrialization. Moreover, piecework left laborers too much freedom over their time from the perspective of new capitalist managers. Pro-industrialists frowned upon the tendency for people to complete the minimum work necessary to earn a living wage, and no more. Reformers believed that, left idle too long, the public was prone to the vices of drink, prostitution, and crime. Thompson notes the sharp increase in histrionics in the Victorian era about the immoral leisure activities of the poor.[17] The wage was important, then, not only to regularize workers' time, but to instill in them the notion that time equals money, that time was to be "put to use" and not frittered away unproductively. Leisure was to be isolated into short, bounded moments in the week, rather than interspersed throughout one's day. The only way to ensure such discipline was to rely on increasingly intense surveillance by managers.

Energy offered one way to access work quality and to make it visible to managers: by equating work quality with productivity and efficiency. As a measurable unit, energy could integrate the two existing modes of labor discipline: piecework and wage labor, one dealing with time and the other with matter. Energy provided a more granular unit by which to measure laborers' efforts—how much energy did they convert toward commodifiable forms, and how efficiently? But as an abstract and universal unit, energy could be applied to any type of process or effort, regardless of outcome (unlike measuring by the piece).

Thermodynamics was thus central to the development of the European and American sciences of work, including Frederick Winslow Taylor's widely influential "time and motion" studies, which aimed to translate the maximum daily work of a healthy man into "foot-pounds of energy."

In a marriage of evolution and thermodynamics, Taylor's scientific management sought maximum efficiency and productivity by "selecting" and training workers best suited to each task to new "scientific laws" of work (derived from the time and motion studies of energy), a notion that "is directly antagonistic to the old idea that each workman can best regulate his own way of doing the work. And besides this, the man suited to handling pig iron is too stupid to properly train himself."[18] Indeed, as Taylorism illustrates, the energetic model of work was above all useful to industrial managers, who struggled to control labor in factory settings; Taylor writes approvingly of moving responsibility from the workmen and "plac[ing] a great part of it upon the management."[19]

With the science of energy deployed as a science of work, humans could be governed as energy-transforming machines—it was an attractive prospect not only to capitalists, but also to some Marxists intent upon a more rational organization of labor.[20] As chapter 3 described, the machine was already popular as a metaphor. But it was only with the advent of thermodynamics that the operations of heat engines, the preeminent industrial prime movers, could be explained in any detail. Henceforth, heat engines could be treated not only as metaphor, but as a practical model. They were functionally analogous to any other organ or body that transformed energy from heat into motion, and they could be governed as such. A machine's inputs and outputs were systematically related as forms of energy, and the optimization of energy flows ensured both time well spent (now measurable as efficiency) and the maximal transformation of energy into commodity form (captured by productivity).

THE VICTORIAN WORK-LIFE BALANCE

By the end of the nineteenth century, historian Anson Rabinbach observes, the enemy was no longer just idleness—a moral failing—but fatigue, or a lack of energy, such that "a more scientific evaluation of work, often materialist in emphasis, gradually displaced the old moral discourse." Work remained a moral concern for social reformers, but it was also approachable as a physiological problem, with "each aspect balancing and reinforcing the other to create an internal equilibrium between the needs of the body and the soul, an economy of physiology and morality."[21] A science of work emerged in which energy offered a universal unit for analyzing the various inputs and outputs of human activity—eating, sleeping, exercise, posture, illness, air flow, friction. It was a science that came with "a modernist politics, the politics of a state devoted to maximizing the economy of the body" and to "a new kind of productivism—the optimum deployment of all forces available to the nation."[22] While this knowledge was often produced in the biological and medical sciences, and in studies of the human body, underlying it was an understanding of energy as the "vital force" that animated a living organism. Rabinbach observes that the new science of ergonomics, or efficient movement, was not located "in the debates over time and space, but in a scientific approach to the conservation of energy as labor power."[23] Instead of measuring output, or time worked, an employer would thus need to take into account a host of energy flows through the system, in pursuit of moral and physiological optimization—the birth of the work–life balance as a tactic of governance.

The notion of balance addressed the two interrelated problems posed by the industrial work project in the nineteenth century: on the one hand, too much work, and on the other, too little. Both were endemic threats to industrial capitalism. Industrialization operated on the promise of full employment, but did not, and would never, actually achieve it. There was always a surplus of labor beyond the needs of capital, and this unemployed "residuum" was often stigmatized by the state as consisting of vagrants, criminals, and ne'er-do-wells. Meanwhile, many of those fortunate enough to obtain employment suffered from cruel and debilitating hours.

Overwork and underwork were already understood as social problems. Through an energetic model of work, though, they could now be approached as a problem of imbalance that was curable through adjusting inputs and outputs. Energy was the optimal unit for balancing, but it required a fine-grained analysis of each working part. One could balance time spent at work and leisure, but how would we know the optimal time for each, which would surely vary by industry and body? A Goldilocks balance of work would push each human body or machine to its limits, but no further. Bodies working either too much or too little could become blockages in the industrial system. Workers must have just enough leisure to recuperate their stores of energy for maximal work, while engaging in just enough work to ensure morally commendable leisure.

Energy had featured in moralistic accounts of work prior to thermodynamics, but in these it retained a mystical quality. If someone lacked energy, it was often understood to be a moral failing with little recourse for improvement. When posed as an energetic equation, the treatment of laborers appeared as a technocratic problem rather than as a problem of morality or of the just distribution of wages and labor. As Taylor insisted, workers could be taught to maximize energy efficiency, but it would require replacing the traditional foreman with a planning department, as well as at least eight overseers, to include the "time clerk," the "speed boss," the "route clerk," and the "disciplinarian."[24] Energy thus neatly tied together older, moralistic codes of work with fossil-fueled machines. If fossil-fueled labor was problematic, the answer was to acquire more energy, and to surveil it more rigorously.

OVERWORK

Labor movements, too, learned to frame their concerns in terms of work time, as they first accepted the discipline of the clock and later the ideals of energeticism. Thompson describes the evolution of the modern labor movements toward a focus on time: "The first generation of factory workers were taught by their masters the importance of time; the second generation formed their short-time committees in the ten-hour movement; the third generation struck for overtime or time-and-a-half. They had accepted the categories of their employers and learned to fight back within them. They had learned their lesson, that time is money, only too well."[25]

The two key demands of labor movements were higher wages and reduced work hours, evident in the Factories Act of 1847, otherwise known as the Ten Hours Act because it limited working hours for women and youth to ten hours daily. Reports on working conditions tell of children working twelve- or fourteen-hour days, or even overnight in busy seasons, or railroad workers on shifts for up to forty hours straight, sometimes resulting in horrific accidents.[26] Marx, a serious reader of energy science, analyzed this inevitable tension between capitalists, who sought, "vampire-like," to extract as much labor as possible from workers, and workers, who aimed for a sustainable amount of daily work according to their physical and "moral" limits.[27] The capitalists' "vampire thirst" was for "the living blood of labour,"[28] blood that was kept flowing and vital by the availability of things like food, fresh air, and rest. And in addition to the physical needs of eating, bathing, and sleeping, Marx notes that workers have "intellectual and social requirements."[29] Like the soil, which needed the cyclical return of waste, as fertilizer, in order to stay healthy, Marx points out that human bodies, too, require organic care. He rails against the nearsightedness of capitalists who work their laborers too hard. While there may be immediate benefits, overwork degrades the "commodity" of a worker's labor-power by shortening her working life.[30]

Socialists were not alone in their concern. The mid- to late nineteenth century was rife with government commissions and investigations on working conditions. Reformers bemoaned the long hours, low wages, poor diets, and detestable conditions. These tracts echoed Marx's sentiments, chastising the employers for failing to properly ensure that their workers stayed healthy and capable of laboring. With the additional heft of the science of energy, the notion of overwork could be approached more holistically than ever, with working hours only part of the problem. The energy spent in labor must be replenished, just as the soil must be revived, and just as steam engines must be returned to an original position, and refueled, in order to do work again.

The logic of energy thus involved a care regime, but it was care extended in the pursuit of maximizing work. In critiques of overwork, the value of work itself was rarely, if ever, in question. For capitalists and many reformers, the goal in reducing work hours was to produce dedicated laborers who would perform their tasks with alacrity. Calls for better nutrition, more breaks, or shorter hours were often advertised as methods for increasing productivity. Lethargy and sloppiness were not sins, as idleness had been, nor resistance to hard toil, but understandable physical reactions to a poor balance of energy, whether as a result of malnutrition, inadequate sleep, or a lack of recreation and spiritual education. They were the equivalent of friction in an engine requiring oil, or from the vibration of a loose part. As such, a poor work ethic could be approached as a problem in need of an engineer's care, fixable not only by moral education, but by carefully attending to the energetic requirements of workers. Unlike converting sinners, energy reforms were as simple and achievable as new nutritional guidelines, with the results measurable in increased profits. Energy was a magical unit of equivalence—more granular than time, and more seemingly natural than money—by which to connect a laborer's breakfast, her walk to work, her children and their demands, and the output of her labors.

Reformers, therefore, were keen to show how improved diet, sleep, and housing could result in tangible gains in productivity. Marx drew heavily on such reports, including one conducted in 1863 by J. N. Radcliffe, a medical doctor, who studied the conditions of women working in West End millineries. Radcliffe describes the physical "lassitude" of the women, which he blames upon "a monotonous and sedentary occupation pushed to excess."[31] The women complain that "they are regarded . . . as mere machines from which the employers obtain the greatest possible amount of work at the least cost of working."[32] Another woman quips that late-night work does not even pay for the gas lighting it requires, as the women are so exhausted that they "work sluggishly and indifferently. Any excuse to idle a moment is too readily seized upon," while other women simply fall asleep mid-stitch.[33]

In his investigations, Radcliffe is particularly interested in a manager who had added protein to the hatmakers' breakfasts. According to Radcliffe, the manager recouped the cost of the protein in the additional work that the women could henceforth complete.[34] On the basis of such experiments, the doctor prescribes a homelike atmosphere for the women, with reasonable work hours and good food. The focus on laborers' energy levels did not leave room for more dangerous musings about work. The pleasures of leisure, of frittering away an afternoon in the park, or an evening dancing, which their wealthy clients indulged without censure in their new hats, went unmentioned, as well as the extremely unequal distribution of drudgery. The milliners' position of daily toil could be improved at the margins, but not transformed. An egg at breakfast, a walk on Sunday—these were the little joys that working women could aspire to be granted. With their little pleasures, the women were more likely to engage in efficient work during the day, and also to avoid "distressing lapses from morality" to which workers are predisposed if there is an "absence of home feeling."[35] For overwork and underwork were also understood as bodily obstacles to morality. As historian Daniel Rodgers explains, labor was both a cure for, and an escape from, temptation, and "the truly moral man was at once a person of strength and a *perpetuum mobile* of repressing energy," one whose busy-ness ensured that there was no energy left for vice.[36]

This energetic model of work morality—with its emphasis on balance—was built upon, but distinct from, the Calvinist morality that Weber located at the heart of the Protestant work ethic. Weber theorized that the extreme asceticism of Calvinist theology had helped capitalism take off. In particular, the Calvinist belief in predestination led to a harsh abstinence, a rejection of "all sensual and emotional elements in culture and subjective religiosity—because they were of no use for salvation and they promoted sentimental illusions and superstitious idolatry."[37] Because salvation had been decided in advance by a God who was unavailable to earthly pleas, redemption could not be earned by good works. One must work hard, not in order to gain salvation, but as an act of pious obedience to a distant God who was beyond worldly comprehension. Weber surmised that predestination led Protestants to live frugally, reinvesting their savings into work projects and, mostly inadvertently, fueling capital accumulation.

While this downplays the role of violence and land enclosure in capital accumulation, Weber's analysis remains important for its early insights into the religious foundations that were crucial to achieving a widespread public commitment to waged work. Nineteenth-century work advocates were no less biblical than Weber's Calvinists in their beliefs, but as social reformers, they were more sympathetic toward the bodily dispositions that made work possible in the first place. The state bore some responsibility for providing industry with bodies that were ready to work. If people were ill, tired, underfed, poorly housed, and unchaperoned, then they simply would not have the energy for hard work. Not only would they be unable to work; their lassitude would also predispose them to vice. In contrast, a well-balanced energy account resulted in active and disciplined people prepared for hard work.

An appropriate work balance also promised a more compliant public. Reformers strategically argued that shorter working hours would blunt labor unrest. First, shorter hours could create additional jobs, reducing the ranks of the grumbling underemployed. Second, reformers feared that overwork made people vulnerable to demagogues. An 1885 pamphlet submitted to the U.S. Senate in support of an eight-hour work day argues that

> constant work for long hours, or over-exertion, causes exhaustion, and creates a desire for strong artificial stimulants (such as alcoholic liquors), produce [sic] mental incapacity, general insensibility, grossness of feeling and perception, with disease and shortened life. That the intelligence of the working classes would improve with the advantage of more leisure time we have every reason to believe, and that political tricksters and shameless demagogues would no longer turn their ignorance to the advantage of political party power. . . . [I]nstead of considering machinery a detriment to labor, [the working classes] would realize it as the greatest benefit to them.[38]

The evils of overwork could be cured by putting oneself into the right relation with machinery. Breaking the machines was never in question.

Thanks to a knowledge of physics, good employers could help to induce lively, diligent workers. Blockages in the system were simply sites that required better energy accounting. Work was a prophylaxis. Energetic people made hard workers, good Christians, and docile citizens. But not everyone could be cured through energetic governance. Overwork was a problem amenable to reform: workers were creaky machines who needed adjustments to their energy balance. However, the opposite problem, underwork, was feared as a veritable scourge on civilization, and one that appeared much more intractable. Here were energy sinks, sites where energy sat unused or, worse, was frittered away, wasted. Applying more energy risked compounding the problem, as any extra energy invested—in the form of welfare or meals, for instance—might still fail to result in a productive worker. If too much work exhausted people, leaving them vulnerable to the temptations of alcohol or protest, then too little work practically ensured it. And if the state was understood as a great organic machine, then these were the sites of waste to be managed, where energy was consumed in the form of food or benefits, but nothing was produced in return.

Consequently, those without work were perceived as the gravest threats to society and were subject to the harshest condemnation. If a person could not be made to work, then many European managers believed that they were to be left to starve; no more food (energy) was to be wasted upon them. As an 1860 plea for homeless children intones, with reference to a biblical maxim, "'He that will not work should not eat.'"[39] It is a verse that remains popular among critics of public welfare today: at least three U.S. Republican lawmakers have quoted it in recent years to oppose food benefits for the poor, who are figured as parasites taking advantage of hardworking citizens.[40]

Then, as now, social reformers who wanted to rally support for public benefits were consumed by the need to categorize the different varieties of unemployed people, with the underlying impetus to exclude the undeserving. Support could only be extended if policymakers had designed a robust system for rejecting those whom current U.S. policy refers to as ABAWDs (able-bodied adults without dependents). The British Workmen's Act of 1905, for example, takes pains to make this point, declaring that "the desire was to exclude loafers, work-shyers, intermittent workers whose case was not exceptional, and any workman out of work from fault of his own."[41] Before the government could justify aiding anyone, they needed to reassure the public that they could identify the idlers.

The threat posed by the figure of the idler is so grave that no one can be permitted to survive the refusal of work without being made to suffer, lest their lifestyle prove contagious. One minister, Thomas Guthrie, pleads for aid to educate homeless children in "ragged" schools, but his sympathy for the children does not extend to their lazy parents. The parents deserve nothing, Guthrie argues, and are a perpetual threat, as "we have not here the miserable consolation that the infected [those who refuse work] will die off. They are mixed with society,—each an active centre of corruption. Around them you can draw no *Cordon Sanitaire*. The leaven is every day leavening more and more of the lump."[42]

Even if the state refused to help work-shyers, it could not rely upon their extermination, as they would keep reproducing ragged children in their image, who must be rescued by the church or state as they appeared on the streets. It was a game of Whac-a-Mole. Like many reform-minded pamphleteers, Guthrie perceived work-shyers as not just moral threats, but imperial threats, as they were weakening the vitality of British industrialism. He warns that if the idle "are left in active operation," the British Empire "shall sooner or later fall like some majestic and splendid iceberg," which will bury "the unhappy mariners who had sought safety in its shelter."[43]

It was not only high-minded ministers who railed against the idle. The threat of lassitude was also the main theme of the influential 1909 *Minority Report* on the Poor Laws, authored by socialists Sidney and Beatrice Webb, which aimed to modernize the existing British system of workhouses and harsh poor laws. The *Minority Report* is often considered to be the first major proposal for a modern welfare system. While the report treated poverty as a structural, rather than a moral, problem, it nevertheless spent considerable effort to reassure the public that a welfare scheme would not be abused by laggards. However, these laggards were not to be left alone in the Webbs' scheme. Work refusers did not usually starve to death, as they could survive on the streets by stealing and "sponging," and so the report argues that it is preferable to keep them under the control of a state administrative apparatus. The authors reasoned that "whilst an able-bodied man remains a loafer and a wastrel, it is urgently desirable that he should be in hand and under observation rather than lost in the crowd."[44]

Why were work-shyers perceived to be such an existential threat to the state? In short, the work-shyers were dangerous to the project of industrial capitalism because they illuminated the rotten core at the heart of waged work. In surviving, and in seeming to succeed in their choice to avoid work (whether or not this was the case), they had publicly rejected work as necessary to the good life. The work-shyer was thus at once a figure of resistance and an invention of the liberal state—the bogeyman that aroused the jealousy of her fellow workers. In other words, while unemployed people certainly existed, and suffered, it was also necessary for the state to invent the work-shyer precisely to address the great weakness of the industrial project—that the real experience of work, for so many, was hell. Work was not for the workers—and not only in the Marxist sense that workers were alienated from their labor. Even for capitalists, the energetic model of work meant that work was not primarily judged according to whether it served life (human, capitalist, earthly, or otherwise), but according to productivity and efficiency. The work-shyer could not be allowed to enjoy herself, as her jollity would bring the discordance between the needs of life and the needs of industry into starker relief.

Accordingly, a chief anxiety, then as now, was that if government assistance were too generous, people would stop working. Again, it was not so much that industrial capitalism needed everyone to work, but rather that industrial capitalism needed the work ethic in place to paper over its exploitative tendencies. There was no quicker way to defeat legislation that aimed to assist the poor than to describe the carefree life of the idler, with a special focus on waste—the central enemy of energy accounting. The more fanciful this description, the better. The *Minority Report*, for example, admits that existing workhouses offered "attractions to the indolent," who could "find themselves in conditions that were certainly more agreeable, if not more 'eligible,' to the apathetic loafer than working continuously for long hours at the low wages of the unskilled laborer . . . leaving him free to come and go as he chose, and to live as he pleased, without even the curb of official cognizance and observation of his doings."[45] This is representative of Victorian fantasies of the idler's life: while meant as condemnation, the idler narratives thrum with desire for the idler's life of living "as he pleased."

In the very admission of the possibility of work refusal, visions of merriment and liberation are inevitably induced. Work-shyers skip puckishly across the horizon, rearing up even in the midst of scolding reform pamphlets. The *Minority Report* describes at length the unseemly pleasures for those who abuse the kindness of the workhouse, where most men finish working by midafternoon, and then "spend their time together as they please, in the yard or in the day-room, with games and gossip." One workhouse master reports that the men treat it "as a kind of club-house in which they put up with a certain amount of inconvenience, but have very pleasant evenings."[46] The intention here is to arouse the jealousy of an audience who must work twice as long, with no afternoon gossip, no pleasant evenings, and no hope of help from the state.

Unfortunately for the state, separating those unable to work from those who simply preferred not to was difficult, if not impossible. Work resistance was often illegible to the state. As Guthrie, the minister, worried in the quotation above, the work-shyers are "mixed" in with the others and cannot possibly be cordoned off.[47] The identities of the unemployed were constantly changing, despite fears of a fixed class of drifters. The state attempted to classify citizens into clearly demarcated zones of virtue, but these zones did not reflect actual dispositions to work. Disability and resistance to waged work were not mutually exclusive and, after all, almost everyone was daily tempted to shirk work. One's ability to work might also shift over time or prove inscrutable to administrators, as with mental illness. (Hence the army of overseers required by the Taylor system.)

Even more disconcerting to the state's classification system were those living outside heteronormative family structures, who did not have a stereotypical male breadwinner to support them, but at the same time, whose age and/or gender blocked them from earning a living income. What were reformers to do with healthy young women who were able to work but were also the sole parents to infants and small children—a job that was certainly necessary to the state, but unpaid? At what point could the single mother be expected to return to waged work, which would even then be underpaid?[48] These concerns, rife within the *Minority Report* and other pamphlets of the era, would lead to the various social welfare schemes that are familiar to Western liberal democracies today. At their core, though, these schemes for assisting the poor are deemed justifiable only to the extent that they have convinced the public that idlers can be, and have been, excluded.

What is important to the concerns of this book, and its focus on the energetic turn in the work ethic, is the way in which work-shyers became reinterpreted in the language of energy. Even where energy terminology is not explicitly used, energetic sensibilities sometimes appear in the insistence upon efficiency and productivity as primary work values. Understood energetically, work-shyers were fearful manifestations of entropy, energy sinks that were incapable of transforming state handouts (energy additions) into productive work. As a representative example, the *Minority*

Report quotes a clerk who bemoans that unemployed men in the labor yard "suffer from overwhelming inertia."[49] The dominant logic of energy helped to reinforce the Western preference for dynamism and productivism that pervaded efforts to discipline laboring bodies. One should not aim to merely survive, or to be satisfied with working just enough to achieve subsistence. As a workhouse administrator grumbled, "a certain proportion of mankind would rather have an assured subsistence, though it is a very small one, than have to work in the open market for their living."[50] Not only was this anathema to capitalism's temporal horizon of endless growth, but it would also be to revert to the linear clunkiness of classical machines, rather than to serve the exponential outputs afforded by fossil fuel burning. If dynamism was the ideal, and the path to civilization and abundance, then the inertia of the work-shyers must be made to appear deathlike and undesirable.

Most importantly, through the lens of energy, work-shyers were not merely localized instances of moral failure. Whereas work-shyers had once been itinerant figures who might have occasionally abused the hospitality of local towns, but otherwise inhabited a shadow world of street corners and alehouses, work-shyers were now enemies of the state who required surveillance and expulsion. They were sites of waste in which the precious energy of a nation could be lost forever. It was unwise for the state to ignore them. Shirking work, and living to tell about it, was a threat to the industrial organism, a rusty gear resisting its smooth operation. The depiction of the state and the workers as an organism similarly relied upon energetic metaphors and knowledge, albeit often implicitly, as the next chapter shows. The notion that idlers were infectious, and could not be left to their own devices for fear of undermining the entire industrial project, relied upon ecological tropes in which the management of energy flows was of primary significance.

When energy and work are understood as historically intertwined in this way, it becomes clear that the reign of fossil fuels is not only about our addiction to fossil fuels and their exponential power. It is also about addiction to the ideology of work, as well as to a particular way of distributing, compensating, and valuing work. Wage labor and fossil-fueled capitalism are certainly part of the formula. Historically, fossil fuel addiction helped to attach humans to the project of wage labor and the advance of global capitalism. However, the attachment to work also operated on a broader and more philosophical plane than is captured by the capitalist systematization of wage labor. The embrace of energy—as science, as worldview, as labor governance—went hand in hand with a privileging of dynamism over stasis, of activity over stillness, of change over stability, to the point that the bare achievement of dynamic change was more important than the outcome of that change.

Energy science thus joined the modern cultural upheaval in which the ideology of progress reigned. Energy become one valence according to which Westerners could measure, and enhance, their progressive activities, especially in labor settings. Energy science itself is not necessarily progressive, though. Just as evolutionary science does not advocate a progressive teleology (evolutionary change is not always progress, and so-called progress has not always ended well), neither does thermodynamics. A thermodynamic perspective understands all activity as energy transformed, but, as Percy Bridgman quips, the universe does not care if one arrangement of energy can do work for humans and another cannot. Both evolution and energy theories were amenable to multiple political interpretations. Nevertheless, the interpretations that came to dominate, most famously with work sciences like Taylorism, were those aligned with progress, which best served the interests of the imperial, capitalist states in which they emerged.

While the influence of Taylorism is well known and has been exhaustively studied, my aim is to put these modern sciences of work into the context of the larger human relationship to energy. Such an approach positions Taylor and his ilk as particular instantiations of the ruling logic of energy, alerting us to energy's power as a traveling concept, a ruling metaphor that imbues a single-minded focus on efficiency and productivity far afield of Taylorist factories. By historicizing energy, we also appreciate how the embrace of a dominant, northern British logic of energy, with its stress on engineering principles and work, reflected only one possible interpretation of energy and its optimal flow through metaphorical machines and organisms (a metaphor further elaborated on in the next chapter). Managers like Taylor could only assert, but never satisfactorily prove, that the maximization of work was in the interest of the well-being of the state or laborers. The assertion was buttressed by its reliance on the seemingly universal, and apolitical, physics of energy. This allows us to appreciate not only how energy infused the governance of work (as in how Taylor deploys thermodynamics), but also how work infuses the governance of energy/fuel. In other words, in disturbing the work/energy nexus, we are carried forward to the concluding claim of this book: that our relationship to fossil fuels has been governed by a singular ruling logic of energy, and delimited by its idealization of work, its unquestioned drive to put the world's materials to use for human profit.

CONCLUSION: FOSSIL FUELS AND THE END OF WORK

The intensification of work in the nineteenth century is often taken as a sign of its increased importance—of the feverish frenzy by which every person, every mountain, every river, and every clod of soil was to be put to work in the service of fossil capital. While this is accurate, it is only part of the story. The Victorian obsession with work reflected the expansion of the domain of work, but also its ongoing vulnerability as a site of governance. Measuring work was difficult, and in disciplining bodies, machines, forests, and oceans to serve industrial work, too much was able to escape. The power offered by fossil fuels also suggested other possibilities to humans besides never-ending toil.

Amid the celebration of work, the nineteenth century also entertained new visions of the possibility of the end of work, at least as a democratic goal that was not only for a select elite, and that did not require asceticism. Prior to industrialism, many had imagined the transformation of work, as in Thomas More's *Utopia*, where work becomes playful and pleasurable, and/or the simplification of work, as in Romantic notions of pastoral and artisanal life, as described in William Morris's *News from Nowhere*. However, these visions of work required a twofold maneuver. First, work must be more equally distributed; elites must work more so that others could work less. And second, consumption must be restrained and administered. It is only with fossil-fueled machines that humans could begin to conceive of everyone working less, and possibly without limiting consumption, as a real possibility. Fossil fuels animated the dream of having our cake and eating it too, a fantasy that refuses to die. After all, fossil fuels, with their exponential power, suggested a solution to the persistent problem faced by the state and exacerbated by demands for democratic rule: unfree or exploited labor has been elemental to nearly every successful state. The famed ancient Greek polis and the revered American founders espoused egalitarianism while ruling over patriarchal slave states. Fossil fuels could instead replace unfree human labor with more powerful inorganic slaves.[51]

On the other hand, there was no guarantee that fossil fuel systems would inevitably lead to a world beyond work. Fossil servitude could simply be integrated into existing styles of domination, spawning new modes of exploitation while simultaneously hiding them behind the veneer of high-tech labor substitution. The vulnerability at the heart of the project of industrial work remains—its resistance to measurement, the many activities and desires that escape its boundaries—as do visions of a post-work future in which the contradictions of labor might be smoothed out.

PART II   ENERGY, RACE, AND EMPIRE

5 | ENERGOPOLITICS

Energy is the ability to do work. This definition has achieved the status of common sense. Part I offered a genealogy of this truism, examining the broad contours of the first wave of energy logics—that of thermodynamics—through the genres of intellectual history and geo-theology. Energy, that multifaceted, amorphous signifier, was captured by thermodynamics, producing a political rationality appropriate to an industrial science of steam engines. By energy logic, then, I do not refer to all possible meanings or connotations of energy. Rather, I am highlighting how energy, as a site of governance, is commonly understood through this one particular interpretation of energy, a logic that has tended to dominate the human relationship to fuels in the Anthropocene. And as part I showed, this political rationality of energy, or its logic, is not simply given by thermodynamics, but also reflects the admixture of Protestant, industrial interests with which energy was overlain from its Victorian inception.

While part I described the contours of this early energy logic as it emerged in northern Britain, part II explores how this energy logic operated politically, as a study of energy as a mode of domination. More specifically, I am interested in examining how energy reinforced the already circulating hierarchies of race, gender, and class that animated the new imperialism, an era of European imperial acceleration that began in the 1870s with the so-called scramble for Africa, and lasted until the disintegration of European empires at the end of the Second World War. New imperialism was driven by the desire to put the world to work according to the rhythm and intensity of fossil-fueled systems. Energy logics contributed new metaphors and accounting tactics to the ethos of work and waste, a long-standing Protestant paradigm that was amplified by thermodynamics, which could be deployed to justify the moral valuation of work with physical laws and mathematical equations.

This evidence will necessarily be partial and suggestive, rather than comprehensive. My intent is not to make an overarching historical claim that posits energy as the central figure in the imperial governance of labor. Energy and thermodynamic terms appear frequently in late nineteenth-century texts, and yet at the same time energy's very universality dilutes its meaning. Energy could explain everything and be advanced in the name of many, contradictory purposes, in much the same way that evolution was embraced for an array of otherwise opposing political movements.[1] And as part I showed, energy did not so much invent new ethical programs (work and waste), or new metaphors (machines), but translated them into appropriate governing tools for a world of multiplying fossil-fueled technologies. Moreover, energy was not the only nascent field of knowledge that offered to explain the relations between humans, machines, and nature. Energy arose alongside evolution and an explosion of new social science and economic disciplines, including neoclassical economics and geopolitics.[2] By the late nineteenth century, energy itself had multiplied and diffracted as a category in physics, with the emergence of electromagnetics and statistical mechanics, as well as later theories of relativity and quantum mechanics.

While these are important caveats that situate energy within the Victorian fervor of new concepts and industrial systems, nevertheless thermodynamics made important contributions to an energetic regime of labor governance in this period. Energy's role as a political logic has been underappreciated, and this only reinforces the still-present assumption that energy enters the field of political reason as an objective unit, untethered to specific values and interests. By offering vignettes of energetic governance, part II continues this book's effort to historicize energy, to submit it to a critique that unsettles its seeming universality. If energy is allowed to stand for unquestioned natural law, unmoored from its Victorian birth as a leitmotif for industrial politics, then it is all the more difficult to challenge the necessity of efficient, productive work as the key to human well-being.

Before examining how energy logics appear in new imperialism, the subject of chapters 6 and 7, this chapter pauses to consider *why* thermodynamics has received less attention as an imperial scientific logic. The simple answer is that the logics of energy were often deployed through, or alongside, biological and ecological metaphors, and therefore energy does not always appear as explicitly in the archives. Many of the energy metaphors also played on older, commonsense judgments in the West about the value of work and activity, and so did not always reference modern physics. But in the wake of thermodynamics and the so-called discovery of energy, these older metaphors were invested with new meanings that intensified the drive toward efficiency and productivity. These new meanings are easy to overlook if the recirculation of energy metaphors is not appreciated in the context of the history of science and the novelty of energy as an object of physics.

Thermodynamics often operated through the more well-known imperial sciences of evolution and, after the turn of the twentieth century, the nascent field of ecology. Like evolution, ecology has long been recognized for its contributions to imperial practice, as well as for the debt that it owes to the ecological and scientific knowledge of those living in the Global South. Because thermodynamics was often subsumed into these biological sciences, the absence of any systematic study of imperial energy logics is not so surprising. After all, evolution, ecology, and the many other biological sciences appear frequently in the imperial archive, while thermodynamics is rarely mentioned. For instance, in the influential 1938 report, *Science in Africa*, which claims to cover the breadth of scientific research on Africa, the chapters span geology, meteorology, soil science, botany, entomology, medicine, anthropology, and more—but there is no mention of thermodynamics.[3] And unlike ecologists or botanists, who traveled widely in the colonies and even served as imperial administrators, and who engaged with local knowledges of flora, fauna, and medicine, Africa and the tropics did not as often feature as primary laboratories for physicists studying the motion of gases.

Nevertheless, this chapter emphasizes how ecology rested not only upon the biological sciences of life, but more importantly upon the *integration* of biology and physics, and in particular, of evolution and energy. Ecology achieved this integration through the reigning metaphor of the organism and its metabolism, a metaphor according to which colonial flora, fauna, and peoples could be researched and governed.[4] The organism was obviously a biological entity, but beneath the harmony of its living form, which botanists, zoologists, or medical doctors could study, lay the constant exchange of energy. Energy was the fundamental unit of the organism; it was the thing that was exchanged in the organism's metabolism, representing the possibility of motion, of activity, of growth. And as work became represented by the unit of energy, so too the organism, composed of energy flows, became governed by assumptions about the importance of work and waste.

When applied to politics, this meant that evolution might sketch the overarching narrative (the progressive ranking of civilizations) as well as the genre (the struggle for survival), but it was thermodynamics that gave the plot: the *specific activities* by which Europeans had struggled, adapted, and advanced. Europeans had reached the top rung of the civilizational ladder by maximizing productive work and minimizing waste, with fossil fuel use as the shining achievement of this goal. In offering a scientific authorization for fossil-fueled work as a paradigm of evolutionary success, thermodynamic logics of energy thus smoothed the way for the Victorian shift "from an industrialism based on imperial slavery to industrial imperialism based on waged labor."[5]

The organism evolved successfully by increasing the volume of energy through its parts while successfully evacuating the waste "outside" its skin. In other words, the organism metaphor was often infused with, and directed by, the energetic logics of work and waste. This was a somewhat counterintuitive deployment of the organism, as most ecologists had intended to accomplish the opposite subsumption. Ecology, after all, could be heralded as the master science of human–nonhuman relations, at least in its explicitly political applications,[6] and it strove to incorporate physics as the minor motif in its biological symphony. In the ecological imagination, thermodynamic principles were meant to serve the well-being of the organism, and not the other way around. Interpreted this way, ecology generates ethical principles that are much more attuned to sustainability. However, the thermodynamic tactics of measurement and efficiency held great appeal for new imperial administrators, mine managers, and industrial capitalists; when combined with a Protestant-tinged work ethic, energy logics helped to blur the line between work as a means to an organism's health, and work as the evidence that proved an organism's health. Troublingly, the boundaries of the organism are open to redefinition, such that the pursuit of work could always be considered "healthy," even as other things and bodies had to be sacrificed and ignored. Through work and waste, Victorian energy logics reinforced the double accounting trick that remains integral to global industrialism in the twenty-first century—counting productivity and concealing waste, or sending waste "away" from the metaphorical organism.[7]

It is worth clarifying that I am not arguing that thermodynamics is false, but rather that the energy–work connection cannot claim to be a reflection of the whole truth of energy, much less of the cosmos. This is never more obvious than when compared with the multiple interpretations made possible by the new biological sciences. In other words, thermodynamics does not simply describe a preexisting thing called energy, but rather *invents* energy as a unit of accounting (and work and waste), thereby offering new governance strategies that were particularly useful to Victorian industry.[8] While energy comes to inhabit the same universal realm as matter, what counts as more or less "useful" forms of energy, or as useful energy transformations, is not given in advance by nature, but is open to political contestation. The valorization of productive, waged work as the highest mode of energy transformation represented a happy marriage of physics, Protestant sensibilities, and the European demand for scientific knowledge with which to address the multifaceted crises of labor resistance in the metropolis and the colonies.

Before evaluating how energy logics appear in new imperialism, which is the subject of chapter 5, this chapter first establishes the energetic assumptions at work in the emergent science of ecology and its metaphor of the organism. It shows how thermodynamics became integrated into organic health through the concept of metabolism. After gesturing toward the alternative organic ethics that emerge from ecology, I argue that the energy logic of work and waste nevertheless tended to dominate the political application of ecological metaphors. This is important because political efforts that draw upon ecological knowledge remain at risk of being coopted by work-based energy logics that often undermine sustainability.

Finally, the chapter concludes by applying this biology–physics integration to Foucault's speculations about biopower, which emphasize biological regimes of truth but underappreciate the role played by physics in the rationality of governing populations-as-organisms. Energopower, a concept first proposed by anthropologist Dominic Boyer,[9] offers an important complement to biopolitics in that it helps to explain how the governance of populations could be directed toward the project of productive work, not only at the expense of the bodies expelled as wasteful, but even at the expense of the life of the population itself. This is more than a necropolitics—Achille Mbembe's concept of sovereign domination in deciding who can be exposed to death—but a political rationality that is not centrally motivated by life at all, even for the most elite.[10] Rather, energopower aims to put the world to work, and to sacrifice any and all who are in the way of that vision.

ORGANISMS: CHEATS IN THE GAME OF PHYSICS

Ecology became a popular field in the first half of the twentieth century, but it had its roots in the Victorian era. Through the influential metaphors of the organism and the system, ecology integrated physics and biology, and drew together the two major fossil knowledges of the nineteenth century: evolution and energy. Ecology and the metaphor of the organism emphasized interconnected webs of living things emerging out of chaotic nonliving energy flows. From the perspective of evolution, thermodynamics was easy to incorporate into its theories of change. Thermodynamic knowledge, and the fossil-fueled technologies upon which it worked, could be interpreted as an astounding adaptation, a novel set of abilities by which human civilization had advanced in complexity and survivability. For many, energy and its use, understood as the ability of living systems to harness work from available energy stores, thus appeared to play a foundational role in driving evolutionary change.

In contrast, thermodynamics was in dire need of an ecological intervention in order to be applied to the governance of living systems. The laws of thermodynamics have little to say about the unfolding of life on Earth, and the second law alerts us to its extreme improbability. If entropy spontaneously increases, the persistence of life seems contradictory, given that life entails little pockets of highly ordered, low-entropy patterns that resist energy dissipation—at least for a time. This paradox between the second law and the emergence of life, and attempts to resolve it, was widely discussed then and now.[11] In his 1926 book *The Anatomy of Science*, physical chemist Gilbert Lewis colorfully describes living creatures as "cheats in the game of physics and chemistry," given that "it seems like animate creatures alone are striving for distinction in the midst of the almost overwhelming leveling forces in the great democracy of the atoms."[12] Meanwhile, Max Planck, the theoretical physicist of quantum theory, observes that, "biologically interpreted, this principle [of entropy] points towards degeneration rather than improvement. The chaotic, the ordinary, and the common, is always more probable than the harmonious, the excellent, or the rare."[13] Notably, in describing life amid entropic dissipation, Planck and Lewis both fall back on metaphors of political hierarchy: life is imbued with aristocratic status, where "the great democracy of atoms" is contrasted with the more rare and elite instances of life, "the harmonious, the excellent." It is yet another example of how energy and its organization become useful proxies for judging value. These more poetic generalizations about life are consistent with the careful categorization of people and things according to their ability to use energy effectively.

Such value judgments are in part made possible by an organic metaphor that, by synthesizing thermodynamics and evolution, offered one solution to the puzzle of life amid entropy. Of course, there was no single organic metaphor to which all scientists or policymakers subscribed at the time. By an *organic metaphor*, I am instead referring to an array of loosely connected manifestations across science, politics, and academic thought, many of which contradicted each other, but which nevertheless drew upon similar combinations of physics and biology for understanding human civilizations as organisms, as bounded, organized patterns of matter-energy and information exchanges. *Organic* points to those things involved with the life of organisms, but also to the fields of science that study the molecular, and often nonliving, components of life (e.g., organic chemistry, which studies carbon-based compounds that are the basis of life on Earth). Like ecology, the organic metaphor has its own rich history, drawing most immediately on so-called Romantic traditions of the eighteenth and nineteenth centuries, which rejected the reductionist and mechanistic explanations of life that had arisen out of the Enlightenment and Newtonian sciences. Through the sciences of energy and evolution, some of these Romantic intuitions about life were recuperated and given a more authoritative expression such that, by the early twentieth century, organic metaphors flourished. Energy, in particular, lent mainstream scientific authority to organicism, as thermodynamics employed a more mechanistic, and quantitative, physics (the first law), while still leaving room for mystery in explaining the emergence of life (in the strangeness of the second law).

While the organic metaphor's parameters were imprecise and shifting, as a lexicon for understanding human life on Earth, organicism was widely influential. The organic metaphor and its kindred concept—systems thinking—pollinated almost every field of human thought and endeavor in the Western metropole in the first half of the twentieth century.[14] The organic metaphor and its energy–evolution admixture appeared in philosophy and the philosophy of science, as well as in the later advent of cybernetics. It was also closely conjoined to the systems-based theories that fed the parallel emergence of the "economy" as an object of politics in the first half of the twentieth century. The related systems metaphor inspired themes in anthropology (cultural systems), sociology (society as system), and politics (political systems).[15] Later, in the mid-twentieth century, systems theories proved central to the climate sciences and Earth systems sciences that spawned modern environmental movements worldwide.[16] The recent turn toward new materialism and geopolitical thinking has also inspired a revival of interest in the explosion of creativity among thinkers who came of age around the turn of the twentieth century, and whose work integrated energy and evolutionary sciences with politics and philosophy, including Alfred North Whitehead, William James, Niels Bohr, H. G. Wells, John Dewey, Norbert Wiener, and Henri Bergson.[17]

Given the immense scope of organic and systems theories in this period, and the multiple modes in which energy appears, it would be impossible to comprehensively review them all here. Instead of aiming for a general overview, in this chapter I have narrowed my focus to an empirical study of one particular, albeit significant, imbrication of organism, evolution, and thermodynamics: in its service to new imperialism. This has relevance for global energy politics today because it reveals how thermodynamic ethics can dominate energy governance even in the midst of ecological approaches to the human–energy relationship.

The organic theories of the early twentieth century incorporated energy physics but revised the nineteenth-century science of energy to take into account not only evolution, but also in some cases the theory of relativity and quantum mechanics. Organic metaphors therefore offered a variety of new resources for thinking about energy, work, and waste, and, more broadly, suggested a planetary ethics that diverged from the Scottish Presbyterian roots of thermodynamics, with its obsessive and laser-like focus on productive work.

THE ORGANIC METAPHOR AND METABOLISM

The organicist philosophies of the early twentieth century rejected the mechanistic explanations of life that were increasingly gaining traction as physics rose in stature among the sciences. Organicists situated themselves somewhere between the vitalists, who had been increasingly marginalized, and the mechanists, and their aim was "to show that even a purely material system, if sufficiently complex and coordinated, could exhibit properties that could never have been predicted on the basis of physics and chemistry."[18] J. S. Haldane, a leading organicist scientist in the early twentieth century, describes organicist theory as the belief that "the living body and its physiological environment form an organic whole, the parts of which cannot be understood in separation from one another."[19] Going further, Haldane argues that "in conceiving what is living we do not separate between matter or structure and its activity. The structure itself is conceived as active—as alive."[20]

However, in pursuing this aim, the organicists stopped short of the vitalists, who maintained that there was some extra, even supernatural, force that distinguished living and nonliving structures, and that exceeded scientific laws. Organicists accepted the applicability of the physical laws of matter-energy but emphasized biological organization as the key to truly understanding living organisms. It was the mechanists, they argued, who failed to explain the complexity of life and its self-organizing and emergent properties, and this was due to their emphasis on physical laws over biological entities. The organicists intended that, "if one area of science was going to swallow up the other, it would be biology swallowing physics, not the other way around as the mechanists predicted."[21] One aspect of physics that was to be swallowed up by biology was energy, which played a central role in the development of organicism and its differentiation from vitalism. On the one hand, organicists noted that the law of energy conservation provided evidence against vitalism. In his 1913 *Mechanism, Life, and Personality*, Haldane argues that Hans Driesch's notion of entelechy, a vital principle, "implies a definite breach in the fundamental law of conservation of energy," which is "a principle which has been verified again and again under all sorts of conditions."[22] Instead, organicists embraced energy, but integrated it into their understanding of life through the concept of metabolism, which denoted the "exchange of material and energy, as exemplified in growth, development, maintenance, secretion and absorption, respiration, gross movements in response to stimuli, and other excitatory processes."[23]

Energy and metabolism arose in the same decade, the 1840s, and were intertwined from the start.[24] One of the so-called discoverers of energy, the German doctor Julius von Mayer, even arrived at the notion of the conservation of energy through a metabolic (and imperial) approach, observing sailors' blood on a Dutch colonial ship and hypothesizing that human bodies required less oxygen to maintain blood heat in the tropics. Metabolism, from the Greek μεταβολή (metabolé), or change, yoked the nineteenth-century fascination with change to the continuity of specific forms of organic life. The overriding stability of organisms relied on constant chemical and physical changes. By the early twentieth century, metabolism had become the central theme used to connect physics to biology. In 1913, Harvard biochemist Lawrence Henderson defined metabolism as "the term applied to the inflow and outflow of matter and energy and their intermediary transformations within the organism," and noted that "among other achievements [of metabolism] is the proof that the principle of the conservation of energy applies to the living organism." Henderson also referred to the "total metabolism" of an organism as "the balance sheet of the body," demonstrating the historical connections between metabolism and notions of "nature's economy," which must also be managed according to the latest scientific principles of thermodynamic accounting.[25]

Because energy was the unit of accounting for the metabolic "balance sheet of the body," more energy could be associated with more growth, and growth with complexification and evolutionary advance. The concept of metabolism thus subordinated energy as the means to achieving organic ends (growth, development, activity), another example of biology's intent to swallow physics. Such a "biophysical economics" applied energy and evolution to the governance of the economy, and posited human civilization as a history of increasingly efficient use of nature's energy.[26] Thermodynamic knowledge showed how energy could be harnessed more prolifically and efficiently, which would increase the metabolic input and, in turn, potentially hasten evolutionary progress.

Adopting thermodynamic insights could also help the preindustrial civilizations that purportedly needed to catch up with Europe. As Wilhelm Ostwald, a German chemist who was a key proponent of the energetics movement, argued, thermodynamics was the "foundation of all sciences,"[27] and evolution was simply the history of increasingly productive conversions of the "native energy" offered by nature.[28] This translated directly into ethics, as "every machine, every process, in fact every intelligent person who improves this coefficient of transformation is valuable, and the greater the improvement and the more important for mankind the kind of energy upon which the improvement is devoted, the more valuable he is."[29]

Ostwald was not alone in arguing for the preeminence of energy flows in understanding life, as well as human civilization. The ecologists' desire to follow energy through living systems turned energy into "a unifying concept for social, political and economic analysis" in the early decades of the twentieth century.[30] So while many ecologists drew heavily upon biological sciences and never cited physics texts, the underlying assumptions of thermodynamics and energy pervaded almost every early work of ecology.[31] Representing this trend, Arthur Tansley, a biologist who engaged extensively with imperial politics and who developed the term *ecosystem* in 1935, mixes metaphors and argues that "all living organisms may be regarded as machines transforming energy from one form to another."[32] Similarly, Frederick Soddy, a radiochemist who advanced an early, ecological economics, affirms that life "is dependent for all the necessities of its physical continuance upon the principles of the steam engine. The principles and ethics of all human conventions must not run counter to those of thermodynamics."[33]

Of course, energy transformations could include everything from cell repair to cello playing, and from tossing and turning in bed at night to sunbathing. But as Soddy's analogy to the "principles of the steam engine" makes clear, the energy exchanges charted by many prominent early ecologists were often interpreted through the value-laden prism of the industrial work ethic and its partner category, waste. One of the most influential social theorists to popularize this interpretation was Herbert Spencer, who fashioned an energetic theory of society that combined evolution, thermodynamics, and industrial capitalism. Spencer was widely read in his time, and became influential to early ecologists, but is little known today, though sociologist Andrew McKinnon argues that it is worth revisiting Spencer as one of the few classical social theorists "for whom energy is central to social organization."[34] For Spencer, a former railroad engineer, energy—or Force—was the key to understanding evolution. Through thermodynamics, Spencer drew connections between the evolutionary patterns of inorganic, organic, and social systems, from planets to crustaceans to nations, all of which moved toward greater complexity, "from indefinite, homogeneous motions to definite, heterogeneous motions."[35] Furthermore, Spencer makes a direct correlation between the rising complexity of organisms, from protozoa to hydra to crustaceans, to the rising complexity of human societies, from the "Bushmen" (the protozoa of human societies) to "aboriginal tribes" (hydra) and, finally, industrial Europeans.

Crucially, Spencer makes frequent use of industrial understandings of work and waste as key analogies in his texts. In his 1860 essay "The Social Organism," Spencer insists that it is the "division of labor" among an organism's parts that distinguishes lower organisms and societies from higher ones.[36] Moreover, organized work is the activity that leads to growth; just as the animal "is developed by exercise—by actively discharging the duties which the body at large requires of it," so the social body "begins to enlarge when the community devolves on it more work."[37] Growth also depends upon an organism's ability to get rid of the corresponding waste, which Spencer compares to the need for blood to flow to active organs, bringing nutrients and carrying away unneeded things. Waste is an inevitable byproduct of growth, and increases as growth accelerates, meaning that more "advanced" civilizations needed to develop the capacity to process ever more waste so that they could continue growing. Spencer concludes that "whence it is manifest that what in commercial affairs we call *profit*, answers to the excess of nutrition over waste in a living body."[38] In this organic depiction of commercial growth, waste is figured as something to be washed away by the blood, just as the kidneys extract waste to be excreted as urine.

As Spencer's explanations show, the organism metaphor did not position work or energy as ends in themselves. It relied upon a number of unstated assumptions: that work ineluctably leads to growth, that growth is unquestionably good for an organism's overall well-being, and that waste could be endlessly excreted into some external "away" place where it would no longer affect the organism. In practice, these assumptions were easily accepted and required little justification, in part because of the influence of the work and waste ethos, which had its own justifications for the virtue of work. Indeed, when faced with evidence that the imperial organism might not be healthy—urban smog, workers' intransigence, rampant disease in the new urban slums—it was more comfortable to tinker with waste processing than it was to question work and energy maximization itself. Still, the organic metaphor and its ecological implications did force a wedge into the Victorian industrial assemblage, leaving a placeholder in early Anthropocene thinking for posing uncomfortable questions to the fossil fuel enterprise.

Energy exchange, as metabolism, might be the central phenomenon of living organisms, but many organicists insisted that life could not be completely understood by a narrow study of energy exchanges. Instead, these metabolic exchanges, rather than being determined by simple physical and chemical inputs, were organically determined; that is, they were determined by the organic structure or pattern of life in which they were situated. Organicism, therefore, imported energy physics into biology in a way that validated the application of thermodynamic measurement, but at the same time subordinated it to organic determination.

The ethical consequences of this subordination were potentially radical. Because the organic metaphor subordinated energy and matter flows to the study of biological organization, it meant that the exchange of energy, the inputs and outputs of work and waste, were not ends in themselves, but rather served the evolutionary pattern of what Alfred North Whitehead referred to as the "endurance" of organisms (whether cell, body, or, for some, ecosystem, state, or planet). Energy exchanges indicated organic activity, but these proxy measurements of inputs and outputs were not to be confused with the ends of organic activity itself. Politically, an organicist understanding of life therefore enshrines the resilience of life—and not the maximization of work or energy exploitation—as the defining goal. The question that this suggests for governance becomes: Which exchanges of work and waste, and energy and matter, best extend the organism?

Importantly, and in contrast to much of Victorian and Edwardian thinking, this does not necessarily suggest a zero-sum competition for a fixed set of fuels, wherein the victors in the game of evolution are the organisms that appropriate the most fuel and produce the most stuff. This more common approach to evolution as a "general scrimmage for available energy" is best reflected by the work of Alfred Lotka, a mathematical biologist who posited that evolution favored species that increased the "total energy flux" of an organic system. Indeed, Lotka is worth quoting at length for his representative synthesis of thermodynamics (and its work-and-waste maxim) and evolution (as survival of the fittest) in support of a politics of industrialism. Lotka reduces animals to "catalysers, oiling the machinery, as it were and assisting energy in its downhill path to levels of lower availability (higher entropy)." However, humans are special in being able to do more than just competitively divert energy. As a result, Lotka proposes that

This at least seems probable, that so long as there is an abundant surplus of available energy running "to waste" over the sides of the mill wheel, so to speak, so long will a marked advantage be gained by any species that may develop talents to utilize this "lost portion of the stream." . . . Every indication is that man will learn to utilize some of the sunlight that now goes to waste. The general effect will be to increase the rate of energy flux through the system of organic nature, with a parallel increase in the total mass of the great world transformer, of its rate of circulation, or both.[39]

Lotka's admittedly extreme description of waste is emblematic of the thermodynamic approach: all energy exchanges on Earth that are not being exploited by human industry can be considered waste, including waterfalls and each ray of sunlight. The underlying spirit of Lotka's argument continues to inform the human relationship to energy, and is evident in the ongoing construction of indigenous lands, as well as desert or swamp ecosystems, as "marginal," "empty," or "unused" in order to justify modernist energy projects, including mega-solar arrays or agrofuel plantations.[40] Lotka's prediction—that humans would seek solar power as a further effort to gain "a marked advantage"—is prescient, though his assumption that this will, indeed, confer an evolutionary advantage, at least over the long term, appears increasingly flawed in the late Anthropocene.

As opposed to this popular, "struggle for existence" interpretation of evolution, Whitehead, for example, highlights the "neglected side" of evolution, that of creativity and cooperation among organisms that participate in "creating their own environment."[41] Such an approach to evolution recognizes that "the single organism is almost helpless. The adequate forces require societies of cooperating organisms," and this in turn "alters the whole ethical aspect of evolution."[42] It is a marked ethical alteration indeed, not only from the struggle for existence ethic, but also from Lotka's embrace of thermo-ethics. As Whitehead's philosophy suggests, the process of defining the boundaries of the organism as a site of governance becomes a key political question from the perspective of organic and systems theorists. If the resilience of the organism is the true aim, then this raises several questions. What are the boundaries of the organism to be made resilient, and what is the meaning of resilience? What are the organism's functioning parts to be worked upon? What are the inputs and, most significantly in the Anthropocene, what gets labeled as waste? For instance, if the organism is defined as the community of human bodies, we can eliminate plastic waste that is ejected outside the organism (into the oceans, underground, into space) as long as it can conceivably remain bracketed from human well-being. Once the waste accumulates, however, these bracketing efforts become increasingly difficult. And if the organism to be made resilient is the whole Earth, waste begins to look different. Moreover, resilience means more than adequate human employment, though this assumption that work results in the well-being of human civilization remains common. Because the desired outcome is not the sum total of productive work, which can be measured easily through motion or money, but is rather a more complicated pursuit toward organic endurance, it is necessary to appreciate the many interrelationships that contribute to organic success across expanded horizons of space and time.

So while the organism to be governed could be defined as narrowly as particular groups of human bodies, organic metaphors inevitably open up toward ever larger, more ecological understandings of humans as enmeshed in lifeworlds that extend to the planet (and beyond). It should be clear by this point why these early organicist intimations have become attractive to eco- and geopolitical theorists today. If resilience and human–nonhuman entanglements are taken into account, burning fossil fuels makes little sense, as its consequences seriously threaten the resilience of life on Earth, and not just for humans. Whitehead's warning echoes from the early decades of fossil-fueled industry: "any physical object which by its influence deteriorates its environment, commits suicide."[43]

THERMO-ETHICS REIGNS

However, despite the alternative fuel ethics suggested by the organicist metaphor, the energy logics of thermodynamics remained dominant. Although organicists endeavored to subordinate energy to biology, in imperial deployments of organicism, the reverse more often happened. The thermodynamic tool kit—efficiency statistics, productivity measurements—proved too attractive for governing elites, and the embrace of the maximization of productive work dwarfed the organicist preference to put energy exchange into the context of living organisms.[44] The energy logic of thermodynamics, in turn, sidelined other ways of knowing energy, as well as alternative governance strategies for industrial life. Human well-being continued to be made equivalent to measurements of energy and work.

But why did thermodynamics tend to crowd out other ways of knowing, governing, and valuing life and energy? One reason is that thermodynamics not only ratified the Victorian preference for productivist economics;[45] it also suggested avenues for revitalizing the work ethic in light of new industrial demands. While variations of the work ethic predated thermodynamics, as described in chapter 4, new energy logics played a role in the adaptation of the work ethic to industrialization and the rise of quantitative accounting to govern workers in the last half of the nineteenth century.[46] Indeed, it is likely that the intensity with which work was proselytized in this period (note that Max Weber, for example, introduced the notion of the Protestant work ethic in 1904, in the midst of imperial labor debates) is related to the increasing vulnerability of the great industrial labor project in the face of the growing recognition that it was producing strikingly ambivalent effects for humans and the planet. If the accumulating waste and the requisite exploitation of humans and nonhumans were not to overwhelm what Mary Kingsley called the "industrial mission,"[47] they required new governance strategies.

Another reason for the dominance of thermodynamic approaches is that, as a governance strategy, energy was attractive. Thermodynamics offered easily applicable tools for making the environment legible, and thus governable.[48] Biological organization, or resilience, is a great deal murkier than the inflows and outflows of matter and energy, which can be counted and tracked. In contrast, while evolution similarly catalyzed the eugenicists' desire to measure and compare human bodies, there was little else in Darwin's work that could be easily converted into data on which the state could apply itself. Joseph Needham acknowledges this problem in his 1941 essay "Evolution and Thermodynamics," when he muses that "the nature of holistic organisation is certainly not susceptible of the same kind of measurement as thermodynamic mixed-up-ness, but we have no reason whatever for supposing that its measurement is impossible. When such a measurement has been achieved, it would be feasible to apply it also to human social evolution. I see no reason for doubting the possibility of this."[49] Although Needham expresses hope here for the "possibility" of such measurement, the above quotation betrays its absence vis-à-vis thermodynamic measurement as late as 1941.

There is a noteworthy historical resonance here between work and money as legible units that enabled an intensification of scientific management of the state. The energy–work–money connection runs through the nineteenth century; Bruce Clarke notes that "the rhetorical substitution of money for energy" has been "commonplace" since energy's discovery. The assumed equivalence of energy and money remains prominent today. Even Einstein described energy through an economic metaphor, explaining how the ubiquity of energy had been "missed" for so long because it was not always "given off externally," just as when "a man who is fabulously rich should never spend or give away a cent; no one could tell how rich he was."[50]

The new field of economics was also deeply indebted to thermodynamics. Philip Mirowski connects thermodynamics to the rise of neoclassical economics, which drew upon analogies between energy and money as measures of value.[51] Similarly, just as work makes energy legible as an object amenable to technocratic control, Timothy Mitchell argues that the legibility of money drove the formation of econometrics in the early twentieth century. Following World War I, administrators found it difficult to measure Germany's wealth, and Mitchell shows how this event provoked a shift from economics as a measure of wealth to economics as a measure of money exchange.[52] Wealth did not translate as well as work or money into units of measurement of industrial accounting. Economics—like energy—became the study of holistic relations underpinned by money exchange, drawing upon the organic and systems metaphors of ecology.

This helps to explain why organicism, which integrated both evolution and energy, had, and continues to have, a mixed ethical legacy. In practice, as the next chapter will show, the tantalizing temptations of energy accounting—which could be conducted almost entirely through the rubric of work, already a revered site of state policy—meant that work maximization tended to dominate organic thinking. Lip service was paid to the organic ideal, in that almost all Europeans, whether labor unionists, abolitionists, or colonial merchants, shared the belief that work and energy maximization were the key to the organic health of European empires. Nevertheless, as evidence mounted to the contrary—in the multiple social and economic crises of depressions, fluctuations in resource prices, unemployment, labor strikes, and outright labor resistance in Britain and the colonies—the response was almost always to double down on work, rather than to question whether work maximization actually led to social well-being. There might be disputes as to the methods to be employed in the colonies, and even a growing anti-imperialist sentiment in Britain, but it was exceedingly rare to question the pursuit of work and energy itself. With metabolism as the reigning metaphor, energy and work remained unquestionably vital to the imperial organism, just as breathing and eating were to animal bodies.

At the same time, because the organic metaphor insisted on including ever-wider processes as relevant to the organism, organicism was also instrumental in the rise of a global environmental consciousness. In other words, the organic metaphor could, on the one hand, speak to the necessity of energy and work maximization as metabolically necessary, while on the other hand making it increasingly difficult to bracket the cruel and destructive consequences of industrialization. Because ecology drew on fields including botany, forestry, zoology, sociology, medicine, and psychology, it was also at the forefront of studying the environmental and social consequences of industry from deforestation to "invasive" species, women's "hysteria," and unemployment.[53] The threat posed by the people and things who suffered in the name of energy maximization, and who were conceivably part of the imperial organism, was neutralized by producing them as waste to be excised or cured, whether by making them invisible altogether or by treating them as diseased parts to be improved by work. The organism was thus consolidated through an active process of treating or, in the last instance, amputating those bodies and materials that undermined industrial goals.

ENERGOPOWER

Terms such as *energy logic* or political rationality draw upon concepts of governance introduced by Michel Foucault in his study of modern power. Readers familiar with Foucault's notion of biopolitics will likely see its echoes in the above discussion of organic metaphors, which served in the governmentality of individual bodies, societies, and empires. Until now, I have not made this debt very explicit. In this section, I propose that the superposition of thermodynamics and ecology through organic metaphors can tell us something new about biopolitics. This involves appreciating energy logics as a kind of energopower, a concept first proposed by Dominic Boyer as a partner to biopolitical modes of sovereignty, as "power over (and through) energy."[54] Boyer argues that one cannot understand the biopolitical projects of Foucault's prisons, schools, and factories without attending to their dependence on industrial energy apparatuses to supply building materials, light, and heat, such that "power over energy has been the companion and collaborator of modern power over life and population from the beginning."[55] This nascent energopolitical project can be further enriched by focusing on the birth of energy in thermodynamic science. Such a focus reveals that the very notion of the possibility of "power over (and through) energy" often mobilizes an energy logic that dictates which energy is most useful, and which is to be minimized or expelled.

Foucault introduced biopolitics[56] to describe the rise of a modern practice of governmentality, starting in the eighteenth century and culminating in the nineteenth century, where "power is situated and exercised at the level of life, the species, the race, and the large-scale phenomena of population."[57] Rather than the older model of sovereignty, wherein the sovereign exercises a negative power over life, deciding who must die and who can be allowed to live, biopower takes life itself as its site of action, "exert[ing] a positive influence on life, that endeavors to administer, optimize, and multiply it, subjecting it to precise controls and comprehensive regulations."[58] While it seeks to work productively on life, biopower simultaneously must protect life by constructing norms, and by marginalizing those deemed outside of them, sometimes to the point of death: the insane, criminals, the poor, sexual deviants.[59] And so the project of making populations live does not lead to the subsiding of mass death; war and genocide indeed become ever more totalizing, but they are now waged in the name of the life of a species, rather than in the name of the defense of a sovereign.[60]

According to Foucault's genealogy of biopower, industrialization played a key role in its emergence: "it is as though power, which used to have sovereignty as its modality or organizing schema, found itself unable to govern the economic and political body of a society that was undergoing both a demographic explosion and industrialization."[61] In other words, capitalism required not only institutions and "the great instruments of the state" for advancing industrialization, but also the techniques inaugurated by "anatomo-politics" (the discipline of individual bodies) and "biopolitics" (the governance of populations and species), which operated through census data, medicine, and social institutions such as schools, hospitals, and families. Foucault observes that "the adjustment of the accumulation of men to that of capital, the joining of the growth of human groups to the expansion of productive forces and the differential allocation of profit, were made possible in part by the exercise of bio-power in its many forms and modes of application."[62]

Biopower draws heavily upon modern science for the construction of its norms, constituting a "physics of power, or a power thought of as physical action in the element of nature."[63] The state was interested in studying and acting upon the socio-material milieu, which was "the intersection between a multiplicity of living individuals working and co-existing with each other in a set of material elements that act on them and on which they act in turn."[64] Evolutionism, for example, and not so much Darwin in particular as a "bundle of notions" such as the "struggle for existence" and natural selection, is flagged as crucial to thinking about late nineteenth-century power. Foucault writes rather damningly that evolutionism became "a real way of thinking about the relations between colonization, the necessity for wars, criminality. . . . Whenever, in other words, there was a confrontation, a killing or the risk of death, the nineteenth century was quite literally obliged to think about them in the form of evolutionism."[65]

But despite Foucault's emphasis on biological sciences such as medicine and evolution, and his reference to a "physics of power," he gives little attention to the physical sciences. This mirrors the tendency, chronicled in this chapter, to overlook the assumptions drawn from physics—including from the science of energy—that played a key role in structuring the application of governing metaphors like the organism, a sister metaphor to the population or species. Appreciating the science of energy helps us to understand how biopolitics so often turns to genocidal, and even suicidal, projects, by adding another layer of complexity to sovereign efforts to produce docile bodies for the project of waged work.

First, energy helps to construct the norm of efficient work, so that working processes can be policed as energy flows. Where biopower aims for a healthy human population by separating the living from the dead, and the sane from the insane, energopower seeks to increase the metabolic rate of the organism by maximizing work and evacuating waste. This requires the definitional separation of work from waste, of ordered energy use from disordered entropy increase, which infers a more active governance of the environment than that assumed by Foucault's milieu.

Second, energopower is not practiced on human populations alone. Biopolitics, and likewise evolutionism, offered strategies for governing humans as populations or species, with sex becoming a significant political problematic because it is "located at the point of intersection of the discipline of the body and the control of the population."[66] Meanwhile, the knowledge of energy is focused on a different fulcrum. Rather than traverse human bodies and populations, with sex as the waypoint, energy connects human–technological apparatuses to the energetic transformations of the cosmos. The key problem posed for energetic governance is not sex and its regulation, but instead the provision and use of fossil fuels and other material resources that make possible the production and reproduction of populations.

The science of energy thus concerns itself with human actions in a milieu that includes not just populations, but also nonhuman energy exchanges. By extracting and burning fossil fuels, in particular, humans were brought into contact with larger, dynamic Earth flows. This is a different kind of milieu than that described by Foucault, who sometimes treated the "physical" aspects of the environment as "material givens"[67] that act upon humans only in a relatively static, "inert" manner. Geographer Bruce Braun argues that although Foucault attended to the relationship between humans and territory, and noted the impacts stemming from industrialization, "in Foucault's work 'territory' merely contained a set of pre-given 'things'" that were assumed to be already legible and available to the state, and "forms of economic and political calculation" that would then "[regulate] the relation of people *to* those things."[68] Foucault's inattention to the remarkable shift in the physical sciences in the nineteenth century, which no longer viewed the material world as "inert," is thus a lacuna that energopower addresses.[69]

Third, while the object of biopolitics is life, the object of energopolitics is more circumscribed: work. Although the object is narrowed, the targets of governance are expanded from organic bodies, assembled as a population, to sociotechnical systems, both human and more-than-human. You do not have to be alive to do work; the only real requirement is energy, paired with a channeling or transforming apparatus. Biopolitics is not always in service to life and, as described below, often deals in death; however, it always justifies itself as in service to *some* population, somewhere. In contrast, energopolitical strategies are not ultimately about maximizing (some) life, but about maximizing (some) work. The apex of work—fossil-fueled, productive, efficient, commodified—does not always accord with life; not even with the life of the most privileged populations. As a result, energopolitics is not required to justify itself in terms of the life of a population in the final instance. Energopolitics claims success through measurements of productivity and efficiency, and by its ability to manage waste.

Waste is the ghoul of energopower, just as death is biopower's nemesis. From the perspective of biopower, which is exercised over life, "death is power's limit, the moment that escapes it; death becomes the most secret aspect of existence, the most 'private.'"[70] Accordingly, the central puzzle of biopolitics becomes one of distinction, of judging what serves the life of the population, and what does not. Racism helps to organize these decisions by inserting "the break between what must live and what must die."[71] Racism is a technology for sorting out those humans whose extinction must be allowed for the health of the species.

Energopolitics also makes ample use of racism for its governing distinctions. But the limit of energopower, that which escapes it, is not death writ large, but that which travels under the more specific sign of waste, a commonplace interpretation of entropy. Death and entropy are kindred phenomena. Life is negentropic (low entropy), and sustaining a low-entropy state is a feat set against the spontaneous increase of entropy everywhere else, which led the early scientists of energy to fear the heat death of the universe. With maximal entropy, energy would be evenly distributed, difference would be erased, and life would theoretically be impossible. But while death and waste are kindred phenomena, they are not synonymous. They have distinct effects as political technologies of sorting. Most importantly, the category of waste extends far beyond human and other living bodies, beyond the organism, encompassing all activities on the Earth that might hamper human enterprises, or whose potential energy is not being put to work—everything from friction to idleness, and from nonindustrial ways of life to pipeline leaks, oil left in the ground, gas trapped in rock, terrain left uncultivated, "invasive" species, crops that are vulnerable to pests, or forests managed by indigenous techniques.

Energopower thus describes a valence of biopower that is not directed toward the life of a population but toward the project of fossil-fueled work. The question is not which humans are allowed to die for the good of the population, but rather which waste—a more-than-human entity— can be made more useful, and which waste is intractable and in need of expulsion. Waste is produced both literally (spent fuel, pollution, trash) and as a manufactured category marking that which is in need of improvement or, barring that, disposal. Entropy, or waste, can be governed, and even minimized, but never eliminated altogether, as waste is an inevitable outcome of work. Making order in one place creates disorder in others. Energopower aims to quarantine waste from the work project, and in the process, ideally render it invisible to privileged humans.

To say that waste is produced by energopolitics is not to say that it had no history prior to the nineteenth century. Before being taken up in thermodynamics, the sin of waste had already enjoyed a glorious career in disciplining Christians, as is apparent in early Protestant tracts or in Benjamin Franklin–style self-help texts. The modern understanding of waste is built upon the ancient Christian sin of *acedia*, or sloth, which Thomas Aquinas defined as "*an oppressive sorrow*, which, to wit, so weighs upon man's mind, that he wants to do nothing."[72] Aquinas and other early Christians considered sloth as a complicated problem that particularly preyed upon monks and ascetics—the "noonday demon" that left them sluggish and weak. Idleness and laziness also appear in these theological texts, but they are treated more as the effects of a sorrowful, apathetic state of mind, which Aquinas opposes to joy. The sin of waste can only be cured by the grace of God and must be confronted by spiritual tactics that work upon one's disposition and faith.

With energopolitics, waste, which had largely functioned as a moral technology of the church, the manor, and the workshop, gets intensified into a scientific technology of the liberal state. To borrow Foucault's formulation of biopower and its use of race, energopower "inscribes [waste] in the mechanisms of the state." Waste becomes a governable target in need of elimination, a central obsession of modern power. Machines, factories, and machine-knowledge deliver this transition; historian Daniel Rodgers writes that the new factories "brought the disciplinary strain in the work ethic, its call to constant busyness, out of the realm of moral abstractions and into nineteenth-century social reality."[73] In energopolitics, the useless energy must be separated from the useful in service to work. If the human conduct that proved so puzzling to biopower was suicide,[74] then the human conduct that appears most vexing to energopower, and that constantly exceeds its disciplinary efforts, is indolence.

CONCLUSION: WORKING TO LIVE, LIVING TO WORK

As with the organic metaphor, which intended that biology "swallow" physics, so too energopower is often meant to be subsumed beneath the overriding goal of biopower. Work is justified as the means to making populations live. When the goals of life and work can be made to appear harmonious, biopower and energopower reinforce each other. Work often needs living bodies (though this is less and less the case), and living bodies need energy, or fuel. In order to work, bodies need to be kept alive and reproduced from one morning to the next. Governing work thus involves the biopolitical tasks of gathering demographic statistics about the health, fertility, natality, or nutrition of populations. In addition, mass consumerism relies on living humans to produce and consume things. We travel in circles, from energy to life to work and back again, that inscribe us as modern subjects who make up governable populations. This is why, for Foucault, the governance of labor is central to the biopolitical project of making a population live. From this angle, energopower can be analyzed as one particular expression of biopower.

At other times, though, the project of work is in tension with the project of life, and not just for sacrificial lives but for all life, human and otherwise. These moments reflect the tension at the heart of capitalism itself, the problem that formed the basis of Marx's critique: that capitalism ultimately does not serve life, but preys upon it. Liberal governance, often through biopolitical regimes, attempts to soften the predatory effects of capitalism on collective life, but ultimately does not resolve them. Energopolitics has less need for liberalism's hypocrisy, for it does not ultimately aim to serve life, but work. Energopower refers to sovereignty practiced not over the life of a population, according to biological and medical sciences, but over the operations of industrial systems, according to physical sciences and engineering. When energopolitics dominates, the tension between human life and capitalism is less problematic. In the logic of energopolitics, life—*all* life, even the most elite and privileged lives, and certainly all nonhuman life—becomes secondary to making things work. Indeed, industrialization, heat engines, and the economy begin to appear as having their *own* lives, and as needing a version of medical tending and prioritization. In a report to the 1885 Industrial Remuneration Conference, a prominent British mill owner named William Houldsworth warns the state against addressing the human problems of wages and unemployment. Instead, he encourages the state to become a doctor to the life of industry, respecting its natural laws of change and turbulence. Industry needs the "freedom to spring where it likes, to flow where it likes, to alter its course as it likes, to disappear if it likes. . . . If you meddle with it you will most likely kill it altogether. History is full of examples. Give it fresh air and perfect freedom to move."[75] Houldsworth's prescription for industry precisely echoes the advice for improving labor conditions in the period, as if industrial systems, like human workers, also needed gentle care. Energopower in this sense is a mode of biopower over a population *and* its dynamic milieu of multispecies industrial apparatuses. The state's role is to remove the obstacles that block the flow of putting fossil fuels to work.

The political rationality of energopolitics is important in making sense of the Anthropocene, an era so saturated in death as to allow life no quarter. Many wonder at its suicidal impulses: How can we continue with activities that we know to be risking the life of the human species, much less countless other species facing extinction? How can we continue when all we can hope for is to become resilient in the wake of disaster, the main biopolitical tactic on offer?[76] These questions appear less contradictory from the perspective of energopolitics, which does not aim to make live, but rather to make work. The Anthropocene does not disturb energopolitical projects that, after all, aim to make troublesome human workers redundant. So long as mass deaths and species extinctions do not stop the process of putting energy to work, nor impede the flows of fuel and money, energopolitics can claim some success. Energopolitics may then step in as a backstop to biopolitics. In other words, when the cycles of life–energy–work grow bumpy, or break, energopolitics reflects the governance of populations toward an alternative goal—if not for life, then for work. The final connection—the presumption that the work of sociotechnical systems will bring human well-being—can hang suspended, a dotted-line fantasy, as intangible as a rainbow. Life can be signed over to the trust of productivity and efficiency, to the faith that, by sucking up more and more energy, progress will one day ensue. This is no longer necessarily the progress of any living species, but the progress of work.

Biopolitics: to make live. *Energopolitics*: to put all energy on Earth to work. Biopower, invested with energopower, culminated in the late nineteenth century, and was crucial to the new imperial zeitgeist. As the next chapter will show, the logics of energy—metabolic accounting to draw up the imperial "balance sheet" of matter-energy inflows and outflows—infused the political rationalities that took aim at the problem of colonial labor, and the desire to capture useful energy, and all of the wasteful, inefficient Earth processes, and put them to work.

6   THE IMPERIAL ORGANISM AT WORK

> From all this it follows that the easiest, most natural
> and obvious way to civilize the African native is to give
> him decent white employment. White employment
> is his best school; the gospel of labour is the most
> salutary gospel for him.
>
> —JAN CHRISTIAN SMUTS,
> *Africa and Some World Problems* (1930)

Victorian empires were steeped in energy. This is most obvious when energy is taken to signify fuel. The use of fossil fuels was tied up with political domination from its inception, both within Great Britain and globally; Andreas Malm describes how "a clique of white British men employed steam power as a literal weapon against the best part of humankind, from the Niger delta to the Yangzi delta, the Levant to Latin America."[1] Fossil-driven technologies of transportation and communication helped in the creation of new European colonies, as in Africa, as well as in the extension of greater control over already existing regimes, as in India or Southeast Asia. Fossil fuel–driven capitalism required an unjust circulation of materials and bodies; the concentration of wealth in some sites occurred at the expense of other people and things, necessitating authoritarianism in certain sites and moments, a phenomenon that has been exhaustively catalogued by postcolonial theorists and thinkers in the Global South.[2]

The material capacities released by fossil fuels are central to the story of nineteenth- and twentieth-century imperialisms. However, this chapter extends the study of energetic empire beyond a consideration of fuel power. Instead, I continue to approach energy as a historical figuration, asking how energy became a traveling metaphor that reinforced the material and capitalist relations of empire in the period following the birth of thermodynamics. Of course, these two questions, premised upon two facets of energy—as fuel and as a ruling logic—are enmeshed. The larger argument of this book is that energy contributed to a Western master code of work and waste that infected the human relationship with fossil fuels, imbuing the drive toward efficiency and productivity with an aura of natural timelessness. The study of fossil-fueled empire can be enriched by an understanding of how energy contributed to the rapacious productivism that galvanized imperial domination.

In order to discern energy logics at work in fossil-fueled empire, this chapter focuses on exhuming traces of thermodynamics in the discourses and practices of the new imperialist era, stretching from the 1870s to the early decades of the twentieth century. I focus particularly on the case of British new imperialism in Africa, both because of the British-based popularization of the science of energy, and because of the significance of Africa and the racist mythologies of African labor to new imperial logics, especially following the dramatic British loss in the First Boer War (1880–81) and in the aftermath of the abolition of slavery. The next chapter will expand beyond the British Empire to consider how energy appears in the new imperial practices of the U.S. technical education movement of this period, both as a settler colonial state (schools for Native Americans) and a former slave state (industrial schools for enfranchised Black Americans).

The new imperialist era, stretching from the 1870s to the end of World War II, witnessed the emergence of a more information-heavy, administrative approach to imperial governance, one that drew upon the sciences and presaged later notions of global development. I have chosen to focus on the new imperial era because it was the imperial moment most marked by fossil-fueled industrialization, and by the birth of energy as a logic of domination, following its so-called discovery by thermodynamics in the 1840s. However, it is worth emphasizing that European imperial domination preceded fossil-fueled industrialization by centuries. Postcolonial theorists like Sylvia Wynter, Walter Mignolo, and Irene Silverblatt look to the Renaissance, and to the Spanish colonization of the New World in the sixteenth and seventeenth centuries to understand the early configuration of what Mignolo calls "colonial difference."[3] Only by first defining themselves against the peoples of the New World did Europeans begin to think of themselves as "European," and as the central agents of world history.

While European imperialism did not originate in the nineteenth century, its intensity and style underwent a significant shift in this period. Wynter, for example, analyzes this shift as the invention of a new "genre" of humankind. Genres of humankind contain "descriptive statements" of what it means to be human in that period. In describing humankind, they also inscribe a "space of Otherness," those who fall outside the human genre. The distinction between the human and the Other, according to each era's genre, ordered European notions of justice and sovereignty in its colonies. Wynter locates the first genre shift in the Renaissance-era move from the "True Christian Self" to the "Rational Self of Man," or what she terms Man_1, which was closely connected to Newtonian physics and Enlightenment sciences. The Christian Self had been defined against the infidel or heretic, but Man_1, the European political subject, now required that the Other be transformed from the spiritually damned to the "politically condemned," which would include categories like "the interned Mad, the interned 'Indian,' the enslaved 'Negro.'"[4]

Man_1 inaugurated the modern self, but Wynter notices that its meaning continued to morph over time. In the nineteenth century, social Darwinism and new biological definitions of the human species contributed to the invention of "Man_2."[5] With Man_2, the human now appears primarily as an *economic* subject whose activities, according to the laws of the market, abide by the laws of nature. Drawing on Fanon, Wynter observes that the elite economic subject announced by Man_2, the "Breadwinners and Investors," defined the Other as the "economically damnés," no longer the politically condemned, the Mad, interned, or enslaved, but "the jobless, the homeless, the Poor," and the "underdeveloped," organized along a global color line.[6]

As is evident in Wynter's analysis of Man_2, the importance of biological sciences such as evolution and ecology to the new imperialist mindset is well established,[7] and was also acknowledged at the time, with mixed feelings. In 1906, a French diplomat named Victor Bérard chastised Britain for its misapplication of Darwinism, writing that "the English people are steeped in this doctrine, which they believe to be in strict keeping with the latest discoveries of science, especially with the latest theories of the great English thinkers, such as Darwin and his followers, which, above all, they feel to be in keeping with the temperament of the race. *It is this doctrine which has really created the Imperialist frame of mind in the nation"* (italics mine).[8]

Energy and its metaphors do not appear as explicitly, nor anywhere near as frequently, as do the biological sciences in the "descriptive statements" of what it meant to be human, nor in the archives of the new imperialism. But while evolution supposedly explained European racial superiority—Westerners had crafted tools that enabled them to better survive their environment—it was the science of energy that specified exactly how civilizational advancement had been achieved. Understood through the logic of energy, Western technological superiority did not arise as a result of better art, truer faith, or liberal government, much as these might have been understood as necessary preconditions. It was by a superior work ethic, imbued with an energetic disposition that sought efficiency and productivity above all other measures of value.

As with older work ethics, this diagnosis had less to do with celebrating European labor than it did with disciplining it. The preoccupation with spreading a gospel of labor reveals the anxieties of a powerful elite in the face of the ever-present recalcitrance of workers. Labor posed a continual problem to those aiming to profit from fossil-enabled power; Malm argues that "fossil fuels necessitate waged or forced labor—the power of some to direct the labor of others—as conditions of their very existence." As a result, Malm traces the origins of fossil economies to the "sphere" of laborers, the contested sites "where biophysical resources pass into the circuits of social metabolism."[9] It is not surprising, then, that energy logics appear most intensely in the governance of laboring bodies and things. The central argument of this chapter is that global struggles over the problem of labor, an omnipresent obsession for European imperial managers, became animated by energetic assumptions. Victorian labor politics are familiar to historians of empire, but I emphasize how thermodynamics contributed to this broader historical development, in particular through an energetic racism that reinforced hierarchies of gender, race, and class.

While energy appears in multiple ways, here I build upon chapter 5, focusing on ecology as a central vector through which thermodynamic metaphors reinforced new imperialist practices. Like energy, ecology was also a child of empire, "[growing] out of the imperial administrative and political culture" of the turn of the twentieth century.[10] And thanks to ecology's preference for systems-level thinking, for taking the view from above (sometimes literally, as in the frequent use of aerial surveys in the colonial world), ecology was often presented as a master science for imperial administration.[11] Historians of ecological imperialism have largely ignored or minimized the role of energy science. Peder Anker, for example, writes that "the natural sciences such as physics and chemistry played little role in the ecologists' understanding of the natural world, despite their use of mechanistic and chemical terminology."[12] However, as chapter 5 showed, energy did play a significant role in the development of ecological thinking. Even a "terminological" adoption of energy physics could and did have political significance thanks to the seductive nature of energy accounting. Through a reexamination of the operations of ecology as a new imperial science, this chapter makes the case for energy itself as a political rationality that served imperial domination, as providing yet another framework, or "Western code,"[13] with which to organize a world of different, and usually subjugated, people and things.

At the same time, it is important to couch energy in an understanding of empire that is multiple and plural: empire was "shaped by various colonial contexts, and worked on different aspects of British society in multifarious ways," such that "we need to be wary of basing wide generalizations upon limited case studies."[14] Energy and work, too, were practiced and interpreted in multiple ways. However, my aim here is less to explore alternative energy logics—a field that deserves further research—and instead to map the contours of how energy emerged as a Western logic of domination, one that claimed itself to be the only possible epistemology of fuel.[15] I follow a dominant logic of energy that valorized productive work, and that was indebted to the Presbyterian synthesis of early energy scientists, as it assisted in the violent capture and transformation of alternative possibilities of valuing work and relating to fuel.

This was not a case of a smooth transferral of European knowledge from core to periphery, but rather of a struggle over how people should organize their activities and energetic accounts. Dominant energy logics were constituted by their engagement with people and things who resisted the European work project. Indeed, the European work/energy nexus, despite its claim to hegemony, faced significant resistance from soils, forests, waterways, and lifeways, as "the apparent ineluctability of 'nature' gave rise to repeated tensions within the colonial medical, scientific and technical services, or proved, as in the case of agriculture and forestry, that what was standard practice in Europe was neither feasible nor desirable in a very different African, Asian or Caribbean environment."[16] Intransigent peoples, forests, and animals only intensified desires to control energy, animating an energy zeitgeist that underlies the more familiar imperial tropes of labor, social Darwinism, and ecological metaphors.

The chapter follows energetic metaphors as they emerge in imperial discourse, first showing how the problem of labor was interpreted through the metaphor of the organism. Categorizations of work and waste depended upon thermo-political judgments that assumed that energy fueled the metabolism of the imperial organism. Energy intake allowed for work—and growth—but only if waste could be adequately processed. In order to process waste, it had to be discovered and labeled, and this occurred through hierarchies of race, gender, and class. When thermodynamics is superposed onto these intersecting hierarchies, fossil fuel expansion could be connected to the virtues of work, and pollution to the sin of sloth, connotations that continue to haunt ideologies of global development.

THE NEW IMPERIAL ORGANISM AND ITS PROBLEMS

The British Empire reached the apex of its power in the nineteenth century, during the new imperial moment, when it "forged one of the largest and most powerful empires in the world."[17] Historians offer a number of explanations for the acceleration of empire in the late nineteenth century, including the rise of Germany and the United States as industrial and military competitors, the global depression of the 1870s, the discovery of diamonds in South Africa, the rise of labor unions and socialist parties in Europe (and, by the 1880s, in Great Britain as well), fluctuating resource prices, soaring unemployment, and the humiliating British losses in the 1880–81 Boer War in South Africa. Regardless of the precise cause, the sudden revival of interest in imperialism was remarkably abrupt.[18] Within the space of a decade, the scramble for Africa was launched and the British claimed roughly two million square miles of new territories in Africa. In 1891, Lord Salisbury reportedly quipped of the "sudden emergence of African questions" that "when he left the Foreign Office in 1880, no one thought of Africa. When he returned to it in 1885, the nations of Europe were effervescing with new African interests."[19]

New imperialism differed from its older variants in part because of the proliferation of steam technologies. Fossil fuels exploded a number of constraints of space and time exponentially beyond what sociotechnical assemblages like the stirrup, sailing ships, or slavery had enabled in the past. The steamships of empire were still constrained by the availability of coal, and the location of coaling stations, but no longer by the much more restrictive vagaries of animal muscle, wind flow, or ocean currents. Fossil fuels are also subterranean, and so transcended the long-standing land constraint of biomass/muscle energy systems that required extensive acreage for forests, grazing, and agriculture. By breaking free from these constraints, Matthew Huber argues that "fossilized time-space compression represents the conditions of possibility for the very ideas of global markets, global civil society, and global states."[20]

However, breaking free from material constraints required a great deal of painful breaking for humans and nonhumans everywhere on the planet.[21] While fossil fuels themselves required less land, land was still necessary to supply the materials for industry, as well as to feed a burgeoning European population with solar-driven agriculture. Much of the new demand for land and material resources was met by extending control over territory outside of Europe, which had to be committed to sustaining European industry and populations. In his 1911 poem "Big Steamers," Rudyard Kipling warns as much, telling the British people that "For the bread that you eat and the biscuits you nibble, / The sweets that you suck and the joints that you carve, / They are brought to you daily by All Us Big Steamers / And if any one hinders our coming you'll starve!"[22] The prospect of industrialization in the Global South was threatening; if the colonies were permitted to industrialize, their land would be needed to feed their own factories, rather than to feed European laborers.[23]

In tandem with colonial land and resources, European industrialization also depended on underpaying colonized peoples. The advancement of productive work, which already governed European industrial life, was an inherently global goal; from the start, British administrators and the public perceived colonial labor as inextricably wound up with British labor and well-being. For some, imperialism, in inciting nationalism among the working class, could also temper the threat of socialist revolution in Europe. Alluding to these difficulties, Charles Sydney Goldman explained in 1905 that "seeing in England an old, crowded, and complex society, with little room for internal development, [the Imperialist creed] sought to open a wider horizon to its view, and to remedy some of the greater evils of the social organism by means of the wide, untried territories at its command."[24]

In order to manage globally distributed lands, things, and bodies, the new imperialist period experimented with new governance styles, shifting from the laissez-faire attitudes of the eighteenth and earlier nineteenth centuries to a more technocratic colonial apparatus in the twentieth century that aimed to "develop" Africa, beginning with the "constructive imperialism" of Joseph Chamberlain, the British secretary of state for the colonies from 1895 to 1903.[25] Britain thus turned from imperial expansion to colonial administration, where "the problem was now one of consolidating British power, of making the Empire more united as well as more efficient."[26] Development by the state produced what historian Thomas Richards calls the world's first information society, in which "much Victorian thought participated in seeing the state as central to human life, and more, in imagining a kind of complete documentary knowledge of human life that would exist solely for the state."[27] Richards documents a host of private-turned-public institutions that arose to process the avalanche of knowledge being collected about the empire, including the museum, the archive, and ecological surveys. The accumulating information about plants, mines, laborers, disease, population, and animals worldwide had to be not only collected but analyzed, and the state increasingly turned to the new fields of modern science to do so. Historian Helen Tilley notes that British colonial administrators "were acutely aware of the complexities involved in holding the empire together in the face of both white settler nationalism and indigenous anticolonial resistance," and they openly called on scientists to assist them.[28]

Ecological science seemed especially well suited to the study of colonial terrain, flora, fauna, and peoples, given its desire to map interrelationships within larger systems. The prominence of ecology is evident in the ubiquity of one of its master metaphors—the organism. As British imperial regimes expanded, and the complexity of governing their diverse parts often bewildered the Colonial Office, new imperialists increasingly came to understand the empire as a living, complex organism. The organic metaphor drew upon older, organic theories of the state, which were of "ancient vintage" in politics, reaching back to Plato and Aristotle.[29] However, alongside the general craze for organic thinking in the Victorian and Edwardian eras, discussed in chapter 5, theories of the organic state likewise experienced a resurgence in the nineteenth century, most influentially in the Romantic-Idealist thought of Hegel and Schelling. For them, the organic theory of society was an alternative response to the eighteenth-century revolutions, and a rebuke to "the Enlightenment idea that the state was voluntarily produced from a state of nature, mechanistic in its function, and atomistic in its orientation."[30] This rejection of mechanistic approaches, and the preference for more holistic thinking, paved the way for the incorporation of modern sciences like ecology, evolution, and energy into politics, all of which feature prominently in organic theories of new imperialism.

By understanding the empire as an organism, it became easier to make sense of how new imperial governance should relate to its restive colonies. In 1902, British politician R. B. Haldane referred to "a new conception of the Empire as an organic whole, with a common life and end pervading and guiding the action of all its members. No longer do we think of our colonies as governed from Downing Street. Downing Street is but the ganglion in which the stimulus derived from contact in different parts is translated into movement in the interest of the common life."[31]

Given the organism's ultimately unknowable complexity, Haldane concludes that the organism must be governed by elites with scientific knowledge of its inner workings, functioning as the "ganglion" that could accumulate and interpret the data, and then translate messages from one part of the body to the other. Haldane's ganglion mirrors Maxwell's demon, an influential thought experiment proposed by James Clerk Maxwell, a key proponent of classical thermodynamics. The demon was an imaginary, intelligent being who could overcome the second law of thermodynamics, the spontaneous increase of entropy. In his 1871 text *Theory of Heat*, Maxwell imagined a vessel filled with gas, with two sides and a trapdoor between them; the demon sits by the door and observes the passing gas molecules, opening the door to allow only "swifter" molecules to one side. Over time, the demon could therefore raise the temperature of one side of the vessel—and recall that a temperature difference is necessary for work—without doing work. Maxwell's demon had far-reaching implications, especially in later information theory, as Maxwell posited that *information* about the molecules could function as a kind of work. However, Maxwell also notes that such molecular detail is "at present impossible to us," given that we can only know about gas molecules through statistical calculation.[32]

The concept underlying Maxwell's demon resonated with the Victorian shift toward scientific governance. The demon revealed both the promise and the limitations offered by thermodynamics, and by modern science more generally. With more information, one could stem the tide of entropic chaos, and potentially approximate the kind of order that Maxwell's demon achieves. And yet the demonic knowledge of each and every molecule, each and every plant, mine, body, opinion, food calorie, wind vector, ocean current, and the like, ultimately remains forever out of human reach, too massive to perfectly compute. The demon, with its sinister overtones, contrasts with the only other "intelligent being" exempted from the second law—God. Meanwhile, humans are left only with their imperfect approximations of energy knowledge. So just as physicists could only comprehend the behavior of gases, and thus heat, through statistical calculations of amassed data, so too administrators in the imperial ganglion, faced with immensely complex governance problems, must resort increasingly to mathematical methods. Hence, Haldane's reading of Downing Street as less the sovereign ruler from which decrees emerge, and more the centralized information processor trying its best to gather ever more energy data and guard the trapdoor between the swift and the sluggish, the workers and the waste.

Indeed, in governing the organism, it was understood that the very breath, bone, and blood that sustained the organism was labor, while many of the organismic forces of illness and death were likewise to do with problems of labor. Through the metaphor of the organism, sustained by the metabolic exchange of energy (read: work), it thus became possible to explain the relationship of Black labor to the well-being of both Africans and Europeans.[33] Turning African men into wage laborers was not just a civilizing mission, and not just to the advantage of some far-flung mine, but instead was recognized as integral to the health of the empire and of white laborers in Europe. Two parts could be different, as the eye and the leg or the root and the branch, but they could also be harnessed to the same organizational pattern or program, to the life of the organism. In 1905, journalist James Louis Garvin claimed that "our Colonies are no longer 'fruits which cling 'til they ripen,' but banyan-shoots spreading with repeated root from the parent-trunk to strengthen the system they extend."[34] In other words, Britain, perceived to be weakening vis-à-vis Germany and the United States, needed to appreciate its colonies as feeding the health of the British imperial banyan, rather than as fruits that would suck away nutrients and detach themselves. In this metaphor, the imperial administration would serve as banyan gardeners.

This notion—that by promoting and developing the colonies as parts of the whole, the British empire would likewise profit—was widely cited. Jan Smuts, a military leader in the Boer War and eventual prime minister of the Union of South Africa, was a proponent of the new ecological sciences and argued that "African progress is one whole organic problem and has to be viewed as such."[35] The goal was to govern the organism's parts so that the health of the whole organism was ensured. As Chamberlain declared in a 1903 speech, the empire could be "self-sustaining" with "decent organisation and consolidation," and in turn, "it is absolutely impossible that anything which contributes to the prosperity of the Colonies, which fills up their waste land, which makes them richer, will not react and add to your prosperity also."[36] Or, as Charles Bruce, a prominent imperial administrator, testified in a 1906 essay, "Indeed it may be said with truth of some of the most important industries in the United Kingdom that they have their roots in the labour of the coloured races, while the trunk, branches, flowers and fruits represent the labour and profits of the white man. It is only the low wage-rate of the tropical area of production of the raw material that enables the manufactured article to be turned out at a price that ensures a large market and yet allows an adequate wage for the British workman."[37] Smuts, always a reliable source for unvarnished defenses of imperialism, proclaims that "the easiest, most natural and obvious way to civilize the African native is to give him decent white employment. White employment is his best school; the gospel of labour is the most salutary gospel for him."[38]

In reality, the so-called gospel of labor was difficult to spread. Labor was the lifeblood of the imperial organism, and at the same time its chief problem.[39] Somehow, cheap labor must be extracted in the colonies in a way that could be consistent with the trumpeting of freedom and democracy in Europe. W. E. B. Du Bois exposed the method by which this was achieved, describing how empire depended on exploitative labor across the global color line, a notion that was openly acknowledged in the imperial jingoism that surrounded him.[40] Du Bois went so far as to call labor "the Problem of Problems" for global politics, by which he meant "the problem of allocating work and income in the tremendous and increasingly intricate world-embracing industrial machine which we have built."[41]

For although the British had officially renounced slavery and had joined the global abolition movement earlier in the nineteenth century, they (as well as other European empires) still relied upon, and desired, laborers whom they paid far less than they paid white laborers. A Ghanaian abolition newspaper observed in 1900 that "the old slavery is dead, but a more subtle slavery may take its place. The demand of the capitalist everywhere is for cheap and docile labour." Most importantly, the newspaper gestured toward labor problems in Europe by noting that low-paid labor was performed by bodies of color so that the capitalist could "rescue himself from the demands of white labor."[42] British imperialists in Africa were thus charged with devising methods to secure cheap Black labor that could pass muster with abolitionists, who largely shared their faith in the virtue of work provided that workers were ostensibly free.[43]

Du Bois encapsulates the imperial puzzle best: "Thus with a democratic face at home modern imperialism turns a visage of stern and unyielding autocracy toward its darker colonies. This double-faced attitude is difficult to maintain and puts hard strain on the national soul that tries it."[44] The hard strain that Du Bois notes, the disjuncture between democratic ideals and forced labor in the colonies, was further exacerbated by widespread African resistance to the venerated gospel of labor, whether through armed resistance, mass migrations, boycotts of European goods, labor strikes and unionization, or refusing to pay colonial taxes. Some of the most well known resistance movements, such as the Nigerian Women's War of 1929, were direct refusals of imperial labor experiments. The intransigence of Black labor is a frequent complaint of European administrators and travelers. As Henry Callaway, a bishop in South Africa, bemoans in an 1859 letter, "There is apparently abundance of *hands*; but to get labour out of them is quite another question. . . . How are 8,000 widely scattered whites to compel 200,000 coloured to labour, against their will?"[45]

In the context of dissent in both Africa and Europe, the new imperialists were left with a crisis of governance.[46] Throughout the period, administrators clamored for scientific knowledge with which to manage Britain and its empire, and many scientists were eager to provide it. As late as 1924, *Nature*, reporting back from the British Empire Exhibition, noted that "the fundamental condition for success [of the commercial development of the colonies] is a systematic investigation, on scientific lines, of the natural resources of the countries concerned," including "the development of a central clearing-house of imperial economic information."[47] This, too, would serve the empire-as-organism, as the journal describes how "each group of cells in this organism performs its particular functions independently, yet all are correlated in the scheme of growth, and their activities affect not alone the vitality of the corporate whole but all other human communities."[48]

The partnership between science and politics, already intimate, solidified considerably in this period. Evolution, ecology, and other modern biological sciences certainly fed this partnership, with fields such as tropical medicine[49] leading the way and providing a moral justification for the benefits of imperial science.[50] Meanwhile, thermodynamics directly addressed work, the problem of problems for imperialists. It made possible an energy logic that valorized a particular kind of work: productive work, work that increased the metabolic activity of the organism. Productivism was aligned with the desire for constant, unending growth. Productive work was in contrast to much of the work activities performed by humans throughout the history of civilization, which diverted energy toward survival or reproduction. Such work was necessary, of course, but a subsistence style of energy exploitation had not led to civilizational advance, where civilization was understood as an effect of accumulation and growth. Since the advent of fossil-fueled technologies, humans could now radically increase the volume of energy influx through the organism of human civilization. Work that lent itself to this metabolic goal was thus the most prized as an activity of evolutionary superiority.[51] Ted Underwood points out that Victorians had already cherished productivism, but in thermodynamics, which became wildly popular, they found the mathematical equations that "ratified" this economic preference and "proved that economic production and natural force were two names for a single power"—energy.[52] Through thermopolitics, productivism took root in the "economic logic" that motivated British imperialism, where "imperial officials viewed African populations less as prospective political actors and more as potential producers."[53]

Just as energy seemed to ratify productive work, it also constructed waste through a productivist framework. In the energy–work nexus, waste was anything that was not productive, or that harmed productivity. Waste was amenable to measurement and improvement, but ultimately unavoidable, as waste would accumulate as organic throughput increased. As a result, so long as waste was tied up with productive work, it did not signal a failure of industrialization, but rather useless detritus that required constant surveillance and excision so as not to slow the organism's growth. Resistance to work was translated as more data to be governed by the colonial demon at the trapdoor. Maxwell's demon had sorted the swift molecules from the sluggish in order to concentrate energy, and the logic of energy governance similarly aimed to sort the more productive workers from the lazy and indolent. Those who refused work needed to be separated and excised.

Violence and outright theft of land remained popular solutions to the puzzle of putting Africa to work. The pillage of King Leopold and the

Belgians in the Congo provides the most famous, but certainly not an exceptional, example. However, in other sites, new labor policies were invented that seemed to better correspond to the ideals of liberal democracy. For example, through the biopolitical tactic of the census, imperial administrators tallied households, wives, and property in order to impose hut taxes. Taxing households was intended to destabilize subsistence economies by forcing many people, especially those from poorer households, into wage labor in order to raise cash to pay the tax. According to Smuts and other imperialists across the continent (against much evidence to the contrary), Africans cheerfully accepted these hut taxes "as their contribution to good government."[54] Administrators in many regions also required Africans to engage in periods of forced (often unpaid) labor for "public" projects such as railroads, dams, and roads, many of which served the needs of private European industries, though they claimed to be advancing the health of the imperial organism.

Rather than being clear-cut categories, the gradations between forced and free labor lie at the heart of imperial debate, as "the British people had come to believe that maintaining the line between free labor and enslaved labor was fundamental to legitimate commerce and government both at home and abroad. . . . Indeed, in the humanitarian politics of the British Empire, no issue was of greater importance than labor."[55] In other words, new imperial logics of domination needed to operate through the grammar of free labor. The mere existence of a wage, even if unequal, became an indicator in the British public's imagination that demarcated the line between slavery and free labor.

ENERGETIC RACISM

According to the energy logic that we are following, colonized peoples were told that if they wanted to receive equal pay and treatment, and eventually to be deemed fit for self-governance, they must first prove themselves to be efficient, productive workers. This is how abolitionists and purported European defenders of "African rights" could rail against slavery but at the same time subscribe to the industrial mission of putting the world to work. Thermodynamics could be deployed through new modes of scientific racism that effectively delayed equality until the far future, the not-yet.

Historian Jürgen Osterhammel briefly suggests the possibility that energetic distinctions informed racist ideology in his sweeping history of the nineteenth century, when he observes that there was also an "energetic racism" at work: "the racism of the age did not end with skin color: it classified the human 'races' on a scale of potential physical and mental energy."[56] An energy discourse motivated "young patriots" to "revitalize" their societies, making nationalist and socialist projects in Asia, for example, into "a vehicle of self-energization."[57] Osterhammel records the preference for vitality and dynamism but does not consider how such amorphous values were often described through the metaphor of the organism, and were reinforced by a new energy knowledge that coded it as metabolic input and output. Taking the history of energy into account makes it possible to expand upon the notion of energetic racism as a conflation of physics and Protestantism in the service of European industrial capitalism.

Scientific racism had become a powerful tactic by which imperial labor projects advanced. The ground had been prepared by earlier theologies that had found ways to justify centuries of pillage, slavery, and exploitation in the colonies. As Hortense Spillers observes, such frameworks constitute "a *semiosis* of procedure" that make possible racialized technologies of violence. The violent act is made possible by violent signification, as "the marking, the branding, the whipping—all instruments of a terrorist regime—were more deeply *that* [the semiosis]—to get in somebody's face that way would have to be centuries in the making that would have had little to do, though it is difficult to believe, with the biochemistry of pigmentation, hair texture, lip thickness, and the indicial measure of the nostrils, but everything to do with those 'unacknowledged legislators' of a discursive and an economic discipline."[58]

Social Darwinism famously served as one such legislator, providing a schema through which races could be distinguished and marked hierarchically according to vague justifications of superior "fitness" and survivability on the Earth. Social Darwinism had an ecological interest in "contrasting the extremes of savagery and civilization," where civilized people were conceived of as more independent of their environment.[59] While such judgments of race referred to biological knowledge in order to mark which bodies were deemed human, subhuman, or nonhuman, thermodynamics also played a role in making these distinctions. In other words, racialized subjects were not only "atomized" into body parts and fleshly pieces to be categorized or experimented upon, as in nose widths, cranial shapes, fleshy wounds, infectious status, or organ providers;[60]

they were also atomized quite literally as carriers or digesters of chemical and physical elements, like food, air, and water.

Energy functioned as a master metaphor by which to understand how these elemental flows traveled differently in racialized bodies. Accordingly, the human, or what Wynter calls Man$_2$, could be described biologically, but also energetically, according to logics of efficiency and productivism. As with biological systems of racism, energetic codes, too, depended upon close observation of the struggles of the Other in the face of colonization, "with this population group's systemic stigmatization, social inferiorization, and dynamically produced material deprivation thereby serving both to 'verify' the overrepresentation of Man as if it were the human, and to legitimate the subordination of the world and well-being of the latter to those of the former."[61]

The European pursuit of work and waste, and its reliance on racist justifications, predated the science of energy, but energy reinforced them by mapping these virtues onto the efficient operations of fossil-fueled machines. The maximization of work and the proper use of the divine gift of energy appealed to ideals of exactitude, progress, novelty, experimentation, measurement, calibration, punctuality, efficiency, and discipline. Consider the way that an energetic engagement with the world functions in the triumphalism of Richard Cobden, a British manufacturer and politician, who wrote in 1854 that "England, with her steam-engine and spinning-frame, has erected the standard of improvement, around which every nation of the world has already prepared to rally. . . . England's industrious classes, through the energy of their commercial enterprise, are, at this moment, influencing the civilization of the whole world, by stimulating the labor, exciting the curiousity, and promoting the taste for refinement, of barbarous communities."[62]

Meanwhile, the category of waste informed Orientalist stereotypes of Africans and Asians as mostly "devoid of energy and initiative,"[63] lazy, stagnant, untimely, and in general unable to either mine their own resources or inventively use them. In his "Occasional Discourse on the Negro Question," for instance, Thomas Carlyle complains that European capitals are taking measures "to get its rich white men set to work; for alas, they also have long sat Negro-like up to the ears in pumpkin, regardless of 'work,' and of a world all going to waste for their idleness!"[64] As these common depictions illustrate, energetic judgments did not always have to be technical to benefit from the new veneer of thermodynamic scientific authority.

Energy's meaning could remain slippery, traveling back and forth between mystical notions of vigor and virtue, and industrial traits of efficiency and fossil-fueled invention.

The civilizing mission was not just about putting the "indolent, tradition-bound, and fatalistic peoples"[65] of the colonies to work; it was also putting the Earth and its forests, terrains, animals, and oceans to work, in order to improve upon the "waste places of the Earth."[66] As Osterhammel observes, "the land-clearing settler, big-game hunter, and river tamer were emblematic figures of this drive to civilize the whole planet. The great opponents to be defeated were chaos, nature, tradition, and the ghosts and phantoms of any kind of superstition."[67] The logic of energy sketched out a method for taming the chaos of nature: the second law of thermodynamics depicted a world of always-increasing entropy, or diffusion of energy, against which hard workers must strive to hack out a little corner of industry.

Energy therefore became one standard by which to assess the vivacity of ecosystems and human civilizations alike. The goal was to yoke other societies to the accelerating fossil energy flows of the West. In more stark terms, energy helped in the moral and sociotechnical organization of good and bad activity, of engine performance and resource extraction, and also of laborers in British factories, of states, of the Earth, and of humans worldwide. The belief that European peoples were technologically advanced, and were better able to conform their bodies to the demands of a work and waste ethos, affected the "allotment of tasks in the global economy," where Europeans supplied the know-how and expertise while the colonies were left to "supply the primary products, cheap labor, and abundant land that could be developed by Western machines, technique, and enterprise."[68] These inequalities contributed to a deepening "global energy gulf" between the Global North and South.[69]

Crossing that gulf required that colonial states imbibe the "valorization of bourgeois traits" and the drive for capital accumulation, "unbound productivity," private land ownership, and environmentally destructive practices, all of which were believed to lie at the heart of Western civilizational advance.[70] Northern Europeans were charged with teaching the way of industrial work to the rest of the world, who were widely figured as culturally and racially indisposed to such toil. Kingsley, for example, observes that although Africans may have "common sense," "they are notably deficient in all mechanical arts: they have never made, unless under white direction and instruction, a single fourteenth-rate piece of cloth, pottery, a tool or machine, house, road, bridge, picture or statue."[71] Aimé Césaire satirizes the dangerous hypocrisy of industrial missionaries like Kingsley, who, alongside "so many valiant sons of the West, in the semi-darkness of dungeons, are lavishing upon their inferior African brothers, with such tireless attention, those authentic marks of respect for human dignity which are called, in technical terms, 'electricity,' 'the bathtub,' and 'the bottleneck.'"[72]

Césaire is an important foil to the story of a dominant energy logic in that he, too, draws upon organic metaphors to analyze colonialism. However, Césaire rejects the pro-industrial association of health with work; his use of the organism is not in service to the energy–work matrix, and is an example of an alternative imaginary of organic vitality. In his 1955 *Discourse on Colonialism*, Césaire memorably connects the violence of European imperialism to the fascist moment of World War II, arguing that Europeans "tolerated that Nazism before it was inflicted on them, . . . because, until then, it had been applied only to non-European peoples; that they have cultivated that Nazism, that they are responsible for it."[73] The practice of horrific violence and sadism abroad could not help but degrade Europe itself, and be returned to Europe "with a terrific boomerang effect."[74]

In addition to the boomerang metaphor, Césaire makes great use of the metaphor of the organism to understand how imperial practice would sicken Europe. He begins with a more ideal vision of circulation and the "redistribution of energy," one that is not centered on work and profit: "I admit that it is a good thing to place different civilizations in contact with each other; that it is an excellent thing to blend different worlds; that whatever its own particular genius may be, a civilization that withdraws into itself atrophies; that for civilizations, exchange is oxygen; that the great good fortune of Europe is to have been a crossroads, and that because it was the locus of all ideas, the receptacle of all philosophies, the meeting place of all sentiments, it was the best center for the redistribution of energy." Europe did not take advantage of this "great good fortune," of course, but instead proceeded according to domination and profit. While it may have understood itself to be healthy and growing, all the while the imperial organism was putrefying from within. In order to describe imperial decay, Césaire reverses the florid descriptions of the imperial administrators, quoted above, who described colonized labor as the flowers, fruits, or banyan-shoots attached to the great roots of the imperial core. In place of flowers and fruits, Césaire piles up the eyes put out, heads cut off, and bodies tortured in the name of "proletarianization," each of which becomes "dead weight" upon the organism, as "a gangrene sets in, a center of infection begins to spread; . . . a poison has been instilled into the veins of Europe and, slowly but surely, the continent proceeds toward *savagery*" (italics in the original).[75]

With his emphasis on European hypocrisy, Césaire reminds us that the gospel of labor and the industrial mission were intimately connected to Europe's own labor problems and social inequalities. The racial and gendered tropes of work and idleness were not simply a contrast between the metropolis and the periphery, or bodies classified as black and white. The imperial organism, fed by work and waste according to a dominant energy logic, was a paradigm that related these different sites of work to each other. Instead of only insisting on one distinction between Europe and the colonies, then, the British Empire also worked through a circulation of affinities between workers and waste in the colonies and in Europe. Britain sought to interpret the colonies through the prism of its own troubled society, and in turn, the new British industrial cities, crowded with poor and disaffected workers, were compared with the "dark continent" and people of color.[76] For instance, in the simplified story of Victorian racism, Europe distinguishes itself from its colonies according to the equality of its own society. However, David Cannadine argues that most people in Britain viewed their own domestic society as hierarchical and unequal, especially as industrialization took hold. Cannadine therefore argues that "the British Empire was about the familiar and domestic, as well as the different and the exotic: indeed, it was in large part about the domestication of the exotic—the comprehending and the reordering of the foreign in parallel, analogous, equivalent, resemblant terms."[77]

As Cannadine's more complex interpretation reminds us, there was never one unified approach to imperial governance, nor any single opinion on industrialization, for that matter. The new imperialist period, while it involved an acceleration of land grabs and labor projects in Africa, was characterized by vigorous dissent over imperial policy, ranging from colonial intellectuals who resisted imperial rule to jingoistic triumphalists and abolitionists who railed against the "new slaveries" in Africa.[78] Added to this was a "broad-based anticapitalist and anti-industrial backlash" in Europe that targeted "the ascendancy of a profit- and productivity-obsessed elite of industrialists, financiers, and technicians."[79]

Nevertheless, it is possible to pick out common thematic elements in the metaphors of rule. The central place of energy in these ruling logics is apparent in that, even among the most vociferous opponents to British imperialists, few railed against the virtue of work itself. Missionary and abolitionist John Harris might call upon imperial administrators in a 1927 essay to "eschew" slavery and forced labor, but he still wanted them "to encourage the indigenous producers by means of secure land tenure, education, and instruction in agricultural science, to an ever increasing volume and quality of raw material."[80] Meanwhile, anti-industrialists were proud of British scientific and industrial advances, even if they resisted the commercialism it had birthed.[81] A notable exception was Marx's son-in-law, Paul Lafargue, who wittily eviscerates the "strange delusion" of work and imagines a post-work socialist utopia in his 1880 essay "The Right to Be Lazy."[82] But although Lafargue's text was popular with some socialists, it remained an outlier in the otherwise work-obsessed white European culture—and even among socialists, who preferred to mobilize around the dignity of labor rather than the right to be lazy.

Amid the swirling debate over imperial politics, then, it was widely agreed that the British were a superior race in terms of evolution, and that their fossil-fueled machines were the evidence of that superiority. Whereas the "civilizing mission" discourse had relied more heavily on religious claims in earlier periods, by the latter half of the nineteenth century, Michael Adas notes that most Westerners (and even most critics in the colonies), "shared the conviction that through their scientific discoveries and inventions [they] had gained an understanding of the workings of the physical world and an ability to tap its resources that were vastly superior to anything achieved by other peoples, past or present."[83] Energy neatly connected these two registers of modern science and religious ideology as justifications for imperialism. Some of the leading scientists of energy, after all, had already managed to stitch together Scottish Presbyterianism with fossil fuel use. In many ways, thermodynamics was a far more comfortable synthesis for imperial ideologies than was the science of evolution, which seriously challenged Christianity and so could not logically reconcile industrialism to older arguments about religious proselytizing.

Technological achievement thus became a measure of civilizational superiority. Typical were the observations of imperial travelers like Kingsley, who wrote in 1899 that "when I come back from a spell in Africa, the thing that makes me proud of being one of the English is not the manners or customs up here, certainly not the houses or the climate;

but it is the thing embodied in a great railway engine."[84] This pride was also evident in the first world exhibition, held in 1851 in London's newly constructed Crystal Palace, which functioned as a space of imperial spectacle.[85] The theme was "the Industry of All Nations," and it featured a Hall of Machines with engines, presses, and other technological wizardry, as well as an exhibit with dioramas of primitive peoples. Ensuing world exhibitions popularized the notion that the fruits of technical knowledge provided evidence of superiority, as well as of God's grace, conveniently ignoring, and erasing, the technological innovations and scientific advances made by non-Europeans across world history. Anne McClintock argues that the exhibition "embodied the hope that all the world's cultures could be gathered under one roof—the global progress of history represented as the commodity progress of the Family of Man," but that it was implicit that "only the west had the technical skill and innovative spirit to render the historical pedigree of the Family of Man in such perfect, technical form."[86]

A sketch from the 1888 Glasgow Exhibition (figure 6.1) captures this spirit with a biblical verse emblazoned across its arches, from Proverbs 24:4, "And by knowledge shall the chambers be filled with all precious and pleasant riches," and another barely discernible, likely from Psalm 104:24, "O Lord, how manifold are thy works! In wisdom hast thou made them all; The earth is full of thy riches."

In Glasgow's triumphalist exhibition, the missionary zeal of earlier colonization is translated for the industrial age, where Europeans are not simply more virtuous because they believed, but were also more virtuous because of the artifacts wrought from their "knowledge," here interpreted as industrial-technical know-how. Similarly, the inclusion of supposedly primitive cultures in the world fairs was proffered as evidence of European superiority, based on a contrast between the machine halls and non-industrial ways of life. Exhibits of colonized peoples also functioned as a visible reminder of what awaited those Europeans who failed to secure waged work: they would be condemned to the fate of those cultures who were imagined to suffer the Promethean drudgery of mere survival, having failed to use knowledge to reap God's gifts. In other words, they would be consigned to the dissipative natural world of the second law, a Nature that was "fallen," and whose rescue could come only by means of productive work, a goal marvelously eased by coal and oil. Those who could not be saved must be dealt with as waste.

Glasgow and its Exhibition.

GLASGOW EXHIBITION: INTERIOR, LOOKING EAST.

FIGURE 6.1. An interior view of the 1888 Glasgow Exhibition. Credit: Sketch from *The Pictorial World*, June 7, 1888, Bound in International Exhibition 1888, "Graphic" Supplements, GC f606.4 (1888). © CSG CIC Glasgow Museums and Libraries Collection: The Mitchell Library, Special Collections.

According to an energetic rationality, waste was controllable, something that could be concealed, an approach that proved more seductive than the depressing and apocalyptic visions that characterized environmental criticism of the period. Thermodynamics suggested its own environmental apocalypse—heat death, the impossibility of work, and the ultimate triumph of waste—but a geo-theological approach to energy had couched it in the Protestant-tinged promise that hard work could secure a temporary respite for humankind. According to this energy logic, waste is the shadow of work, in much the same way that sin shadows grace. The only way that the imperial balance sheet could be optimized was by concealing or excising those bodies and things that weighed against the benefit of work. The British empire thus perfected the double maneuver—the acceleration of work and the concealment of waste—upon which industrial governance still depends.

According to the organic metaphor, in order for an organism to grow, waste had to be continually filtered and excreted. Recall that Spencer, the popular philosopher of energy, argued that "all action implies waste; blood brings the material for repair; and before there can be growth, the quantity of blood supplied must be more than is requisite for repair. In a society it is the same."[87] For Spencer, the emergence of vascular systems parallels the rise of the middle class, which distributes goods across society; the blood vessels are akin to roads and railroads; the nutrients delivered by the blood are "consumable commodities," and the "blood disks" or corpuscles that circulated are money.[88] Societies lacking such things as roads, money, and a middle class are "lower societies," just as hydrozoa are "lower creatures."[89] The demand for labor was thus always partnered with the need to process the accruing residuum of bodies and forces, to separate them—as the kidneys filter the blood—so that they would not hamper the growth of the organism, which was achieved through work. And rather than see waste as evidence of industrial failure, Victorians treated waste bodies as "irredeemable outcasts who had turned their backs on progress . . . because of an organic degeneration of mind and body."[90]

Victorian Britain urgently set about producing and delineating waste, relying increasingly on state intervention to manage it. To govern waste, the state relied upon what McClintock calls an "unholy alliance" between evolution and "the allure of numbers, the amassing of measurements and the science of statistics,"[91] which, as I argued in chapter 3, was also reflected in the emergence of thermodynamics and statistical mechanics. The urgency was partly a result of the visible accumulation of industrialism's woes, from pollution to unemployment and urban disease, all of which were interpreted through a sieve of racial, gendered, and class distinctions.

However, the urgency surrounding waste stemmed not just from the woes of waste, but also from the woes of work. As industrial labor spread in the nineteenth century, the notion that work delivered independence and democracy clashed with the reality of grueling, dependent, wage labor, which was remaking European life. Whether there were not enough jobs in Europe, or not enough Africans willing to toil in mines for low wages, the promise of work—virtue, industrialization, health, wealth— had proven empty for many. Waste threatened to overwhelm European projects at every turn. It represented all that was lost to entropy and could not be made into work, and it could manifest as smog, polluted rivers, denuded landscapes, tropical climates, outdated machines, urban disease, unruly crowds, crime, indolent (read: resistant) Africans, hysterical women—anything that clogged the arteries of industry and slowed productive work. In addition, the more work done through the exponential powers of fossil fuel, the more waste created, and the more total metabolic activity to be managed in order to bend as much as possible back toward productive work.

Historians of race and labor have observed how white workers responded to these anxieties by ever more feverishly policing the line between slavery and free labor, relying on slavery and Black labor to operate as reminders of the relative good fortune of "free" white labor. For Lionel Phillips, a one-time president of the Chamber of Mines in the Transvaal, racial differences are so necessary that they require a distinction in duties and wages: "the disparity between the scale of payment to the white and coloured workers [in the South Africa mining industry] is so great, and the planes upon which they live so widely different, that the employment of the former in work that, of necessity, would command lower wages than the skilled artisans and overseers receive today, would create a class of 'poor whites' looked down on by, and degraded in the eyes of, the Kaffirs."[92]

A similar phenomenon occurred in the industrializing United States, where the growing white labor class sought to distinguish themselves from Black laborers. As David Roediger reflects in his classic study of nineteenth-century U.S. labor politics, *The Wages of Whiteness*, "the white working class, disciplined and made anxious by fear of dependency, began during its formation to construct an image of the Black population as 'other'—as embodying the preindustrial, erotic, careless style of life the white worker hated and longed for."[93] The racial division of laborers was necessary as part of the uncomfortable adaptation of republican government to capitalism, and Roediger writes that "increasingly adopting an ethos that attacked holidays, spurned contact with nature, saved time, bridled sexuality, separated work from the rest of life and postponed gratification, profit-minded Englishmen and Americans cast Blacks as their former selves."[94]

This role for Blacks, as the "former selves" of Europe, was not just a social role but also a biological status, thanks to both evolution and thermodynamics. Energy provided yet another framework by which to parse waste and justify the virtue of (European) fossil-fueled work, helping to solidify these racial and gendered categorizations of waste as supported by modern science. In this sense, waste was not only accumulating through the faulty engines, inefficient factories, smog, sewage, or scraps left over after the work was done. It was actively produced as an invented, social category that helped to ameliorate the crises of industrialism for the supposedly virtuous (white, Western, straight male) workers, who could at least console themselves with their position as thermodynamic enthusiasts atop the evolutionary ladder.

The elevation of fossil fuels, engines, corporations, and white workers thus required the subordination of waste through what McClintock refers to as the Victorian "invention of idleness."[95] While McClintock focuses on idleness as a human category intersecting with race and gender, energy adds another dimension to the story: idleness also functioned as a category for the Earth and its nonhuman forces and things, which likewise intersected with race and gender. Activities of humans and nonhumans like sex, reproduction, eating, leisure, beauty, weather patterns, forest growth, rainfall, and topography must either be reordered and carefully managed to serve industrial production (organic growth), or else denigrated as wasteful. Not just humans, but nature, too, could be rescued from dissipation. Refusing wage labor that would support the steam economy meant refusing to be rescued from nature, a plight that had long been associated with women, people of color, and indigenous groups.

With the fiction of middle-class Victorian women of leisure as the ideal counterpart to white "economic man," McClintock traces how those who operated outside of the fiction of the "domestic woman/economic man" partnership—working women (especially sex workers, miners, or domestic servants), Jews, gay men, Africans, the Irish, the poor, urban crowds, and so on, both in Europe and in the Global South—were racialized, feminized, and socially ranked in keeping with their supposed indolence, degeneracy, or deviance from the white work ethic.[96] The imperial state set about managing deviant money, sexuality, and race, all of which "threaten[ed] the fiscal and libidinal economy of the imperial state," where deviance was often interpreted through the terminology of idleness or laziness.[97] In inventing idleness, British imperialists were appealing to the remnants of a 300-year-old discourse that associated poverty with sloth, and that had functioned in Europe "to sanction and enforce social discipline, to legitimize land plunder and to alter habits of labor."[98]

The zombified work ethic resonated with imperialists in Africa as well. Indeed, the laziness of Black men is one of the most common tropes in the imperial archive, as well as in the complaints of American slave owners. In a characteristic observation, James Bryce, a British traveler to South Africa, writes of the "Bechuana" men that "the main impression which they leave on a stranger is one of laziness. Of the many whom we saw hanging about in the sun, hardly one seemed to be doing any kind of work. Nor do they. . . . [H]aving few wants and no ambition, they have practically no industries, and spend their lives in sleeping, loafing, and talking."[99]

As is evident in Bryce's description, the British attributed this laziness to a combination of climate ("hanging about in the sun") and innate temperament ("few wants and no ambition"). In this way, energy dovetailed with a related theory of human civilization that circulated in this period: climate as a central factor in explaining which regions progressed and which languished. Climate connected temperature, humidity, rainfall, and wind to human and agricultural health. Extreme climates would hamper civilizational advance. For instance, hot climates hosted more infectious diseases, and it was also inferred that heat tended to induce torpor and passivity.[100] Here again, the logic of energy, and its privileging of dynamism, intersects with metabolic and organic metaphors that relate humans to their surroundings.

More generous imperialists objected to these stereotypes about "natives" and their capacity for industriousness. Some insisted that Africans *could* work hard if only they had proper white management. John Harris attests that "It may be true that he has periods of idleness—he is not alone in that!—it may be true, probably is so, that he labours intermittently. But what is equally true, is, that in spite of the fact that the African race is only now emerging from barbarism, is only now attempting to cross, in a decade, the bridge of centuries, the whole race is not only working, but is working hardest where the hand of a considerate administrator beckons onwards to a higher rate of progress."[101] The considerate administrators of the late nineteenth century institutionalized this poverty–sloth connection with reference to evolution and thermodynamics. Evolution seemed to illustrate the broad contours of the ladder of progress, while the logic of energy could guide those attempting to accelerate across an evolutionary "bridge of centuries."

From our perspective in the late Anthropocene, what is of special interest was the extent to which the invention of idleness relied on concealment. It was sometimes less about bringing torpor and other modes of waste "to light," in order to cure them through work, and more about hiding those threatening economies and ecologies, just as subterranean oil pipelines, refineries sited in poor, industrial zones, and opaque gas pumps help to conceal our sensory awareness of the ubiquity of oil.[102] In the Victorian era, for instance, McClintock asserts that Victorian women were not actually idle, despite the popularity of proclaiming this feminine ideal. Instead, women faced the unprecedented demand that they conceal their labor; thus the erection of immaculate front parlors, the rise of soap as a global commodity, and the obsession with white linens and cleanliness.[103] The goal was to discredit the importance of women's labor, which was ironically increased to meet the demands for cleanliness, such that what mattered was not the "spectacle of leisure," but rather "the undervaluing of women's work that the spectacle achieved."[104] This maneuver— hiding waste, hiding the work of women, of sex workers, and of the most dangerous and dirty jobs, throwing things away, subterranean pipelines, globally dispersed commodity chains—remains central to the practices of global capitalism today.

Likewise, the discourse on African idleness was not about leisure, but "more properly speaking, a discourse on work—used to distinguish between desirable and undesirable systems of organizing labor. Pressure to work was, more accurately, pressure to alter traditional habits of work."[105] Du Bois, in fact, extols Black labor as emblematic of an alternative work ethic to the "mechanical draft-horse" of white capitalism, wherein

the black slave brought into common labor certain new spiritual values not yet fully realized. As a tropical product with a sensuous receptivity to the beauty of the world, he was not as easily reduced to be the mechanical draft-horse which the northern European laborer became. He was not easily brought to recognize any ethical sanctions in work as such, but tended to work as the results pleased him, and refused to work or sought to refuse when he did not find the spiritual returns adequate; thus he was easily accused of laziness and driven as a slave when in truth, he brought to modern manual labor a renewed valuation of life.[106]

Idleness glossed over what was, more accurately, resistance to European work schemes, and attempted to erase alternative economies and work ethics.

The metaphor of the organism, which was laced through with thermodynamic imagery, helps to better explain how all this concealment was achieved. While scholars like McClintock, Roediger, Du Bois, and others note the social function of concealment—to elevate and discipline white workers, to disparage those that might compete with or resist the new economic order—concealment also served a tangible, material function. Because an organism cannot grow without processing its waste, likewise the governance of industrial work must be paired with the active concealment of waste. The contradictions of industrialism could not hope to be so widely embraced without the active removal of its destructive consequences from the sensory experience of middle-class Europe and America. McClintock highlights these maneuvers as the "double-ness" of the Victorian empire, where the ideal of economic man/idle woman depended on making the "deadly labor" of others, which was necessary to production, invisible. Likewise, the Victorian obsession with white aprons, shiny mirrors, and other new commodities of cleanliness sought to erase "the fetid effluvia of the slums, the belching smoke of industry, social agitation, economic upheaval, imperial competition and anticolonial resistance."[107]

Here the theme of double-ness returns. The double-ness of British imperial politics is another materialization of the contradictions to which the two laws of thermodynamics were responding. With energy, the doubled nature of industrialism—how technical marvels rise from belching smoke—reflected the contradictions of life in the cosmos—energy was conserved, and yet entropy continually increased, making life so rare, and such a struggle. A dominant energy logic of work and waste helped to naturalize industrialization, but also its pollution, both of which were only intensifications of already existing physical processes of energy exchange and dissipation. Energy also naturalized the imperial circulation of power, which sacrificed people and things to the project of work, just as coal was sacrificed to the engine. To become a citizen in a carbon democracy was to become a waged worker, a valorized subject-position formed through fossil fuel assemblages.[108] The drive for equitable inclusion in the waged work system would catalyze many citizen movements in the nineteenth and twentieth centuries, including civil rights and women's movements. According to this political logic, a loss of energy, as a threat to jobs, would pose a threat to democracy itself.

CONCLUSION

Work and waste as social categories helped to organize the global circulation of commodities, bodies, and technologies in the period of new imperialism. As waste spewed forth from smokestacks and urban hovels, its grime and depravity had ambivalent consequences: industrial waste catalyzed early environmental and labor movements, but it also served as a visceral threat to be avoided by getting and keeping waged work. Evolution has been duly evaluated for its role in the formation of scientific racism and imperial labor policy, but it was thermodynamics and the fundamental role of energy as a unit of metabolism that reinforced these connections between environmental and socioeconomic categories of waste, between faulty engines and hysterical women, hot climates and indolence, or chaotic entropy and urban crowds.

The drive to put the world to work was certainly founded on the expansion of capitalism and its need for new markets and resources to fuel profit. However, it also reflected a modern understanding of life on Earth wrought by evolution and thermodynamics, and their synthesis in the nascent science of ecology and the metaphor of the social organism. The human exploitation of fossil fuels, and the global injustices that stemmed from it, was therefore weighted with the metaphysical, and often spiritual, meanings connected to work and waste. All the while, the chaotic and unfriendly Earth was a constant goad, haunting industrialism as a specter that could be guarded against only by erecting a fossil-fueled civilization that ceaselessly uprooted energy gifts wherever they appeared. As Donald Worster quips, after Darwin's insights, it was beyond question that nature was fearsome and "an enemy that fully deserved to be routed and enchained."[109]

Industrialism set in motion a dangerous feedback loop; its increasingly visible and disgusting waste in many ways only further confirmed the need to keep conquering nature and to escape its smells, poisons, and unpredictable effluvia through the promise of productive work and the sparkling cleanliness of new global commodities (whether soap in the nineteenth century or the clean, white lines of the newest iPhone in the twenty-first). The violence, grime, and exploitation required to produce these commodities remain successfully concealed. As the first self-aware Anthropocene society, it was Victorian Britain that forged these thermodynamic connections, where waste as human indolence or leisure shared inflections with waste as pollution, both of which deserved scientific management and minimization.

To put the world to work, while properly weeding out waste, required, in Césaire's words, "relations of domination and submission which turn the colonizing man into a classroom monitor, an army sergeant, a prison guard, a slave driver, and the indigenous man into an instrument of production."[110] Instead of talk of progress, or better standards of living, he points to those who have been robbed of their lands and lives, and "millions of men in whom fear has been instilled, who have been taught to have an inferiority complex, to tremble, kneel, despair, and behave like flunkeys," in a "parody of education."[111] Chapter 7 considers how energy logics permeated the parody of education set up by white imperialists, who set about converting students into docile, low-paid wage laborers. Energy appears most glaringly in its moments of failure, when students dragged their feet, shirked their duties, or refused to give up familial relationships or supposedly loftier ambitions. The rationality of work, as with the engine, emerges out of its confrontation with that which it dismisses as waste.

7 EDUCATION FOR EMPIRE

In the fall of 1873, William Ayrton, a "bearded and dashingly handsome" physicist, arrived in Tokyo.[1] Owing to a strong recommendation from his mentor, William Thompson (the "king of physics" and energy), the Meiji government had offered Ayrton a five-year contract as a professor at Tokyo's new Imperial College of Engineering. In accepting the post, Ayrton joined a steady flow of Scottish engineers into Japan.[2] The Japanese government was keen to exploit Western science in order to organize their own tradition of engineering.

This would not be Ayrton's first time abroad. Just before traveling to Japan, he had distinguished himself in the Indian telegraph service, where he helped British imperial administrators locate faults that were preventing communication via overland telegraph lines. Now, in setting up a model laboratory in Japan, Ayrton could engage in "social experiments" that would have been impossible at home, and could "taste and test in the field at first hand the government-directed system of education hitherto associated with France, Germany, and Switzerland."[3] Nevertheless, the infusion of Scottish energy scientists into Japan was not a one-way transfer. While Ayrton's colleague, the Scottish engineer Henry Dyer, praised Japan as "the Britain of the East,"[4] the Japanese retained ultimate control of the new technical schools, and sent their British guests home as soon as the laboratories were up and running.[5] Japan had also made its own scientific advances; Ayrton, for example, studied Japanese advances in seismology while in Tokyo.[6] And when Ayrton returned to London, he sought to infuse the lackluster British technical education system with the principles he had learned in Japan, where colleagues described the Japanese school as superior to any to be found in Europe.

Ayrton's story offers an example of how the norms and practices of the early energy scientists—and particularly British popularizers of energy like Thompson—began to circulate globally through new styles of technical and engineering education. Energy featured centrally in syllabi, but it was not just in the guise of the laws of thermodynamics. Most importantly, energy infused technical education with an emphasis on the necessity of precision and measurement for industrial work. Work, now governable as a site of energy conversion, could be valued according to one's energy use. Unlike time measurements, energy efficiency offered a much more fine-grained picture of the quality of a worker's efforts. Ensuring good work, then, whether by bodies or machines, called for comprehensive energy surveillance and accounting in order to track energy intake and consumption.

Engineers like Ayrton and Thompson are key figures in the history of energy. However, here I want to focus less upon their stature as inventors and teachers, and instead view their classrooms as illustrative products of the new energy regime and its engineering approach to working and teaching. Ayrton and Thompson did not so much originate the new regime of work-as-energy; rather, they served as conduits for its amplification. They modeled how an embrace of energy operated as a matter of scientific principle, personal virtue, and economic common sense. In the industrial engineering framework, to embrace energy science meant practicing a metrics-based approach to human and economic activity, where efficiency and morality went hand in hand, and where arduous work was prized above all other outcomes of energy consumption. Inactivity, purposeless motion, frivolity, playful excess—none contributed much of value to an engineer's balance sheet.

This dominant logic of energy, infused with the ethos of work and waste, became a guiding theme in what Aimé Césaire disparages as the imperial "parody of education,"[7] which aimed to produce docile workers fit for fossil capital.[8] The work ethic was already cemented in industrial culture, but thermodynamics suggested new tactics for controlling fossil-fueled labor. Engineers, who embraced work-centric paradigms of energy, became esteemed as industrial managers in mines, quarries, and infrastructure projects across the colonial world. Even as work changed from human to machinic, from workshop to factory, or from piecework to hourly, thermodynamics was interpreted in ways that validated those changes as progress. Steam engines and coal-burning machinery could be operated in line with Protestant virtues—even as evidence of them. Engineers were thus among the vanguard spreading the gospel of labor, both through pedagogy and through labor management in mines and other industrial sites.

In this chapter, I have chosen to home in on a constellation of technical schools in the United States in order to show how the broader trend—an energetic gospel of labor—was instituted on the ground. These U.S. schools are not meant to be representative of all imperial labor practices in the period. Rather, they offer specific examples that illuminate how the governing techniques of race and energy converged in the imperial effort to administer colonial labor. By following the gospel of labor into American schools, we also echo the movement of industrialization, which increasingly shifted from British leadership toward the United States and Germany. The choice of American schools also diversifies and expands a story that has, until this point, been weighted toward European empires, and foreshadows how the energetic gospel of labor became a global imperial project by the twentieth century.

EDUCATING ENGINEERS

Energy science may have been born in the realm of abstraction and theory, but many energy scientists, including Joule and Thompson, became famous in ensuing decades for inventing better measuring devices. Ayrton, too, made his reputation through improvements in measurement apparatus, including dynamometers, ohmmeters, and wattmeters.[9] He had identified the telegraph problem in India as one of precision and faulty measurement. He seems to have imbibed the central importance of measurement and accounting in part from Thompson, whom he refers to as "the inspiration of our [his students'] lives."[10] Ironically, the value of precision would not have been immediately apparent from Thompson's lectures, which Ayrton describes as conversational and ad hoc, nor from Thompson's surprising ineptness at conducting experiments. Ayrton remembers that "Thomson with all his genius, all his power of advising how an experiment should be made, . . . could not make the experiments with his own hands. We all dreaded his touching the apparatus which we had set up and adjusted. He was too impulsive, too full of exuberant energy. After the apparatus was broken when he had touched it he was profoundly sorry."[11]

But while Thompson may have been clumsy and disorganized, what Ayrton admired most was his ingenuity, which appears to have been motivated by a mania for energy efficiency and an abhorrence of waste. After one disappointing efficiency report, Thompson reportedly declared that "I can not degrade a man by asking him to use his energy so wastefully; I must design something better."[12] Thompson also relied on the principles of the stock market, using the "compound interest law" to build a machine that needed only a tiny initial charge to get going. Ayrton jests that "we who had never invested any money in our lives, indeed, possessed no money to invest, might have been mistaken for budding pupils of a stock broker had any visitor chanced to come into the lecture room."[13]

It was this energy thriftiness, this fascination with precise accounting and measurement, that Ayrton sought to replicate in his own teaching laboratory in Japan. A journalist visiting his lab marveled that "nearly every table in the whole place rests on columns of masonry coming up from the foundations and kept detached from the floors and walls, so that instruments resting on these tables may not be shaken by persons walking about in their neighborhood."[14] Likewise, the energetic racism espoused by Ayrton and other Europeans often centered on supposed cultural resistances to precision. Ayrton regretted that he must teach the Japanese "habits of responsibility which are at present quite unknown in this country," as the Japanese were prone to "relapse into the orthodox small Japanese officer whose fancied knowledge is too vast to allow them to attend to trifles." Importantly, it was these "trifles," Ayrton asserted, that made all the difference in successfully operating new technologies, as "success depends upon trifles: the difference of one hundredth of an inch in the position of a wire means the difference between . . . a telegraph line in good working order and a total interruption."[15]

Students must not only learn the scientific theories of energy and electricity, but also the proper *disposition* of energy, which meant bodily habits of organization and painstaking attention to detail. Above all else, the journalist who visited Ayrton's laboratory remarked on how its order and cleanliness would work upon students' habits and desires, as "the countless drawers, each with its label alphabetically arranged; the cases of apparatus overhead and the general atmosphere of efficiency would have tempted the laziest of men into using files and hammers and shellac."[16] Energy, which threatened to escape from the smallest glitch, from wires misplaced "one hundredth of an inch," demanded an aesthetic of tidy regulation. Such regulation was ideally also meant to be inviting; educational texts of the period repeatedly insisted upon the pleasures of a clean and organized learning space as an inducement to student discipline.[17]

Ayrton was emblematic of an energetic gospel of energy, which combined energy science and a punishing work ethic. He was renowned for the long hours he spent at work, as well as for his "energy, that earnestness, that untiring industry, that hatred of inaction which was his most intense characteristic," in the admiring words of his friend and fellow engineer, John Perry.[18] The journalist who toured Ayrton's Tokyo laboratory marveled that students clamored to continue working after 10 PM, "as they knew that their professor often worked much later every night."[19] Among the things Ayrton carried with him to Japan was his personal notepaper, which was embossed with a single word that encapsulated "his motto for life" and his earnest industry: "Energy."[20]

As Ayrton's example suggests, an important means of spreading the energetic gospel of labor was through new modes of industrial education. Technical and industrial schools proliferated worldwide during the new imperial era, demanding a higher status vis-à-vis the still classically dominated, elite university curriculum. It became a truism among industrial and political leaders in the West that more, and better, technical education was crucial to the ongoing prosperity of their states. Training more people to think like engineers was understood as an "absolute necessity" to ensure industrial success, whether for the spreading American empire or the "endangered" British position.[21]

While noteworthy technical schools had existed earlier, such as the prestigious French system, with the École Polytechnique, founded during the French Revolution, the number of technical schools increased dramatically at the end of the nineteenth century, through the so-called Second Industrial Revolution. In the United States, for example, the Morrill Act of 1862 extended federal aid for the first time to state colleges of agriculture and the mechanic arts; the number of engineering schools in the United States consequently grew from just a handful in the 1860s, to 85 by 1880, and 126 by the First World War. This period saw the founding of the Massachusetts Institute of Technology (1861) and the California Institute of Technology (1891).[22]

There was no single style of technical education in these new schools. Engineering cultures and pedagogies varied considerably by region and across time, from the informality of British engineering to the state-centered *grandes écoles* of France, the university-focused German system, and, later, the mass-production methods and Taylorism of the U.S. system. These distinct cultures were openly acknowledged, as one state's industrial success usually led others to try to emulate its particular style of training and education.[23] Despite this diversity in engineering education—and even in what it meant to be an engineer in a given society or economy—there were important shared features. First, engineering schools almost universally embraced the project of industrial capitalism and its goals of profit seeking and productivity. The primary aim of many schools was not to produce citizen-scholars or scientists, but rather to produce industrial workers and managers, to increase the "industrial intelligence" of workers, as a 1905 Massachusetts Commission on Industrial and Technical Education report explains.[24] Practicality, or the ability to apply scientific theories to the "real world" of technical apparatus, was the overriding goal. John Stevenson, a geographer at New York University, explained in 1908 that "technical schools are not schools for the study of science, but schools in which the principles of pure science are applied to practical operations. . . . [T]hey are to prepare a man to earn a livelihood in honest and honorable fashion, to do well that which formerly was done in slipshod fashion."[25] The professional engineer, a "new social type" that emerges in the nineteenth century, slipped easily between the laws of science and the needs of capital.[26]

This posed no intellectual conflict as, in the eyes of the engineer, capitalism reflected natural laws. Historian David Noble explains that the engineer's work "was guided as much by the capitalist need to minimize both the cost and the autonomy of skilled labor as by the desire to harness most efficiently the potentials of matter and energy."[27] In the cruder words of Henry Towne, a prominent engineer of the period cited by Noble, "the dollar is the final term in almost every equation which arises in the practice of engineering in any or all of its branches."[28]

Second, and hand in hand with embracing capitalism, engineering promoted a thermodynamic understanding of labor. In their magazines, textbooks, and publicity materials, these schools treated work as energy conversion, and labor governance as the striving for disciplined efficiency over those energy flows. Many early technical schools articulated a world-view that drew upon energy physics, stressing dynamism and productivism as ideals drawn from knowledge of natural laws. Energy, the sign for the ability to do work, underlay dominant assumptions about nature and industry. As earlier chapters have shown, the development of engineering, and the study of steam engines, was deeply entwined with thermodynamics and the ensuing studies of energy. The first scientists of energy, including Sadi Carnot and William Thompson, were later recuperated as key figures in the historical canon of engineering. The connections between energy and engineering were more than conceptual: as the chapter-opening story of Ayrton shows, some of the first technical schools in Japan and the United Kingdom were set up by students of Thompson, the reigning king of thermodynamics, and by this point a national hero due to his improvements on imperial telegraph cables.

As in other reports from the imperial archive, however, thermodynamics, or even energy itself, is easy to miss. Energy only appears as a trace, smuggled into the more explicit, and ever-present, obsession with work. This helps to explain why physics receives less attention as a contributor to imperial governance. Ironically, in this case, the absence of energy physics from such texts may point to the degree of its influence. Energy, as understood by thermodynamics and utilized by engineers, appears to have become such a commonsense foundation for certain sectors as to need no explanation or direct reference.

Indeed, by the late nineteenth century, energy had been successfully established in science, even as its meaning remained in flux and continued to produce multiple, alternative fields of energy studies. Amid these multiple ways of doing energy, the spread of technical education reflected the rising dominance of an engineer's approach to energy—one focused on efficient work and minimal waste for the benefit of industry—as the guide for organizing industrial economies. In contrast, other possible sciences and cultures of energy were less useful to industrial purposes.

Although most technical schools shared an affinity for energy and capitalism, their programs were markedly different depending upon the composition of the student body. Education reformers believed that technical education was necessary not just for engineers, who would become managers, but also for the working class and colonized peoples, whose bodies were to be folded smoothly into industrial schemes. A two-tiered system of industrial education emerged, mirroring the wider pattern of school divisions by race, gender, and class.

Engineering schools, often affiliated with universities, were the most elite, and were intended "to prepare people for a life of managing labor"[29] by producing industry-friendly engineers. These almost entirely white, male pupils were to become the managers of energy flows—those who would ensure energy was spent efficiently and productively. Engineers trained in the United States quickly became favored by mine managers worldwide. American engineers were popular not only for their technical acumen, but also for their ability to address "the thorniest problem of all facing any large-scale mining enterprise involving low-grade ore (as in the case of Rand gold): access to a plentiful and steady supply of quasi-servile low-cost labor."[30] Their experiences managing (and struggling against) indigenous Americans at mines in the American West and Mexico lent them an expertise in racialized labor that was attractive to colonial rulers attempting to discipline low-paid labor elsewhere.[31] This was especially true for mining in South Africa, where U.S. engineers imported a "culture and ethos of the emergent corporate industrial capitalism in their penchant for cost-cutting efficiency and scientific economies-of-scale production."[32] On an 1896 trip to South Africa, Mark Twain marveled that "the capital which has developed the mines come from England, the mining engineers from America. . . . South Africa seems to be the heaven of the American scientific mining engineer."[33] It was certainly heaven for men like William Hall, the state engineer of California for ten years, who profited by consulting with the South African mining industry, and whose report takes particular pains to address the problem of unreliable and resistant "kaffir labour." Hall argues that the mining companies are not as profitable as U.S. mines because of "the shortcomings of man, not the obduracy or unkindness of nature," and that "the problem is to get the gold out of the ground at the least possible cost." This requires managers to make the indolent "kaffir" into a human, where a human is defined as someone who works hard and docilely for wages.[34]

White managers were therefore reliant upon a second kind of industrial education, which ranked below their own engineering schools: those industrial or technical schools that aimed "to prepare people for a life of labor"[35] by producing ideal workers. These bodies were to be the energy transformers who needed to be disciplined to efficiency and productivity. The second-tier technical and industrial schools often advertised themselves in the language of the engineering schools, suggesting that they would confer expertise in the machine arts. However, the promise of technical education could be deceptive: engineering, science, or technical expertise might make up very little of the daily rhythms of school life. Especially in the case of schools for students of color, industrial schools were more concerned with disciplining future laborers to a life of menial toil, long hours, and docile subservience that was not always so different from preindustrial expectations of labor. At the same time, these schools benefited from the veneer of modernity that the terms *industrial* and *technical* provided.

Such education schemes were the preferred tools of a progressive racism that aimed to improve colonized others. Energy provided one metric by which to gauge status: lower-status workers had not yet proven a mastery of efficient energy flows, and in a feat of circular reasoning, this was supposedly evident in their resistance to menial, waged work. This was a new spin on a much older tradition of work governance. Earlier discourses had emphasized morality, where laziness was a sin to be overcome by spiritual reform. Through energy, work became more a technical operation than a moral practice, one that could be improved through scientific training.

A global survey of technical education is beyond the scope of my argument. Rather, the following examples of U.S. technical schools for Black and Native American students illustrate how a handful of prominent programs adopted an energetic understanding of work in order to reinforce a racialized hierarchy of industrial labor. The energetic approach to work provided another means by which to naturalize white male supremacy in industrial capitalism. However, this was not simply a case of Western knowledge transferring easily to passive, racialized others. Instead, school administrators perceived themselves to be engaged in a struggle against alternative ways of organizing work. Resistance to school-imposed norms of efficiency and productivism were constant aggravations. These schools were also sometimes intended as experimental programs, imposing intensive disciplinary models on students of color that would then be held up as templates for poor and middle-class white schools. So, while this chapter is mostly concerned with describing energy as a logic of domination, it is important to recognize that domination becomes intense in the face of resistance. If capitalists and managers had faced a docile, compliant labor force, then there would have been little need for the extraordinary focus on spreading the gospel of labor. The very existence of energy logics as modes of domination provides evidence that many people refused, resented, and resisted waged work, whether in dodging it, in performing it halfheartedly, or in defending times and spaces of leisure and living otherwise.

During the Second Industrial Revolution, in the aftermath of the Civil War, the United States was an empire on the make. White imperial and industrial managers faced labor problems on multiple fronts, each of which posed challenges to white supremacy. As a settler state, the United States was still making war on indigenous peoples in the American West. As a recent slave state, the country was forced to adjust itself to a new political economy of freed Blacks in the South. And as an aspiring imperial state, it was engaged in overseas governance in Hawaii, Cuba, Puerto Rico, and the Philippines.

At the same time, some Americans in the Progressive Era explicitly rejected the imperial and racist statecraft of the period. From abolitionists who had organized against slavery, to those who expressed sympathy for the historic harms done to Native Americans, many progressive white Americans longed to make amends for abuses against peoples of color. Setting up schools for the children of liberated slaves or Native Americans forced onto reservations became a popular practice among such reformers, an impetus satirized by "School Begins," an 1899 cartoon in *Puck* magazine in which Uncle Sam attempts to discipline his new colonies, while the Native American child reads a book upside down in the corner and a Black child washes the windows (figure 7.1).

Two of the most prominent schools in the progressivist spirit were the Hampton Normal and Agricultural Institute in Hampton, Virginia, opened in 1868, which had the stated aim of training newly liberated Black Americans for industrial work, and the Carlisle Indian Industrial School in Pennsylvania, opened in 1879, which intended to apply the Hampton model to the reeducation of Native American children. But education arranged by white people on behalf of colonized others was rarely so innocent. For one, focusing on education as a civilizing mission played into the narrative that U.S. expansion, if genocidal in its early years, could in the long run become helpful to the people it had dominated. Moreover, despite their professed goodwill toward students of color, many of these schools, and the progressives who raised money to support them, had the effect of merely softening the public relations image of white supremacy. Schools run by white managers often aimed to help their students advance in the world, but only so far. The biggest danger that school administrators feared, aside from outright resistance to wage labor, was that students who were educated would no longer want to work in low-paying

FIGURE 7.1. "School Begins in America." Source: Louis Dalrymple, published in *Puck* 44, no. 1142 (January 25, 1899), centerfold.

jobs and would aspire to clerical and management positions. As a result, while reformers rejected the view of white southern elites, who feared that education would "spoil good field hands," many did so by reassuring elite whites that education would produce "a more productive and contented agricultural work force," and would not lead to more Black people competing for higher-paid white jobs.[36]

This accorded with widespread white anxiety about the threat of Black labor, especially for white workers in settler colonies. Tiffany Willoughby-Herard writes that this fear fed the need "to render black people as incompetent, inefficient racially, incapable of doing 'white jobs,' permanent migrants, natural servants, ugly female beasts of burden, dandies, lazy, criminals, vagabonds, American slaves, strikebreakers—anything and everything, except workers."[37] If Black people were not natural workers, then all the more reason to conceive of Black industrial education as intensive labor discipline under white oversight. Schools like Hampton would replicate the northern model of industrial efficiency and would "upgrade black productivity while preparing blacks for racially prescribed social roles."[38] The contradictory desires of progressive racism, which underlie industrial education for students of color, meant that students were meant to read and write—to advance intellectually and spiritually— but not so much that they would reject the hard, menial toil best suited to their status.

In short, the primary goal of many of these schools was in fact to discipline students to the rhythms of efficient drudge work. Schools that centered on technical and industrial education were especially attractive for this purpose. A technical school could more easily elevate work as the highest value in its curriculum. Teaching work at a *technical* school had the advantage of sounding more modern, and in line with the higher-status engineering schools proliferating in this period, even if students were only minimally engaged in labor that involved new technologies. The preeminence of work, and the minimization of more traditional subjects like reading, writing, and math, could be justified without reference to racism, but instead through an economic ideology that resonated with the new culture of engineering itself. After all, the intimate relationship between engineering and industrial capitalism had already positioned work as a category that was crucial to both science and industry.

ECONOMIC CRUMBS AT HAMPTON

Much of the school day at technical schools for students of color was dedicated to work, which sometimes meant toiling for low wages in businesses owned by, or profitable for, the school and its (white male) masters. Pupils were promised an education in machines and industry. But for poor students, students of color, or women, a technical education was geared toward training for menial jobs, including the care, service, and agricultural work still necessary to reproduce industrial households. Thus, many so-called technical schools set pupils to work in labor whose only technical aspect involved the new styles of labor discipline that would make these tasks more efficient and productive, as in home economics. For example, schools modeled after the Hampton Institute felt that one of their important purposes lay in counteracting the threat of Black intellectuals and spiritual leaders who, some Hampton leaders feared, were demagogues tempting Black folk away from hard work. As Hampton explains in its 1879 report to the Virginia Assembly, the "greatest danger" to its students lay "in the bad leadership of demagogues, whose destiny is not yet assured, and whose future honorable position is secured only by toil."[39]

The founder of Hampton was Samuel Armstrong, a man long familiar with U.S. imperial and racial politics, having been born to missionaries in Hawaii, and having later commanded a regiment of Black soldiers during the Civil War. Armstrong exemplifies the Reconstruction-era focus upon labor as the key to helping freed slaves, as well as the assumption that Black people needed to learn how to become disciplined workers and to embrace work as a moral value. Even Hampton's student teachers were to be trained as promoters of labor discipline: "The race will succeed or fail as it shall devote itself with energy to Agriculture and the Mechanic arts, or avoid these pursuits, and its teachers must be inspired with the spirit of hard work and acquainted with the ways that lead to material success."[40]

Hampton was therefore less interested in the liberal arts—much less in brilliant students, who would be expelled if they did not also work hard[41]—but instead advertised itself to "chiefly country youth who don't mind hard work" and aimed to train them "how to work steadily and regularly, to attend promptly at certain hours to certain duties," such that "the pauper spirit has no encouragement; there is no begging except for more work."[42] As Captain H. C. Romeyn, a commander of the Hampton Cadets, explains, the faculty and its drills were instilling "respect for order and properly constituted authority that, in general, would do much to keep down the dangerously increasing communistic elements in the midst of the population of our country."[43]

Hampton's industrial focus lay at the heart of the disagreement between its most famous graduate, Booker T. Washington, who would go on to teach at Hampton and to found Tuskegee University on the Hampton model, and critics like W. E. B. Du Bois. In a now-famous speech to a largely white audience at the Atlanta Exposition in 1895, Washington declared that "No race can prosper till it learns that there is as much dignity in tilling a field as in writing a poem. It is at the bottom of life we must begin, and not at the top."[44] While Du Bois at first congratulated Washington on the speech, he later grew more critical of this pedagogical style, and in 1903 wrote of "these days when every energy is being used to put Black men back into slavery, and when Mr. Washington is leading the way backward."[45] In *The Souls of Black Folk*, Du Bois devotes an entire section to Washington and his embrace of industrial education, a position that he felt reflected "the old attitude of adjustment and submission. . . . This is an age of unusual economic development, and Mr. Washington's programme naturally takes an economic cast, becoming a gospel of Work and Money to such an extent as apparently almost completely to overshadow the higher aims of life."[46]

Du Bois acknowledges that a Hampton-style industrial education, focused upon training workers, could benefit some students, but he insists that many students also deserve a university education replete with the arts and humanities, whose primary aim was not economic. Du Bois represented the wider spirit of Black-run schools which, in the late nineteenth century, largely resisted the work focus of the Hampton model. However, schools run by the Black community would continue to run up against white corporations and philanthropists who kept the industrial model awash in funding.[47] After all, Black education remained an uncomfortable proposition for whites in the South, as Du Bois observes that "the South believed an educated Negro to be a dangerous Negro. And the South was not wholly wrong; for education among all kinds of men always has had, and always will have, an element of danger and revolution, of dissatisfaction and discontent."[48]

But not only was it politically dangerous to educate freed Blacks—Du Bois also observes that Black education was in tension with the needs of industrial capitalism. In his history of racial capitalism, *Black Reconstruction in America*, Du Bois points out that "the giant forces of water and of steam were harnessed to do the world's work, and the Black workers of America bent at the bottom of a growing pyramid of commerce and industry; and *they not only could not be spared*, if this new economic organization was to expand, but rather they became the cause of new political demands and alignments, of new dreams of power and visions of empire" (italics mine).[49] Industrial capitalism not only needs workers; it needs racialized workers who can be underpaid according to their supposed inferiority. And so, after abolition, a new mode of slavery emerged that maintained the systematic organization of workers by race, to the benefit of capital, which "was adopted, forwarded and approved by white labor, and resulted in subordination of colored labor to white profits the world over."[50]

Again, while evolution, in the form of social Darwinism, was important in justifying the new race-based labor schemes that Du Bois details, thermodynamic understandings of energy also contributed to how industrial managers and school administrators governed industrial work. This is evident in the casual distinctions between energetic and indolent bodies, and in the ideological preference for dynamism, efficiency, and productivity as scientifically oriented values. Again, this is not to say that such values originated in thermodynamics, but rather that the science of energy lent new, objective-seeming justification for these Western preferences.

Energy's function in governing racialized labor is evident in a close reading of one of Hampton's textbooks, *Economic Crumbs, or Plain Talks for the People about Labor, Capital, Money, Tariff, Etc.*, authored by Thomas Bryce, a Hampton faculty member and also the owner of an oyster cannery that employed hundreds of Hampton students. The worldview of *Economic Crumbs* (whose title reflects its paternalistic attitude toward its readers) is saturated with the truisms of the laws of thermodynamics, which it uses to teach students of color that economic hierarchies are natural and necessary. Bryce's chief concern is to head off the threat of labor insurrection and to warn his students against unionizing and strikes. The essays justify industrialism, private property, and wage labor, as well as hierarchies of wages and wealth, by referring to laws of nature, which are mostly colloquial versions of the laws of thermodynamics. It is worth quoting *Economic Crumbs* at length, as it affords a rare view into a classroom, and shows how a mostly white faculty translated thermodynamic visions of energy into a defense of social hierarchies.

The book begins by equating the ubiquity of energy to the ubiquity of work, with the slogan "Labor, Labor Everywhere—All Men Laborers," and a breathless scientific explanation of the world at work:

> Of all the many wonderful things we can see in this world, if we keep our eyes open, perhaps one of the most striking, is the omnipresence of motion. From the sweep of the most distant planet, in its tremendous orbit, to the disintegration of the hardest rock, there is motion; different in degree, but the same in kind. Everything about us is in motion, and all motion is work; but it is not with work in general that this paper has to do, but with that small, yet important part of work, called Labor. What is Labor? Labor is any human exertion, voluntarily put forth in exchange for something desired. The Chinaman, who toils all day for two cents, and the eminent advocate, who receives thousands of dollars for a single plea, are both laborers.[51]

Energy, here figured as "motion," provides the underlying unit of equality—we are all exchangers of energy, and we are all laboring, whether we are field hands or doctors. And because energy has leveled the field of motion, there is also a democratization of work that, strangely, Bryce employs to argue against the existence of a "laboring class" or a racial division of labor. There are no capitalists in reality, Bryce intones. Everyone labors, and so everyone is part of the laboring class, and "viewing labor in this, the only true light, the consideration of the labor question becomes simpler, for there are no class feelings to irritate, no color line to fight over."[52] Instead, we are left with a vast sum of exchanges, as "labor forms a greater or less part of everything that is exchanged; therefore the universal laws governing exchanges, can be applied directly to labor."[53] Those "universal laws" of exchange accord with both thermodynamic and capitalist sensibilities, as "human industry is the algebraic sum of human energies."[54]

While all exchanges have a labor dimension, and all men are laborers, it is also natural that there be some distinctions between these activities, as in the opening contrast between the two-cent "Chinaman" and the highly paid "eminent advocate," that we can safely assume is meant to refer to a white, Western man. Energy democratizes the laboring activity, but Bryce's defense of inequality also echoes the insights of thermodynamics: the steam engine, as well as living bodies, requires energy differentials (e.g., between hot and cold) in order to operate. If energy were uniformly distributed, it would spell death and stasis—the heat death that early energy scientists feared. Bryce equates cosmic, heat-death imagery with communism. All activity is laboring, but at the same time, uneven concentrations of energy (and so, wealth) are necessary for work and life. He warns Hampton students: "that some men should have more capital than others is a necessity from the very nature of things," given that "on these diversities the whole world moves. Perfect equality would be perfect stagnation. . . . The world and its people might as well return to chaos, and in universal nothingness, find the universal equality of property preached by the communist, and practiced by the highwayman."[55]

Alongside this paean to work, *Economic Crumbs* also employs thermodynamic metaphors and the "natural law" of entropy to disparage waste, in many ways echoing the Scottish Presbyterian synthesis of early energy scientists. Bryce calls for an appreciation of matter and energy as gifts from God, who created humans to manage that energy wisely, according to their knowledge of energy transformations. Inevitably, loss (entropic increase) haunts every laboring activity, but people are called upon by God to combat loss to the best of their ability. Bryce offers a folksy version of the gospel of entropy, explaining that "in the economy of nature, nothing is really lost, although apparently something disappears in every change that matter undergoes. If ten thousand cords of wood were burned to ashes, and then scattered in the sea, there would not be an ounce of matter lost: there would have been a change of form, and that is all. The object of transforming any bit of matter, is to increase the utility, or beauty of some part of it: those transformations are best, in which the least apparent loss is noticeable."

The "higher aims of life" that Du Bois calls for have been reduced to work and waste; beauty is reflected by degrees of usefulness. Under this thermodynamic worldview, industrial capitalism emerges as the straightest path toward virtue, according to both righteousness and natural law. It was good and right that Black students should be happy with economic crumbs.

CARLISLE AND THE "MAN-ON-THE-BAND-STAND"

Hampton's adoption of energy science into the industrial governance of labor was representative of technical education in this period, especially as it was designed for students of color. Indeed, Hampton became not only a model for Black technical education in the South; its methods were also transplanted into other sites in which racialized laborers were to be trained, including by German colonizers keen to develop cotton plantations in West Africa. As Andrew Zimmerman writes in *Alabama in Africa*, the Hampton method of "scientific" training for Black students thus acquired global significance, "help[ing] transform the political economy of race and agricultural labor characteristic of the New South into a colonial political economy of the global South."[56]

The "social-biological regime of control" instituted by German colonizers, applying the Hampton model, drew upon a "neo-racism" that was conducive to the needs of fossil capital, a racism "of exploitation and subordination rather than a racism of conquest and annihilation."[57] In an era of supposedly free workers, racism was an important tool in the new apparatus of labor governance. Without the internal, white, Protestant compulsion to work that Max Weber had theorized, external methods of discipline, such as industrial education, would be necessary to get people to embrace work as an end in itself, as a calling to be pursued without regard to wages or hours.[58] Like his German compatriots, Weber was also inspired by the Hampton model, having visited Tuskegee in 1904 with his wife, Marianne, and also corresponding with Du Bois, whom the Webers persisted in describing as only partially Black. Zimmerman shows how the experience of Black workers in the South was instrumental to Weber's analysis of racial and civilizational differences in laboring capacity, a field that Weber proposed as a "psychophysics" of labor.[59]

In describing the neo-racism of German colonizers, as well as Weber, Zimmerman points to a complex mixture of biological and sociological conceptions of race. Weber, for example, sometimes approached race more sociologically, in line with progressives, interpreting racial differences as the result of structures of education and labor that could be reformed. However, a careful reading of Hampton's program shows that there was also an energetic element to the new imperial racism that had as much to do with physics and engineering as it did with evolution or biology. To the extent that the natural sciences are accorded a privileged position as objective and universal knowledges, it is important to recognize the role of energy in upholding labor hierarchies. The relevance of texts like *Economic Crumbs*, which drew upon thermodynamics for its defense of inequality, can be appreciated in this light. Similarly, Weber's psychophysics of labor combined energy and biology, in that it sought to discover the biological traits of raced bodies that produced outcomes of efficiency and productivity.

While German colonizers would attempt to build their own Hampton schools in West Africa at the turn of the twentieth century, Hampton also inspired the construction of reformist schools for Native Americans in the United States, such as the Carlisle Indian School in Pennsylvania, which opened in 1879, and which itself became a prototype for off-reservation boarding schools for Native American children. The idea of Carlisle was born at Hampton; its growing popularity among white reformers inspired those who sought to extend similar "benefits" to Native Americans. Herbert Welsh, the secretary of the Indian Rights Association—a white group whose goal was to help Native Americans gain citizenship by civilizing them—asserts in an 1890 pamphlet on the "Indian Question" that "probably nothing has done so much to change the current of public opinion as to the possibility of civilizing Indians as the experiments in the education of Indian youth at the Carlisle and Hampton schools."[60]

Before acquiring the funds to retrofit the Carlisle military barracks into a school, Colonel Richard Henry Pratt, the founder of Carlisle, brought the first classes of Native Americans to partake in the Hampton industrial training experiment alongside Black students. Many of the early students in Pratt's group were prisoners of war, transported from Fort Sill, in what is now Oklahoma, to a military prison in St. Augustine, Florida, and who had been subjected to Pratt's original education experiment there. Pratt

FIGURE 7.2. Richard Henry Pratt with Navajo students at Carlisle: Before. Credit: PA-CH1-009a, photographed by John N. Choate and acquired from the Cumberland County Historical Society.

had been a military officer in Indian Territory, and in Florida he had garnered the attention of progressive reformers by transforming the prison experience into a civilizing education mission, where he dressed the prisoners in U.S. military uniforms, taught them Christianity and English, and above all insisted on a work ethic that involved hiring them out for local day jobs and putting their wages into forced savings accounts that he personally oversaw. Harriet Beecher Stowe was among Pratt's fans and early assistants, and she observed that "We have tried fighting and killing the Indians, and gained little by it. We have tried feeding them as paupers in their savage state. . . . Might not the money now constantly spent on armies, forts, and frontiers be better invested in educating young men who shall return and teach their people to live like civilized beings?"[61]

FIGURE 7.3. Navajo students at Carlisle: After. Credit: BS-CH-069b, photographed by John N. Choate and acquired from the Cumberland County Historical Society.

Pratt's experiment, and the idea of transitioning from war-by-soldiers to war-by-teachers, became popular enough to garner the resources to expand his idea, first into a new wing at Hampton and then into his own school at Carlisle. Carlisle, the first federally funded, off-reservation school, was part of a wider trend in settler colonial states in which children were separated from their families, often through force and threats, and sent off to day schools or off-reservation boarding schools where they had to conform to Western dress, language, and religion. The aim was to "get rid of the Indian as a separate and peculiar people," in the words of a Carlisle school newsletter.[62] Similarly, Pratt was well known for his dictum: "kill the Indian, save the man."[63] He carefully documented his handiwork with the new medium of photography. In figure 7.2, Pratt is the man on the bandstand, posing with a group of twelve Navajo students who had just arrived at the school in October 1882.

This "before" picture is an example of one of Pratt's favorite marketing techniques—before-and-after photos were staged as evidence of Carlisle's success in civilizing children, and they were widely circulated to donors, politicians, federal agencies, and even as commercially available souvenirs. The photos were carefully arranged to maximize the contrast of savagery and civilization, with the "before" children depicted as what Pratt called "blanket Indians" and often seated on the ground outdoors, while the "after" children wear their mandatory school uniform (a Western military style for boys) and forced haircuts, and are photographed in chairs with Victorian parlor backdrops.

While the schools thus advanced a narrative in which reformers were helping Native Americans and rescuing them from a life of poverty on the reservation, the programs had both economic and political benefits to white rulers. First, as Stowe's argument implied, education seemed to provide a cleaner way to pacify Native Americans. As Pratt insisted to President Rutherford Hayes, "I am at this time, 'fighting' a greater number of the 'enemies of civilization,' than the whole of my regiment put together, and I know further that I am fighting them with a thousand times more hopes of success."[64] Second, and relatedly, Native American children were openly understood as hostages of war who helped to ensure the good behavior of their parents, because "while their children are at school they will not fight."[65] Moreover, education was a more appealing method to progressives in the North who felt the need to compensate the Native Americans for stealing their land and extinguishing their civilizations. However unjust that land theft was, they believed that civilizing Native Americans would be a gift. Once again, the salvation was to be through the gospel of work. Merrill Gates, the president of Friends of the Indian, asserted that "we are going to conquer the Indians by a standing army of schoolteachers, armed with ideas, winning victories by industrial training, and by the gospel of love and the gospel of work."[66] Armstrong, of Hampton, explains the stakes more clearly, positioning education as the only chance of saving Native Americans from extinction: "if the race is doomed in any case, civilizing has the advantage at least of being a cheaper as well as more merciful means of extermination than starving and the horrors of Indian warfare."[67]

Finally, as with Hampton, the industrial education of Native American children had local and systemic economic benefits for white rulers. Native

Americans who refused industrial labor schemes were considered useless to the state, "and the idea of supposedly primitive peoples living independently in the midst of industrializing, modern nations who needed cheap sources of labor seemed to pose an affront to white Americans and Australians."[68] This played out to the benefit of white families and companies located near schools like Carlisle, which hired out students as field hands and housekeepers at low wages; the schools then often kept most of the students' earnings.[69] A 1909 article in *Red Man*, a Carlisle school newsletter, reports that a Carlisle graduate has been assigned to expand the "outing" system in the West, hiring Native Americans to work on railroads, irrigation construction, and in sugar beet fields.[70] As with the Black students at Hampton, and colonial labor in the Global South, the industrial schools for indigenous peoples were for the most part training children for a life of reproductive, care, and manual labor for white households and managers, rather than training them to become managers themselves. For example, the *Red Man* article mentions one exceptional Native American who had become the assistant engineer of an Indian-run power plant, but otherwise, the most skilled Native American workers are promoted to become blacksmiths and mechanics, only sometimes rivaling their white counterparts, while the rest are in "lower" positions.[71]

Indeed, in Pratt's arrival at Hampton, the racialized underpinnings of the industrial education system, which sought above all to reinforce white supremacy, become apparent, as what was deemed appropriate for Black students in the South was judged to be directly applicable to the Native American experience. Armstrong, the founder of Hampton, writes that "I believe that a colored school, on the labor plan, offers better conditions for educating Indians than any others. Both races need similar methods."[72]

The first and overarching goal for civilizing the students thus had to do with work—and not always with *how* to work, but to even *want* to work, as Native American cultures were seen as communistic and lazy. As at Hampton, here, too, an industrial worldview involved an understanding of labor as energy conversion, and the deployment of energy metaphors to support an ideology of dynamism in the name of industrial capitalism. Hierarchies of workers, according to race and gender, were explained by propensities for efficiency and innovation in energy use. Energy discourse appears frequently across Carlisle pamphlets, including in its newsletter, *The Indian Helper*, which describes itself as "PRINTED by Indian boys, but EDITED by The-man-on-the-band-stand, a person of another race and color."

The paternalistic man-on-the-band-stand pops up in many vignettes and serves as a kind of omniscient narrator; he seems to function as a reminder to the students that they are continually under surveillance. One of the favorite pastimes for the man-on-the-band-stand is to report on children whom he spies loafing or complaining. As with *Economic Crumbs*, the newsletters, written by school administrators for student readers, offer a glimpse inside the school's philosophy. *The Indian Helper* is centrally preoccupied with inciting students to dynamism and asceticism (the combination of which is necessary for producing docile, low-paid workers). In an 1888 newsletter, for example, the man-on-the-band-stand reports eavesdropping on two students, one who is a strapping boy "full of good intentions, a body full of energy and a heart full of GRATITUDE," while the other "has a slothful disposition," a distressing penchant for fine clothes, and a desire to go to a better school where he would not have to work so hard to pay his tuition—an attitude that the man-on-the-band-stand dismisses as ungrateful and lazy.[73] Meanwhile, an 1885 newsletter explains the meaning of loafing: "What is loafing? When a boy stands with his hands in his overcoat pockets, or his pants pockets, lazily leaning against something, waiting, waiting, doing nothing, thinking nothing hard, that is LOAFING. . . . A LOAFER is of no account in this world. Last Saturday afternoon, the Man-on-the-band-stand saw too many boys LOAFING around the corners. Of course you don't want to WORK all the time. That is all right. Nobody wants you to work all the time. Nobody wants you to STUDY all the time. But NEVER loaf. Walk, run, play, take exercise, do SOMETHING. DO NOT LOAF!"[74]

The preference for dynamism is coupled with white distress when confronted by stillness, a posture once prized by white aristocrats, and now allowed only in circumscribed sites, as in the fantasy of the idle Victorian woman, although neither figure has much purchase in the new American industrial culture. To loaf is to be ugly, in the worldview of *Economic Crumbs*, because it is to be useless to industrial capital—to be, according to the man-on-the-band-stand, "of no account in this world." To loaf is to become an energy sink, to exit the field of energy transformations and to become akin to death.

More ominously, to loaf is to be on the side of a civilization doomed to extinction, where evolutionary trajectories are impacted by one's efficient use of energy. Humans' efficient use of energy reflected their ability to put the energy of the land and its resources to productive use. The project of industrial capitalism, again, was not only to put colonized people to work for white managers, but to put the entire world to work. What doomed the Native Americans to extinction, in this view, was not just their lazy loafing, but how that loafing contributed to their relatively lighter ecological footprint in North America, which seemed all the smaller in the centuries following the mass die-offs of indigenous peoples after contact with European colonizers in the sixteenth and seventeenth centuries. They did not spread out and work the land as the white man did.

And so in 1829, Andrew Jackson could sanguinely shrug his shoulders at the prospect of the extinction of Native Americans and ask in his congressional address on the Removal Act, "What good man would prefer a country covered with forests and ranged by a few thousand savages to our extensive Republic, studded with cities, towns, and prosperous farms, embellished with all the improvements which art can devise or industry execute, occupied by more than 12,000,000 happy people, and filled with all the blessings of liberty, civilization, and religion?"[75] Jackson's urge to populate North America with white people, and to make every acre useful, would become the pillar of the new imperialism. Putting the world to work remains the dominant ideology of industrial capital, and is evident, for example, in justifications for recent land grabs in the Global South, where corporations argue that local people have failed to maximize the productivity of their land, or categorize some terrain as wild or empty even if it may have been a key dimension of local agro-ecological or pastoral systems for generations.[76] Fossil-fueled technologies, and the energy physics that governed fossil machines, both accelerated and justified the final death sentence for ways of life that resisted Jackson's genocidal sentiment.

CONCLUSION

The industrial school movements suggest one mode through which energy contributed to stabilizing a growing industrial workforce. The purpose of these schools was to teach a mode of science—which was deeply indebted to thermodynamics and ensuing studies of energy—that would be useful to industry. As such, it was allied to the professionalization of engineering, which, likewise, had energy and its efficient use as a foundational principle. These schools understood labor as energy conversion and labor governance as a striving for disciplined efficiency. New modes of discipline were required for enfolding laborers into the industrial project in a way that was safe for capital, but in a Progressive era in which slavery and serfdom were no longer acceptable modes of exploitation. Not only must people of color be made to work at the most menial tasks for a lower wage than white workers, and with few, if any, opportunities for advancement. White imperialists and settlers must also still guard against labor resistance and insurrection, both at home and abroad. Over and again, the labor resistance of colonized peoples was read through the prism of idleness and waste. These came to be understood as no longer just moral vices, but as signs of insufficient evolution that could be accelerated through technical education.

The resulting energy–work nexus has persisted to frame the politics of fuel, leading to an inherent bias toward high energy consumption and fossil fuel extraction so long as the work ethic reigns. Those who resisted the work ethic, and who persisted in multiple lifeways in which activity and leisure were differently structured, posed the most menacing challenge to fossil capital in the late nineteenth century. Across *Economic Crumbs* and *The Indian Helper*, the figures of the lazy Black worker, the racialized dandy, the Native American loafer, and the reservation dancers garner the most vicious condemnation. If workers of color threatened to steal white jobs, it was all the more alarming when they threatened to embody white aristocratic leisure—both are symptoms of bodies who refuse their lot as exploited labor in the global circulation of fossil capitalism.[77]

By and large, fossil capital has continued to target lifeways that refuse the work ethic. It is aided by the fact that energy—as human fuel use—is still wedded to the work ethic, even among left-leaning circles. Most visions of energy transition and fossil fuel divestment remain allied to the ideals of dynamism, efficiency and productivity. The obsession with counting, metering, and saving energy, and putting every unit to good use, which exercised Ayrton in his Tokyo laboratory, have only become more urgent in an era of global warming. The concluding chapter asks what it might mean to resist the thermodynamic disciplining of energy, drawing upon the tropes of lazy, indolent colonial workers for inspiration.

Energy is a problem in the Anthropocene—it is perhaps *the* problem of the Anthropocene. Humans need new energy systems—and likely new energy cultures—that leave fossil fuels in the ground and that instead rely on renewable fuels, coupled with more efficient technologies and, most likely, decreased energy consumption. There is no shortage of ideas as to how this could be achieved, ranging from techno-fixes that would swap out fuels and technologies but otherwise maintain the status quo of capitalist growth, to proposals for a green economy that might involve, among other reforms, monetizing natural resources and pollution costs in order to better "count" nature as integral to a market system.[1]

However, market-based fixes are insufficiently appreciative of the limits of human mastery over the world. In order to live appropriately on the Earth, humans need to reevaluate our commitment to endless growth, productivity, and commodity accumulation.[2] With the publication of such texts as *The Limits to Growth* and *Small Is Beautiful* in the midst of the 1970s oil crisis, this sensibility gained mainstream, albeit brief, appeal in the U.S. before subsiding again in the economic heyday of the 1980s Reagan era. Critiques of productivism remain central to green political platforms, but at the same time, they have always been haunted by fears about their social consequences: that shifting to a slow-growth or no-growth economy would result in massive recession, job losses, poverty, and social unrest. Left-accelerationists Nick Srnicek and Alex Williams assert that, "without full automation, postcapitalist futures must necessarily choose between abundance at the expense of freedom (echoing the work-centricity of Soviet Russia) or freedom at the expense of abundance, represented by primitivist dystopias."[3] Similarly, Clive Lord, a founding member of the British Green Party, recalls his initial reaction to the *Limits to Growth* report in the 1970s, when he asked other greens, "What is your social policy? You are proposing a deep recession. I agree it will be necessary, but every recession to date has caused widespread hardship. What will you do when desperate people start looting?"[4] Since Lord bemoaned the state of oil politics in the 1970s, the problem of energy has only become more intractable, and more urgent, in the so-called Anthropocene, which purports to name a geological era in which humans become planetary agents, setting off irreversible, self-amplifying processes, largely as a result of fossil fuel consumption. The problems of the Anthropocene are distinctly troubling: the interlocking flows of climate, glaciers, species death, plastic accumulation, toxic dumping, deforestation, ocean acidification, and so on appear unprecedentedly disruptive, global, and complex.

In the Anthropocene, humans are glimpsing new Earth problems that exceed our capacity to sense, experience, and understand them. These involve planetary flows that Timothy Morton has referred to as hyperobjects, such as global warming, climate, or oil, that are "massively distributed in time and space relative to humans," and that force us to undergo a radical 'reprogramming' of our ontological toolkit.[5] Global warming can be real and everywhere sticking to us, but "because it's distributed across the biosphere and beyond, it's very hard to see as a unique entity. And yet, there it is, raining on us, burning down on us, quaking the Earth, spawning gigantic hurricanes. . . . [G]lobal warming is real, but it involves a massive, counterintuitive perspective shift to see it."[6]

Of course, big objects have always already been there, nudging those who would listen toward such an ontological reprogramming, but it has been possible for most people to ignore this. No longer. Morton argues that the hyperobjects of the Anthropocene have become visible to humans, largely through the very mathematics and statistics that helped to create these disasters. As we grasp, blind and mole-like, toward snapshots of those higher dimensions in which hyperobjects dwell, our sense of the world and the cosmos is seriously threatened. Indeed, one of Morton's central arguments is that hyperobjects signal the "end of the world," if by world we mean that human reification in which we inhabit the center, and there is a horizon outside that cozy hobbit-hole we call home.[7] Hyperobjects show us "there is no center and we don't inhabit it. Yet added to this is another twist: there is no edge! We can't jump out of the universe."[8]

The ontological shift forced upon us by the Anthropocene also upends our understanding of politics. First, it presents global governance challenges that do not lend themselves to a system of nation-states, nor to global institutions that arise out of state-based collaboration. In their "Planet Politics" manifesto, international relations (IR) scholars Anthony

Burke, Simon Dalby, Stefanie Fishel, Daniel Levine, and Audra Mitchell argue that that IR "has failed because the planet does not match and cannot be clearly seen by its institutional and disciplinary frameworks. Institutionally and legally, it is organised around a managed anarchy of nation-states, not the collective human interaction with the biosphere."[9]

Second, and more theoretically, our understanding of agency, power, freedom, and justice all takes on different inflections when anthropocentrism loosens its grip. This is why many ecological thinkers and activists, like Morton, conclude that the problems of the Anthropocene will demand more radical political change, and that a society that privileges accelerated growth and productivity—even if it runs on more renewable fuels—will be unable to stem planetary destruction and climate change. In a colorful metaphor, Morton writes that "the *Titanic* of modernity hits the iceberg of hyperobjects,"[10] and that capitalism does not seem equipped to save us: the more our engines of accumulation and economic growth churn to escape, the more they seize up in the ice.[11] We need experiments with socialist and democratic modes of government to make them relevant to a new Earth, an Earth that can no longer be taken for granted as hospitable to human habitation. For example, the aforementioned manifesto for planet politics contends that "in the near term, we will have to work with flawed institutions, but the gravity of this crisis means that it is right to demand more profound and systemic change, and to explore, in politics and in scholarship, what that change should be."[12] This might involve new global institutions, such as an "Earth Systems Council," that would incorporate ecological violence into international law, or treating coal as a controlled substance.[13]

The gap is widening between the slow pace of human change and the self-amplifying and irreversible geological and planetary feedback loops. Historic environmental victories, while encouraging, at the same time appear as mere preambles to the changes in production, consumption, and ethics now required by the global population of humans, and particularly Westerners. This is widely evident: Morton's work, for instance, is often steeped in moods of melancholy and horror, while the planet politics manifesto begins from the assertion that IR has "failed" and that "this may finally be the death of Man, but what will come next if this face is lost in the rising tides? . . . We are speechless, or even worse, cannot find words to represent the world and those within it. We do not hope that politics will suddenly change—but it must change."[14] The Western sense of doom is but an aftershock, given that many Earthlings have been losing worlds and civilizations for centuries in the face of imperialism and industrialization. Nevertheless, there is something distinctly frightening about our current moment, in which so many of the disasters have become truly planetary and trans-species in scope.

I write this conclusion in the spirit of a new planet politics, venturing proposals that could help to incite a more far-reaching global movement, a "resonance machine" that could effectively counter what William Connolly has called the "evangelical-neoliberal resonance machine" that advances late modern capitalism and planetary destruction.[15] A key argument of this book has been that our commitment to growth and productivity has been reinforced by a geo-theology of energy that combines the prestige of physics with the appeal of Protestantism in order to support the interests of an industrial, imperial West. While the first geo-theology of energy was particular to a northern British crew and their efforts to improve steam engines, this logic of energy continues to haunt human relationships to fuel. The politics of energy has been captured by the ethos of work and waste, especially in the West. Historicizing energy as a modern logic of domination helps to denaturalize the energy–work connection. This does not mean that engineering equations are wrong: in many sites, energy can be successfully calculated to measure work (as matter moved). But the computing function of those units—energy and entropy—should not be allowed to stand unexamined as the basis for ethical prescriptions surrounding fuel and activity. After all, the physicists themselves remind us that energy and entropy are more epistemological than ontological. Let us affirm that the energy–work rationality is just one epistemology of energy—and not *the* epistemology of energy. Let us, following Walter Mignolo, upset the "Western code," which has recruited support from thermodynamics, and that code's "belief that in terms of epistemology there is only one game in town."[16] Let us be free to multiply energy epistemologies, metaphors, and visions concerning how we participate in and value work, production, and dynamism.

In this conclusion, I explore just one possible path toward living energy otherwise, and toward resisting fossil fuel cultures: putting post-carbon movements into conversation with the post-work political tradition. An alliance with post-work movements would help environmentalists in countering the pleasures of the post-Fordist, consumerist life of high energy consumption with an alternative political vision of pleasure. In particular, such an alliance would respond to the conundrum raised by Clive Lord's question—the fear that a low-growth or no-growth economy would entail, at best, sacrifice and asceticism and, at worst, violence and massive poverty. This is the position taken by many so-called ecomodernists, who reject the notion of limits to growth, and chastise the dominant environmentalist narrative of reducing energy consumption as inherently unjust to those in the Global South.[17] Ecomodernists insist that high energy consumption is integral to escaping poverty, and to achieving modern standards of well-being, and therefore call for a massive, publicly organized expansion in modernization and technological innovation based on the premise that economic growth can be successfully "decoupled" from ecological destruction.[18] In contrast to the ecomodernists, post-work movements would challenge the unquestioned assertion that modernization and high-technology society can be trusted to produce widespread well-being. Instead, they offer an alternative vision of a society that decouples energy from work, and productivism from equality and well-being.

Such alternative visions are urgently needed, given that, despite growing awareness of climate change and associated environmental emergencies, energy consumption and fossil fuel burning continue apace as environmentalists struggle to disrupt dominant fossil fuel cultures and narratives. The appeal of ecomodernism (or accelerationism) is that they rest upon a pleasurable politics that promises the continuation of, or expansion of, consumerism and productivism. A radical planet politics, if it seeks to contest ecomodernist claims, needs its own politics of pleasure. However, this remains difficult in large part because environmentalists are hampered by a dominant energy logic that operates upon the assumption of the virtue of wage labor and economic growth, something that ecomodernism, too, takes for granted. According to this framework— which structures almost every contemporary debate over energy projects and technologies—environmentalists must make their case in the now-familiar terms of work and waste. They must have an answer to the simple, but dominant mantra, captured in the political cartoon advocating for the Keystone XL pipeline in figure C.1: energy means jobs.

As a result, in most energy debates, environmentalists are compelled either to prove that alternative fuels would create more jobs and/or more economic growth than existing fossil fuel systems or, if this is not possible, to prove that the waste associated with fossil fuels outweighs the benefit of fossil fuel jobs. While minor victories can be achieved within a

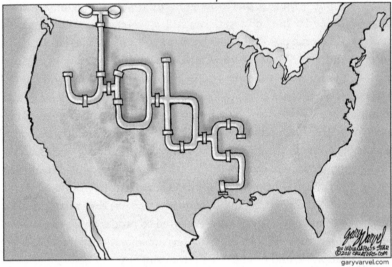

The KEYSTONE XL Pipeline Plan

FIGURE C.1. "Pipelines Mean Jobs." Credit: Cartoonist Gary Varvel, published December 15, 2011. Gary Varvel Editorial Cartoon used with the permission of Gary Varvel and Creators Syndicate. All rights reserved.

work–waste framework, it ultimately stymies the ability to imagine new energy cultures that depart from an endless acceleration of energy consumption and productivism.

First, a work–waste ethos stacks the deck in favor of fossil fuels. If environmentalists operate within a work-based argument, positing that alternative energy will support job growth and a healthier economy, they get mired in a back-and-forth over accounting logics that, in the spirit of neoliberalism, sidelines normative and political claims. Moreover, such an argument invites complacency, in that it encourages the belief that technology alone can save us. Changing only fuels and fuel technologies while keeping in place the globally unequal capitalist growth machine may alleviate some of the carbon accumulation in the atmosphere but will not address the multitude of other ecological problems that humans face. The hope that economic growth and ecological destruction can be reliably decoupled, and that we can achieve a "good" Anthropocene,[19] is ultimately too dangerous a risk to take in light of mounting evidence of Anthropocene crises. In a recent article on the Anthropocene, Donna Haraway asserts that "it's more than climate change; it's also extraordinary burdens of toxic chemistry, mining, depletion of lakes and rivers under and above ground, ecosystem simplification, vast genocides of people and other critters, etc., etc., in systemically linked patterns that threaten major system collapse after major system collapse after major system collapse. Recursion can be a drag."[20]

If humans could switch overnight to run entirely on wind and solar power, leaving all else intact, it would certainly pose benefits for the Earth and its creatures, but it would not come close to resolving many of the other destructive patterns on Haraway's list. Likewise, full automation, even if harnessed to a postcapitalist economy, will continue to imperil the planet if the underlying spirit of productivism remains.

Second, a waste-based critique of fossil fuels has important limitations. Drawing attention to waste arouses fear, sorrow, disgust, and anxiety. Its most popular genres are dystopia, nostalgia, and horror. Alarming doomsday lists have also become common; most environmental texts today begin with exhaustive catalogues of the horrors now occurring on Earth.[21] How many readers, like me, find their eyes skipping over these lists, which now feel redundant, even boring? Ironically, the motivation behind these genres is to shock readers, and especially the world's most privileged humans, by rendering ecological violence visible, to depict in detail that which has all too often remained subterranean, oceanic, filtered, and displaced. Much as thinkers like Haraway strive to resist hopelessness and apathy, her own list of Earthly disasters, cited above, is emblematic of the genre, and her pithy conclusion—"Recursion is a drag"—sums up the emotional effect that such lists make upon the reader, blasted with words like "depletion," "genocide," and "major system collapse."

As an affective strategy, a focus on waste is vulnerable to backfiring. The cultivation of public fear about waste and pollution can easily feed into desires for authoritarianism, militarism, and nationalism, and can reinforce anxieties about racist and gendered connotations of waste. In the United States and other parts of the West, we are already witnessing the effects of a dangerous political merging of "climate change, a threatened fossil fuel system, and an increasingly fragile Western hypermasculinity."[22] In addition, in relying on the collection of waste data, environmentalists are left in the position of needing to "prove" that certain categories of waste exceed a fuel's benefits. A waste-based argument requires that humans *know* about the waste in the first place, and that they can develop the tools with which to measure it, both of which only occur post hoc, and often after the ecological damage is planetary and deeply entrenched.

As an alternative to the demand to amass incontrovertible evidence before making policy changes, environmentalists have long asserted a precautionary principle, where the burden of proof would be flipped, such that one would have to prove that oil is *not* harmful, that fracking does *not* contaminate the water supply, and so on. The precautionary principle is part of a long-standing effort on the part of environmentalists to mount an alternative politics outside the work-and-waste paradigm. Political ecology, pastoralism, ecofeminism, green parties, indigenous groups, simplicity movements, those who strive to live off the grid— all have appealed to more positive, hopeful narratives and emotions in countering industrial modernity. These traditions of environmental thought, drawing upon experimenters in eco-living like Henry David Thoreau or Vandana Shiva, have argued that industrial capitalism has led to the deterioration of community, and has substituted more fulfilling pleasures with a vapid cycle of debt and consumerism. Disconnecting oneself, or one's community, from consumerism and productivity is heralded as more enriching and satisfying. The struggle continues today in countering the bounty of post-Fordist life in the wealthy Global North and overcoming the inertia that keeps people stuck in the grooves of consumerism and productivity. More avenues are needed in inspiring new visions and provoking original experiments in both institutional policy and lifestyles.

My proposition here is that a historical genealogy of energy suggests some insights and tactics that could be folded into this struggle. For one, despite the seeming novelty of the Anthropocene, the Victorians were already thinking in anthropocentric terms. They may not have had a full understanding of the speed and scale of the planetary disruptions set in motion by industrialization, but they nevertheless were duly terrified of the prospect of a changeable planet, a new Earth that cared nothing for human well-being. As this book has argued, a dominant logic of energy emerged in the mid-nineteenth century that provided one guide to handling an entropic, chaotic planet: it reinforced the drive of industrial imperialists to put the world to work.

Energy science, as well as energy metaphors and logics, have morphed and evolved across the intervening decades of modern life; after all, the work ethic itself has transformed with neoliberalism, automation, and the prominence of service-industry jobs. Nevertheless, that early logic of energy, with its engineering emphasis on thermodynamics and its drive to maximize productivism and efficiency, continues to haunt the politics of energy, and limits our ability to imagine alternative energy systems. The history of energy thus shows how energy and work became tethered to each other, and how this connection is continually reproduced in global industrial politics. The contingency and historicity of this binding are rarely acknowledged, much less contested.

However, because the energy–work paradigm must be continually re-produced, it is also vulnerable to disruption. There are other (scientific, political, spiritual) modes of knowing and experiencing energy that do not elevate productivity as a primary goal for human well-being. Reject-ing productivism does not require rejecting technology or automation *tout court*. Contra Srnicek and Williams, who do not question the impor-tance of productivism, we are not forced to choose between full automation, totalitarian planning, or primitivism. This paltry menu has already been circumscribed in advance by the dominant energy logic featured in this book.

In displacing an energy logic that demands productivism and effi-ciency, we open up space to judge technology and automation according to other energy and ecological imaginaries of what constitutes a good life, or a well organism. In preceding chapters, I have pointed to just a few (of many) alternative scientific approaches to energy that have flourished since the nineteenth century, and in which productive work plays a minor role in the well-being and maintenance of organisms and ecologies, or in which the meaning of energy itself is severely complicated and escapes measurement or control. These include approaches within evolution, ecology, complexity theory, cybernetics, neurobiology, relativity, symbi-ology, and quantum mechanics.

I have also gestured toward the many practices of resistance to the dom-inant logic of energy, including an insistence on work refusal and leisure. In her history of British colonial ideology in South Africa, Zine Magubane argues that "the only space of freedom for blacks was in the avoidance of work. Leisure constituted the sole exercise of power in the body."[23] In other words, a genealogy of energy suggests that energy and work (mean-ing human, waged work in the name of productivity) can be untethered for the purposes of ecological politics. Doing so opens up new conceptual, and material, space and time, in which truly alternative energy practices can proliferate. More ecologically generous ways of life on Earth, made unthinkable and unintelligible by neoliberalism, might become attractors for budding movements. This suggests the importance of a sustained partnership between energy politics and political ecology, in which the meaning and culture of energy are challenged alongside and through the revaluation of productive work.

The problem of energy is therefore intertwined with the politics of work and leisure. As Stephanie LeMenager notes in her study of oil and American life, "'Energy' becomes a way to talk about how both humans and nonhumans do work—and avoid it."[24] Without challenging dominant practices of work and leisure, and the high valuation of waged, productive work in a neoliberal economy, it will remain difficult to dislodge fossil fuel cultures. Indeed, the failure to challenge the organization and ethic of industrial work contributes to the difficulty in overcoming fossil fuel systems. If energy remains tightly bound to productive work, and the work ethic goes unchallenged—a work ethic that applies not only to human labor, but also to the fuels, technologies, and nonhumans put to work for humans—then any threatened decrease in energy consumption becomes automatically tainted as dreary, ascetic, and constrained, even if it espouses vitality and hope. This is because giving up energy implies giving up work, which is widely accepted as necessary to the good life, even if, as in left-accelerationism, the *humans* are no longer working. With the work ethic intact, the field of optimism and hope is ceded to more piecemeal reforms or techno-fixes that directly uphold the virtue of work and the promise of either plentiful jobs and/or plentiful production.

Creating space between energy and work could take a number of paths, and in the remainder of this conclusion, I want to highlight just one potential partnership that I suggest is ripe for testing new alliances: feminist post-work politics. I will explore Kathi Weeks's *The Problem with Work*, transposing its insights into the politics of work onto the politics of energy. Putting these two movements—one against fossil fuels and the other against work—into a more enduring conversation can benefit both. A post-work politics suggests one more route by which environmentalists can escape the neoliberal resonance machine, which obliges fossil fuel to be contested from within a work-and-waste paradigm. Meanwhile, by allying more explicitly with environmentalists, post-work movements can expand their relevance beyond anthropocentric critiques of capitalism, showing how not just human life, but Earthly life, is at stake in the contestation of work. And as I have been suggesting, a feminist post-work politics is distinct from the post-work politics of accelerationism, although alliances are possible. Accelerationists like Srnicek and Williams draw heavily upon Weeks, and engage with feminist critiques of work, but their embrace of full automation and productivity leaves energy tethered to work, only gesturing to the desirability of a techno-fix that would make those automated machines ecologically sustainable.

THE PROBLEM WITH WORK AND THE PROBLEM WITH ENERGY

It is no easy thing to mount a critique of work, and Weeks argues that political theory has largely ignored work and its "daily reality." She attributes this to the tendency to reify, privatize, and individualize work, such that "it is difficult to mount a critique of work that is not received as something wholly different: a criticism of workers. . . . [T]hinking about work as a social system—even with its arguably more tenuous private status—strangely becomes as difficult as it is for many to conceive marriage and the family in structural terms."[25] Moreover, the reification of work means that "the fact that at present one must work to 'earn a living' is taken as part of the natural order rather than as a social convention." Our modern system of work has become necessary to secure life, rather than a "way of life."[26]

Already, this analysis of the depoliticization of work is relevant to understanding the depoliticization of energy. Weeks (like many in the anti-work tradition)[27] does not address environmental or energy issues in her text, and yet, because thermodynamics equates work and energy as scientific units, we can gain new insights by transposing energy into the concept of work. First, we might notice that, with work so deeply entrenched as a social convention, its supreme value taken for granted, it is no wonder that the threat of losing jobs is enough to derail the pursuit of new energy cultures. In other words, if it is difficult to mount a critique of work, then it follows that it will be all the more difficult to mount a critique of energy. Another way of saying this is that the depoliticization of work does not just hamper us from reimagining work; it also blocks our ability to imagine new energy cultures.

Energy, like work, tends to be reified, privatized, and individualized when it becomes an object of politics. In relation to work, Weeks notes that options for contesting work have been narrowed to either unionization, whose relevance has waned in the United States and which anyhow tends to embrace the work ethic, or to consumer politics. With the emphasis on consumerism, corporations justify dismal wages and outsourcing by pointing to low prices for consumers (the classic Walmart strategy).[28] Parallel problems plague energy politics. Macroanalyses of energy are dominated by techno-rationality and market reform, both of which eschew normative claims. More political claims about energy, meanwhile, are often relegated to the micro level, to personal habits of energy consumption and individual consumer choices: fly less, bike to work, install solar panels, buy an electric vehicle. While these micropolitical shifts in habit are admirable and important to an "all-of-the-above" energy movement, when they make up the primary or sole avenue of energy contestation, they can leave citizens feeling fragmented and frustrated when set against the magnitude of planetary destruction. Also, parallel to the Walmart strategy, if citizenship becomes consumership, corporations can insist that environmental destruction is justified by low energy prices, with gas station signs serving as important political symbols. Corporations also exploit environmental sensibilities by hawking "green" commodities which, at best, only reinforces consumerism and, at worst, constitutes "greenwashing" in cases where certification and regulation are weak.

Second, Weeks argues that work is not necessary to life, but is instead a disciplinary apparatus through which political subjects are produced.[29] Something similar can be said of energy, although thanks to energy's association with physics, such a statement feels even more counterintuitive. Energy—the energy that I followed in this project, that thermodynamic unit that has been captured by a dominant, fossil-fueled logic of work and waste—is not *necessary* to life. Of course, this does not mean that energy and work in a more multivalent sense do not play integral roles in life, nor have value. Rather, it is to contend that the dominant political rationalities of "energy" and "work" have naturalized the *particular* ways in which Westerners have sought to arrange energy-things and work-activities in the Anthropocene: mostly into fossil-fuel–soaked, waged work for the purposes of productivity and profit.

It is these particular historical edifices of energy and work that have become reified as universal, and thereby removed from political contestation. By making work, and energy, public, it becomes possible to reimagine their meaning for citizenship and sociality, and to invent new practices of energy and work. As Weeks explains, the effort to politicize work and its productivist values "is not to deny the necessity of productive activity. . . . It is, rather, to insist that there are other ways to organize and distribute that activity and to remind us that it is also possible to be creative outside the boundaries of work."[30] Her goal is, first, to deconstruct work and diagnose its problems, but, second, to "generate an alternative mode of valuation—a vision of the work society not perfected but overcome."[31]

This second goal is relevant to energy politics because new ways of organizing work and productive activity, as well as creativity and leisure, will also, by default, constitute new ways of organizing energy, although Weeks does not explicitly explore this possibility. Srnicek and Williams only briefly allude to studies showing that reducing work could lead to "significant reductions in energy consumption," but they do not explicitly consider how working less might induce a transvaluation of work—it is still crucial to their vision that machines are working productively in the name of human abundance.[32]

A genealogy of energy can provide additional analytical support to these post-work visions, while pushing them further in post-productivist directions. A genealogy of energy suggests its own decoupling move, in opposition to the ecomodernist faith that energy consumption can be decoupled from ecological violence. Instead, a history of energy provides the basis for decoupling energy from work. A partnership between post-carbon and post-work politics can also be advantageous to energy scholars. In many ways, the degradations of waged work are more widely felt, and more easily sensed, than planetary processes like glacial melting or ocean acidification. Just as health concerns have served as a key motivation for environmental justice movements in the past, work can also operate as a useful launching point into ecological sensibility, as it touches upon everyday practices of pleasure, pain, and desire. Forging cross-regional alliances that combine these concerns can therefore help push toward further disruption and catalyze public pressure for institutional change. Instead of calling on individuals to save, skimp, meter, and reduce energy, a post-work energy politics calls for the liberation of energy.

ENERGY FREEDOM

The most trenchant critiques of work have emerged from those who have been excluded or exploited in the industrial waged work system, with Marxism as the most well-known example. Work intersects with other practices of domination and subjectification, including gender, race, and empire; this intersectionality was evident in the practices of British new imperialism, discussed in part II of this book. Weeks similarly observes how the class identity of the white, working man in nineteenth-century Europe and the United States was secured through the marginalization of racialized, immigrant, and gendered groups. Not surprisingly, the most fertile sites for contesting work have emerged from among marginalized groups, in the politics of indigenous peoples, of race and slavery, of decoloniality, and of feminist and queer theory.

Weeks draws most heavily upon feminism, which has made significant contributions to unsettling and reimagining the meaning of work. Feminists have shown how the waged work system depends on the exploitation and invisibility of "women's work," which relegates caring labor to the private realm of the family. For women in particular, the rise of waged work, and its association with masculinity, required that "unwaged domestic work [be] reconceived as nonproductive women's work." It also yoked the work ethic to the family ethic, and the woman to the privatized home; Weeks traces how "this family ethic emerged in the Fordist period as an important means by which to manage the production-consumption nexus."[33] Rather than treat work as a social and economic necessity, then, Weeks shows how work functions as a "disciplinary apparatus," where "work produces not just economic goods and services but also social and political subjects. In other words, the wage relation generates not just income and capital, but disciplined individuals, governable subjects, worthy citizens, and responsible family members."[34] The industrial system of waged work thus relied on the marginalization of gendered and racialized others who would work for lower, or for no, wages, serving a crucial, and yet invisible, role in production.

However, in order to locate a truly radical critique of work, Weeks must look to the margins of even these critical traditions. She observes that, historically, both feminism and Marxism have had "productivist tendencies."[35] They have mostly embraced, rather than problematized, the work ethic in order to advance their claims, prioritizing inclusion into the waged work system for groups that have been systemically marginalized. This is true, for instance, of second-wave feminists' emphasis on the importance of including women at all levels of waged work. It is also true of the wages for housework movement, which demanded wages for the reproductive and care work whose value had been excluded from the modern industrial marketplace. While such strategies have been remarkably effective, Weeks also regrets that "all of these demands for inclusion serve at the same time to expand the scope of the work ethic to new groups and new forms of labor, and to reaffirm its power."[36] We can extend this observation to the left-accelerationists, who simply expand the scope of the work ethic onto machines, leaving productivism intact. In other words, by tinkering with the work ethic rather than politicizing it, these movements "[fail] to contest the basic terms of the work society's social contract," and end up limited in what they can imagine or demand.[37]

By politicizing work, Weeks seeks to build upon these older feminist traditions. She does so through a politics of "utopian hope" that feels its way toward other modes of work and leisure. Weeks's reading of utopianism, as well as her proposed "utopian demands" for building post-work societies, is useful for a radical energy politics that likewise strives to combine optimism and radicalism, while resisting nihilism, in weaving visions of the future. Weeks is aware that utopianism has been belittled in political thought, but she seeks to rehabilitate it through her readings of Bloch, as well as Nietzsche. Bloch's utopian hope requires a specific approach to the future, one that treats it not as a linear evolution from the past, but as ripe "with possibilities for significant ruptures and unexpected developments."[38] Even as it seeks opportunities for rupture, utopian hope also requires an affirmational approach to the present. Weeks draws on Bloch and Nietzsche to "claim the present as the site of utopian becoming," as the site containing "not only the artifacts of the past but the seeds of the possible future." This is in many ways an internally contradictory project, one that attempts "both (self-)affirmation and (self-)overcoming; to affirm what we have become as the ground from which we can become otherwise."[39]

Emotionally, such a project triggers both fear and hope. Fear: clinging to the present, to our self-affirmation, to the self we know, and anxious about the future world and the self-to-come, which is unknowable. Hope: acknowledging our self as unfixed, as an artifact of our past experiences, and therefore capable of becoming other, better, through the possibilities of our present experiences. As Weeks observes, "cultivating utopian hope as a political project of remaking the world is a struggle to become not just able to think a different future but to become willing to become otherwise," which entails no small feat of courage.[40] This is why Weeks ultimately warns against the politics of fear, which "disables" subjects from seeking more radical political goals: "whereas the fearful subject contracts around its will to self-preservation, the hopeful subject . . . represents a more open and expansive model of subjectivity."[41] Likewise, the cultivation of fearful subjects in the Anthropocene, attuned to the horrors of extinction and planetary catastrophe, risks pushing publics toward the desire for self-preservation, for contraction around conservative, security-oriented values, rather than toward expansive, more generous ethics and distributions of power.

In order to advance a project of utopian hope geared toward the re-valuation of work, Weeks makes two utopian demands. She describes the utopian demand as a utopian form for politics; it is a partial, fragmented kin to the genre of the manifesto. The utopian demand combines a "conflict between the speculative ideals of utopias and the pragmatism of demands."[42] It therefore resonates with the "paradoxical" relationship of present and future described above, seeking out both the seeds of possibility in the present (pragmatism), and yet also treating the future as capable of rupture and surprise (utopianism). In this way, the utopian demand must combine both some measure of practicality—it should be achievable (even if difficult) in the present—while also opening humans up to radically different visions of life.[43] Importantly, the purpose of the utopian demand is not to map out the precise contours of a future society or set of policies. Rather, it is in the very act of making utopian demands that humans engage in a process of becoming different, of becoming new kinds of political subjects, "thus opening new theoretical vistas and terrains of struggle. The point is that these utopian demands can serve to generate political effects that exceed the specific reforms."[44]

Weeks points to the feminist movement for wages for housework as a prime example of the utopian demand. It is a practical demand, on the one hand, and yet implementing wages for housework would dramatically alter the conditions of capitalism, possibly setting off a domino effect whose outcome would be impossible to predict. Moreover, the influence of wages for housework movements has been less about their ability to offer precise policy prescriptions, and more about how, in the act of making the demand, people began to relate to the system of work and family, and its subordination of women, differently, opening up new choices and agencies for women.[45] While Weeks is inspired by wages for housework, she notes that it was too narrowly fixated on domestic tasks within the family, with the resulting solutions offered (e.g., work–life balance and privatized household services) doing "more to sustain the existing system than to point us in the direction of something new." So while the wages for housework movement was important in revealing how household labor was necessary to reproduce waged work, Weeks now wants to go further, with utopian demands that "broaden the concept of social reproduction" beyond the heavily gendered sites of home and family.[46]

Her utopian demands are meant as "successors" to wages for housework: first, a universal basic income (UBI), and second, shorter working hours.[47] Both are intended to contest productivism, and to develop a "political project of life against work," to free time and energy from the strictures of the work ethic.[48] A UBI uncouples the reproduction of life from waged work, separating the right to food, shelter, and citizenship from one's contribution to economic productivity. Its purpose is also to "create the possibility of a life no longer so thoroughly and relentlessly dependent upon work for its qualities," which "might allow us to consider and experiment with different kinds of lives, with wanting, doing, and being otherwise."[49] Perhaps most provocatively, the demand for a basic income is "anti-ascetic"; it dramatically protests "the ethics of thrift and savings" that Weeks notes forms the basis of most political claims-making, and instead insists on the *expansion* of desires and needs.[50]

While a UBI is meant to be radical, it is gaining increased traction worldwide, among both scholars and social movements, including the "No Jobs" bloc in the UK. Switzerland failed to pass a 2016 referendum on a basic income, but the referendum helped to mark the UBI as worthy of serious public debate. The appeal of a UBI to green politics has deeper roots: the Green Party in the United Kingdom has long championed a UBI, for instance. Lord, the British Green Party cofounder cited above, came to the conclusion that a UBI, whose proponents usually focus solely on social justice, can also "enable a low growth economy to protect the ecosphere." Moreover, for Lord, a UBI that is given to everyone regardless of their work status, staves off the social fears that attach to limits to growth arguments.[51]

Along with the demand for a basic income, Weeks argues that we must also demand more time away from work, starting with shorter working hours. This is a feminist demand in that, in seeking to liberate time from work, it also insists on expanding what we mean by work, to include reproductive and care work, and to demand more time away from those responsibilities as well. It is therefore important to Weeks that the demand for shorter hours does not collapse into a demand for more "family time," a project that tends to reinforce the neoliberal family and has historically only added more work and anxiety, especially for women.[52] Shorter working hours steals back more time for family and community, yes, but should also mean devoting more time to "what we will," to pleasure, to "broaden [our] perspective on the possibilities of nonwork time."[53]

It is the anti-asceticism of these utopian demands that offers the most opportunities for energy politics. Environmental movements have struggled to counter the pleasures of energy consumption without embracing constraint, thrift, or simplicity as an antidote. While such values may be necessary in a post-carbon society, environmentalists would also do well to continue to multiply other pleasurable, desire-based visions for the future. A feminist post-work politics suggests one such mode of hopeful politics, one that shifts from the impetus to save energy, to give up energy, to use it more thriftily and efficiently, toward a practice of liberating energy from work. At the same time, the focus moves from individual energy consumption to the larger problem, the connection between energy and production, a problem that is not satisfactorily resolved by left-accelerationism and full automation. Rather than energy efficiency, which reinforces the bond between energy and the work ethic, what if we posit energy freedom? Energy freedom—by which I mean an attempt to free more energy from the strictures of waged, productive work— would short-circuit the dominant logic of energy and its assumption that freedom is equivalent to a nation's industrial capacity for maximum fuel independence.

Let us pause here for a moment to pursue a thought experiment: How might the realization of post-work demands neutralize the most pressing arguments in favor of fossil fuel burning? Consider, as just one key example, the rampant fossil fuel boosterism in the wake of the 2016 U.S. presidential election of Donald Trump and the conservative capture of Congress. In a short time, the Trump administration and the Republican Party have shored up fossil fuel systems by denying climate change and dismantling a host of environmental policies including: withdrawing from the Paris Climate Agreement, installing a climate denier (Scott Pruitt) to lead the Environmental Protection Agency, taking steps to kill the Clean Power Plan, weakening the Clean Air Act and the Clean Water Act, lifting a moratorium on new coal leases on federal land, ending a study on the health effects of mountaintop coal removal, and moving to open nearly all U.S. coastal waters to offshore drilling for oil.[54]

In analyzing the press releases, blog posts, and interviews of Republicans and allied fossil fuel proponents, it is abundantly evident that most arguments mobilized in favor of fossil fuels begin and end with jobs. As Representative Richard Hudson (R-NC) explains, "As I've said before, my top three priorities are jobs, jobs, and jobs. Our robust energy plan will not only create jobs, but help equip workers with the skills necessary to find employment. It's time for us to seize the tremendous energy opportunity ahead to lower energy costs, empower folks with more good-paying jobs, and get one step closer to energy independence."[55]

Another opinion essay filed in October 2015 as part of the House Energy and Commerce Committee's "Idea Lab" derides the new Environmental Protection Agency regulations on air quality as "equal to putting every worker in Ohio out of work."[56] Meanwhile, Trump's professed love for coal is most often expressed through the discourse of putting miners to work, a promise that resonates strongly with a community primed to associate mining jobs with masculine identity. In other words, Trump and his supporters "dig coal" (a popular campaign slogan) because it is an icon of masculinist empowerment.[57] Again and again, jobs appear in the discourse—"jobs, jobs, jobs."

The job argument has proven to be compelling, and is an incredibly difficult argument to counter, given the unquestioned importance of work to the American notion of hegemonic masculinity and citizenship. Imagine, though, if the United States had instituted the feminist, utopian demands of a basic income and shorter hours, such that full-time, traditional waged work was no longer an economic necessity. It is impossible to foresee the exact outcome of such demands-making, but let us assume that, in making such demands and gaining some autonomy from the late industrial system of organizing work and activity, people were engaged in undermining the supremacy of waged work as a sign of self-worth and morality. In such a situation, the argument of "jobs, jobs, jobs" would be toothless. The threat of lost jobs only works if, in losing one's job, one loses access to the necessities of life, to the respect of society, and to the rights of citizenship. Instead, a post-work politics pries open new possibilities in countering "jobs, jobs, jobs," possibilities in which alternative arrangements of energy and work appear more intelligible and palatable. Without the threat of lost jobs, the fossil fuel argument, at least as outlined by the House committee, would have almost nothing else to say in support of fossil fuels.

Of course, alternative ways of organizing energy and work would not necessarily be more ecologically sustainable, nor more globally just. A post-work politics that stays wedded to productivism, and sited in the Global North, risks inventing yet another idle Victorian woman fantasy, one in which labor is not transformed but simply made invisible. Utopian demands need to be considered on a transnational scale, taking advantage of regional alliances. Challenging work entails not only challenging the work ethic that dominates human life, but also the work ethic that captures nonhuman and machinic activity into its profit, while violently expelling the unemployed, the underemployed, and anything coded as waste.[58] Privileged practices of leisure will also need to be revitalized and reimagined; humans, especially in the Global North, have been conditioned to fill non-work time with unbridled consumption. However, reorganizing leisure will likely be impossible without first reorganizing work and opening up more time, space, and, yes, *energy*, with which to do so, both in the sense of moral and political energy and in the sense of fuel.

My wager is that many alternatives to work and leisure are imaginable that could pose significant advantages to the planet and its creatures. Humans would be hard-pressed to devise new work systems that matched the ferocity with which industrial capitalism has mined and burned fossil fuels. Moreover, the urgency with which we burn fuel is tied to the urgency with which we pursue productivity and hard work. After all, as pleasurable as consumption has been, especially for the Global North, its partner has been an alienating system of modern work that is breaking down.

Work supposedly earns humans the right to consume what they will. Post-work political movements ease us away from the fever dream of work, highlighting its oppressive and exploitative nature, while potentially inaugurating what Lord calls "a totally new culture" that "will also allow people generally to heed eco-constraints, notably climate change, where competitive capitalism does not."[59] By building upon accelerating frustrations with the work system, such a pleasure-based politics stands the best chance of appealing to a broad and diverse public and motivating the kind of radical change called for in the Anthropocene.

INTRODUCTION: PUTTING THE WORLD TO WORK

1. Leslie A. White, "Energy and the Evolution of Culture," *American Anthropologist* 45, no. 3 (1943): 335.

2. Vaclav Smil, *Energy and Civilization: A History* (Cambridge, MA: MIT Press, 2017), 1.

3. Vaclav Smil, "Science, Energy, Ethics, and Civilization," in *Visions of Discovery: New Light on Physics, Cosmology, and Consciousness*, edited by R. Y. Chiao et al. (Cambridge: Cambridge University Press, 2010), 725–26.

4. Figure from the U.S. Energy Information Administration, accessed September 14, 2018, https://www.eia.gov/tools/faqs/faq.php?id=85&t=1.

5. "International Energy Outlook 2017," U.S. Energy Information Administration, September 2017, https://www.eia.gov/outlooks/ieo/pdf/0484(2017).pdf.

6. Richard York and Shannon Elizabeth Bell, "Energy Transitions or Additions?," paper under review.

7. Will Steffen et al., "Trajectories of the Earth System in the Anthropocene," *Proceedings of the National Academy of Sciences* 115, no. 33 (2018): 8252–59, https://doi.org/10.1073/pnas.1810141115.

8. Elizabeth Kolbert, *The Sixth Extinction: An Unnatural History* (New York: Henry Holt, 2014).

9. Gerardo Ceballos, Paul R. Ehrlich, and Rodolfo Dirzo, "Biological Annihilation via the Ongoing Sixth Mass Extinction Signaled by Vertebrate Population Losses and Declines," *Proceedings of the National Academy of Sciences* 114, no. 30 (2017): E6089–96.

10. Steffen et al., "Trajectories of the Earth System in the Anthropocene."

11. Timothy Mitchell, *Carbon Democracy: Political Power in the Age of Oil* (London: Verso, 2013); Matthew T. Huber, *Lifeblood: Oil, Freedom, and the Forces of Capital* (Minneapolis: University of Minnesota Press, 2013); Dominic Boyer, "Energopolitics and the Anthropology of Energy," *Anthropology News* 52, no. 5 (2011): 5–7; Stephanie LeMenager, *Living Oil: Petroleum Culture in the American Century* (New York: Oxford University Press, 2016); Andrew Nikiforuk, *The Energy of Slaves: Oil and the New Servitude* (Vancouver, BC: Greystone, 2014); Dominic Boyer, *Energopower: Wind and Power in the Anthropocene* (Durham, NC: Duke University Press, 2019).

12. LeMenager, *Living Oil*; Sheena Wilson, Adam Carlson, and Imre Szeman, eds., *Petrocultures: Oil, Politics, Culture* (Montreal: McGill-Queen's University Press,

2017); Andreas Malm, *Fossil Capital: The Rise of Steam Power and the Roots of Global Warming* (Brooklyn, NY: Verso, 2016); Imre Szeman and Dominic Boyer, eds., *Energy Humanities: An Anthology* (Baltimore: Johns Hopkins University Press, 2017); Cara Daggett, "Petro-Masculinity: Fossil Fuels and Authoritarian Desire," *Millennium: Journal of International Studies* 47, no. 1 (2018): 25–44, https://doi.org /10.1177/0305829818775817.

13. Barri J. Gold, *ThermoPoetics: Energy in Victorian Literature and Science* (Cambridge, MA: MIT Press, 2010), 4.

14. Joan Martinez-Alier, "Ecological Economics as Human Ecology," in *Dimensions of Environmental and Ecological Economics*, edited by Nirmal Chandra Sahu and Amita Kumari Choudhury (Hyderabad: Universities Press, 2005), 66.

15. Bruno Latour, *We Have Never Been Modern*, translated by Catherine Porter (Cambridge, MA: Harvard University Press, 1993).

16. Donna Haraway and Thyrza Goodeve, *How Like a Leaf: An Interview with Donna Haraway* (New York: Routledge, 1999), 24.

17. Haraway and Goodeve, *How Like a leaf*, 25.

18. Haraway and Goodeve, *How Like a leaf*, 26.

19. Donna Haraway, *Modest_Witness@Second_Millennium.FemaleMan_Meets_ OncoMouse: Feminism and Technoscience* (New York: Routledge, 1997), 11.

20. Cynthia Weber, *Queer International Relations* (New York: Oxford University Press, 2016), 28.

21. Haraway, *Modest_Witness@Second*, 11.

22. Karl Marx, "The German Ideology," in *The Marx-Engels Reader*, edited by Robert C. Tucker (New York: W. W. Norton, 1978), 172–73.

23. Marx, "German Ideology," 171.

24. In disrupting the universality of energy, *The Birth of Energy* also points toward the need for research that would aim to further decolonize energy, which would begin with acknowledging that modern Europe's claims to scientific invention depended on knowledge drawn from, and through, engagements in the Global South. This book is focused on energy as a Western logic of domination, but in disrupting its claim to universality, it points to the need for a more diverse energy studies. Walter Mignolo, *The Darker Side of Western Modernity: Global Futures, Decolonial Options* (Durham, NC: Duke University Press, 2011); Eric R. Wolf, *Europe and the People without History* (Berkeley: University of California Press, 2010).

25. Anne McClintock, *Imperial Leather: Race, Gender, and Sexuality in the Colonial Contest* (New York: Routledge, 2013), 112.

26. Donna Haraway, *Simians, Cyborgs, and Women: The Reinvention of Nature* (New York: Routledge, 1991), 200.

27. Haraway, *Simians, Cyborgs, and Women*, 201.

28. Simon L. Lewis and Mark A. Maslin, "Defining the Anthropocene," *Nature* 519, no. 7542 (2015): 171–80.

29. Timothy Morton, "Victorian Hyperobjects," *Nineteenth-Century Contexts* 36, no. 5 (2014): 489–500; John Plotz, "The Victorian Anthropocene: George Marsh and

the Tangled Bank of Darwinian Environmentalism," *Australasian Journal of Ecocriticism and Cultural Ecology* 4 (2014): 52–64.

30. Haraway, *Simians, Cyborgs, and Women*, 201.

31. Andreas Malm and Alf Hornborg, "The Geology of Mankind? A Critique of the Anthropocene Narrative," *Anthropocene Review* 1, no. 1 (April 2014): 62–69.

32. Dipesh Chakrabarty, "The Politics of Climate Change Is More Than the Politics of Capitalism," *Theory, Culture and Society* 34, no. 2–3 (2017): 25–37.

33. Kathi Weeks, *The Problem with Work: Feminism, Marxism, Antiwork Politics, and Postwork Imaginaries* (Durham, NC: Duke University Press, 2011), 3.

34. Mark Caine et al., "Our High Energy Planet: A Climate Pragmatism Project" (Oakland, CA: Breakthrough Institute, April 2014), http://thebreakthrough.org/images/pdfs/Our-High-Energy-Planet.pdf.

35. William Connolly, *Capitalism and Christianity, American Style* (Durham, NC: Duke University Press, 2008).

CHAPTER 1: THE NOVELTY OF ENERGY

1. Stephen Pyne, *Fire: Nature and Culture* (London: Reaktion Books, 2012); Simon Dalby, "Firepower: Geopolitical Cultures in the Anthropocene," *Geopolitics* 23, no. 3 (2018): 718–42.

2. Aristotle, *Nicomachean Ethics*, translated by Joe Sachs (Newbury, MA: Focus, 2002), viii.

3. For instance, Hans Driesch's vitalism centers upon entelechy as a vital force, though his entelechy differs notably from Aristotle's. Jane Bennett has excavated Driesch, as well as other vitalist thinkers like Henri Bergson, finding in them precursors to a "vital materialism." See Jane Bennett, *Vibrant Matter: A Political Ecology of Things* (Durham, NC: Duke University Press, 2010), 62–81.

4. Bruce Clarke, *Energy Forms: Allegory and Science in the Era of Classical Thermodynamics* (Ann Arbor: University of Michigan Press, 2001), 21.

5. Clarke, *Energy Forms*, 21.

6. Arjun Appadurai, *The Future as Cultural Fact: Essays on the Global Condition* (New York: Verso, 2013), 223.

7. Appadurai, *The Future as Cultural Fact*, 225.

8. Hannah Arendt, *On Violence* (New York: Harcourt, 1970), 26; Pierre-Joseph Proudhon, *Philosophie du progrès* (Brussels: Alphonse Lebègue, 1853), 35, 39; William H. Harbold, "Progressive Humanity: In the Philosophy of P. J. Proudhon," *Review of Politics* 31, no. 1 (1969): 37.

9. Clarke, *Energy Forms*, 2.

10. Dainian Zhang, *Key Concepts in Chinese Philosophy* (New Haven, CT: Yale University Press, 2002), 45.

11. Zhang, *Key Concepts in Chinese Philosophy*, 45.

12. Peter Barker, "Stoic Contributions to Early Modern Science," in *Atoms, Pneuma and Tranquility: Epicurean and Stoic Themes in European Thought*, edited by Margaret J. Osler (New York: Cambridge University Press, 1991), 138.

13. For more on the relevance of conservation to the emergence of energy, see Philip Mirowski, *More Heat Than Light: Economics as Social Physics, Physics as Nature's Economics* (Cambridge: Cambridge University Press, 1989).

14. Arnold Hermann, *To Think like God: Pythagoras and Parmenides* (Las Vegas, NV: Parmenides Publishing, 2004), 158.

15. Historian Carolyn Iltis notes that "such a philosophical conviction [that something was conserved in nature] is not unusual and is important in the development of other conservation laws." Carolyn Iltis, "Leibniz and the Vis Viva Controversy," *Isis* 62, no. 1 (1971): 27.

16. Mirowski, *More Heat Than Light*, 13.

17. Heraclitus, *Heraclitus: Fragments*, translated by T. M. Robinson (Toronto: University of Toronto Press, 1991), 25.

18. Clarence Glacken argues for Lucretius as a harbinger of concepts in modern physics in *Traces on a Rhodian Shore*. Similarly, in *The Birth of Physics*, Michel Serres argues that Lucretius and the Atomists formulated theories that anticipated complexity and relativity. I would like to thank Beth Mendenhall for suggesting that I consider Glacken in order to distinguish the nineteenth century from deeper historical traditions of knowing the Earth.

19. Clarence J. Glacken, *Traces on the Rhodian Shore: Nature and Culture in Western Thought from Ancient Times to the End of the Eighteenth Century* (Berkeley: University of California Press, 1976).

20. Lucretius, *Lucretius: The Way Things Are: The De Rerum Natura of Titus Lucretius Carus*, translated by Rolfe Humphries (Bloomington: Indiana University Press, 1968), 170, v. 369–74.

21. Lucretius, *Lucretius*, 161, vv. 99–102.

22. Lucretius, *Lucretius*, 200, vv. 35–37.

23. Lucretius, 191, vv. 1119–21.

24. Stephen Greenblatt, *The Swerve: How the World Became Modern* (New York: W. W. Norton, 2011).

25. If humans had instead taken Lucretius's advice and imbibed his physics, what would our energy systems look like? Perhaps we should find out.

26. Some historians of science have pointed out that early modern science was indebted to the Stoics, and that Isaac Newton in particular was inspired by Stoic physics. See, for example, Peter Barker, "Stoic Contributions to Early Modern Science," in *Atoms, Pneuma and Tranquility: Epicurean and Stoic Themes in European Thought*, edited by Margaret J. Osler (New York: Cambridge University Press, 1991), and B. J. T. Dobbs, "Newton and Stoicism," *Southern Journal of Philosophy* 23 (1985), Supplement.

27. Iltis, "Leibniz and the Vis Viva Controversy," 22.

28. For an engaging history of Leibniz, his feud with Descartes, and his relationship to the philosophy of Spinoza, see Matthew Stewart, *The Courtier and the Heretic: Leibniz, Spinoza, and the Fate of God in the Modern World* (New York: W. W. Norton, 2007).

29. Iltis, "Leibniz and the Vis Viva Controversy"; Mirowski, *More Heat Than Light*, 18–21; George E. Smith, "The Vis Viva Dispute: A Controversy at the Dawn of Dynamics," *Physics Today*, October 2006, 32–36.

30. Iltis, "Leibniz and the Vis Viva Controversy," 34.

31. Crosbie Smith, *The Science of Energy: A Cultural History of Energy Physics in Victorian Britain* (London: Athlone, 1998), 36.

32. Clarke, *Energy Forms*, 21–22.

33. Rolf Peter Sieferle, *The Subterranean Forest*, translated by Michael Osmann (Cambridge, MA: White Horse, 2010), 1.

34. Dorrik Stow, *Vanished Ocean: How Tethys Reshaped the World* (Oxford: Oxford University Press, 2010).

35. Francesco Berna et al., "Microstratigraphic Evidence of In Situ Fire in the Acheulean Strata of Wonderwerk Cave, Northern Cape Province, South Africa," *Proceedings of the National Academy of Sciences* 109, no. 20 (2012): E1215–20.

36. Berna et al., "Microstratigraphic Evidence of In Situ Fire."

37. Jean-Claude Debeir, Jean-Paul Deléage, and Daniel Hémery, *In the Servitude of Power: Energy and Civilization through the Ages*, translated by John Barzman (Atlantic Highlands, NJ: Zed, 1991), 15; Richard Wrangham, *Catching Fire: How Cooking Made Us Human* (New York: Basic Books, 2009).

38. Mark Bonta et al., "Intentional Fire-Spreading by 'Firehawk' Raptors in Northern Australia," *Journal of Ethnobiology* 37, no. 4 (2017): 700–718.

39. See, for example, James Scott, *Against the Grain: A Deep History of the Earliest States* (New Haven, CT: Yale University Press, 2017), and Barry Buzan and Richard Little, *International Systems in World History: Remaking the Study of International Relations* (New York: Oxford University Press, 2000). Scott amasses archaeological and anthropological evidence that troubles the civilizational narrative by which agriculture leads ineluctably to the rise of the state, a story told as a linear progression of human advancement. Instead, he points out that humans domesticated plants and lived in sedentary communities for thousands of years prior to the rise of the state, and that most were healthier and better off outside the state.

40. Joseph Needham, *Science and Civilisation in China*, vol. 4: *Physics and Physical Technology*, part 2: *Mechanical Engineering* (Cambridge: Cambridge University Press, 1965).

41. Bruce G. Miller, *Coal Energy Systems* (Burlington, MA: Academic Press, 2005), 30–31.

42. Sieferle, *The Subterranean Forest*, 81.

43. Sieferle, *The Subterranean Forest*, 99; Alf Hornborg, "The Fossil Interlude: Euro-American Power and the Return of the Physiocrats," in *Cultures of Energy: Power, Practices, Technologies*, edited by Sarah Strauss, Rupp Stephanie, and Lowe Thomas (Walnut Creek, CA: Left Coast, 2013), 46.

44. Andreas Malm, *Fossil Capital: The Rise of Steam Power and the Roots of Global Warming* (Brooklyn, NY: Verso, 2016), 325.

45. Vaclav Smil, *Energy in World History* (Boulder, CO: Westview, 1994).

46. Sieferle, *The Subterranean Forest*, 135.

47. Smil, *Energy in World History*, 187.

48. Sieferle, *The Subterranean Forest*, 137.

49. Sieferle, *The Subterranean Forest*, 41.

50. Sieferle, *The Subterranean Forest*, 42.

51. Sieferle, *The Subterranean Forest*, 135.

52. Kenneth Pomeranz, *The Great Divergence: China, Europe, and the Making of the Modern World Economy* (Princeton, NJ: Princeton University Press, 2009).

53. Malm, *Fossil Capital*, 101–3.

54. Malm, *Fossil Capital*, 267.

55. Malm, *Fossil Capital*, 117–20.

56. Malm, *Fossil Capital*, 131–36.

57. Malm, *Fossil Capital*, 294–95.

58. Malm, *Fossil Capital*, 148–56.

59. Malm, *Fossil Capital*, 297–98.

60. Malm, *Fossil Capital*, 272.

61. Malm, *Fossil Capital*, 298.

62. Malm, *Fossil Capital*, 308.

63. Daniel Yergin, *The Prize: The Epic Quest for Oil, Money and Power* (New York: Free Press, 2008).

64. Timothy Mitchell, *Carbon Democracy: Political Power in the Age of Oil* (London: Verso, 2013).

65. John Tyndall, "The Constitution of the Universe," edited by George Henry Lewes, *Fortnightly Review* 3, no. 14 (December 1, 1865): 143.

66. Sieferle, *The Subterranean Forest*, 44.

67. William Stanley Jevons, *The Coal Question: An Inquiry Concerning the Progress of the Nation, and the Probable Exhaustion of Our Coal-Mines* (London: Macmillan, 1865), 141.

68. James Scott, *Against the Grain: A Deep History of the Earliest States* (New Haven, CT: Yale University Press, 2017), 5.

69. Gilles Deleuze and Félix Guattari, *A Thousand Plateaus: Capitalism and Schizophrenia*, translated by Brian Massumi (Minneapolis: University of Minnesota Press, 1987), 347.

70. Jürgen Osterhammel, *The Transformation of the World: A Global History of the Nineteenth Century*, translated by Patrick Camiller (Princeton, NJ: Princeton University Press, 2014), 639.

71. Osterhammel, *The Transformation of the World*, 639.

CHAPTER 2: A STEAMPUNK PRODUCTION

1. Michel Serres, *Hermes: Literature, Science, Philosophy* (Baltimore: Johns Hopkins University Press, 1982), 57.

2. John Robert McNeill and William Hardy McNeill, *The Human Web: A Bird's-Eye View of World History* (New York: W. W. Norton, 2003), 213.

3. Barry Buzan and George Lawson also make this point in *The Global Transformation: History, Modernity and the Making of International Relations* (Cambridge: Cambridge University Press, 2015), 17–18.

4. McNeill and McNeill, *The Human Web*, 213–14.

5. Serres, *Hermes*, 56.

6. Crosbie Smith, *The Science of Energy: A Cultural History of Energy Physics in Victorian Britain* (London: Athlone, 1998), 32.

7. M. Norton Wise and Crosbie Smith, "Work and Waste: Political Economy and Natural Philosophy in Nineteenth Century Britain (II)," *History of Science* 27, no. 4 (1989): 392.

8. Norton Wise and Smith, "Work and Waste," 392.

9. Norton Wise and Smith, "Work and Waste," 392.

10. George Caffentzis, *In Letters of Blood and Fire: Work, Machines, and the Crisis of Capitalism* (Oakland, CA: PM Press, 2013), 13.

11. In his influential essay, "Energy Conservation as an Example of Simultaneous Discovery," Thomas Kuhn selects a dozen scientists as having the best claim in the discovery, and they range from across Europe.

12. Philip Mirowski, *More Heat Than Light: Economics as Social Physics, Physics as Nature's Economics* (Cambridge: Cambridge University Press, 1989), 52.

13. Sadi Carnot, *Reflections on the Motive Power of Heat*, edited by Robert Henry Thurston (New York: John Wiley, 1897), 38.

14. Andreas Malm, *Fossil Capital: The Rise of Steam Power and the Roots of Global Warming* (Brooklyn, NY: Verso, 2016).

15. Silvanus P. Thompson, *The Life of William Thompson Baron Kelvin of Largs* (London: Macmillan, 1910), 265; Raymond Flood, Mark McCartney, and Andrew Whitaker, eds., *Kelvin: Life, Labours and Legacy* (New York: Oxford University Press, 2008), 12.

16. Carolyn Iltis, "Leibniz and the Vis Viva Controversy," *Isis* 62, no. 1 (1971): 27.

17. Mirowski, *More Heat Than Light*, 42.

18. Donald S. L. Cardwell, *James Joule: A Biography* (New York: Manchester University Press, 1989), 85; Flood, McCartney, and Whitaker, *Kelvin,* 12.

19. Sandra Harding, *Science and Social Inequality: Feminist and Postcolonial Issues* (Urbana: University of Illinois Press, 2006), 8.

20. Thomas S. Kuhn, *The Essential Tension: Selected Studies in Scientific Tradition and Change* (Chicago: University of Chicago Press, 1977), 72.

21. Harding, *Science and Social Inequality*, 8.

22. William John Macquorn Rankine, "XVIII. On the General Law of the Transformation of Energy," *Philosophical Magazine*, Series 4, vol. 5, no. 30 (1853): 106.

23. Smith, *The Science of Energy*, 139.

24. Mirowski, *More Heat Than Light*, 76–77.

25. P. W. Bridgman, *The Nature of Thermodynamics* (Cambridge, MA: Harvard University Press, 1941), 3, http://archive.org/details/natureofthermody031258mbp.

26. Walter T. Grandy Jr., *Entropy and the Time Evolution of Macroscopic Systems* (New York: Oxford University Press, 2008), 151.

27. Mirowski, *More Heat Than Light*.

28. Richard Feynman, *The Feynman Lectures on Physics*, vol. I: *Mainly Mechanics, Radiation, and Heat* (New York: Basic Books, 2011), 33.

29. Carolyn Merchant, *The Death of Nature: Women, Ecology, and the Scientific Revolution* (New York: HarperCollins, 1990): 4.

30. Feynman, *The Feynman Lectures on Physics*, vol. I.

31. Mirowski, *More Heat Than Light*, 75.

32. I am grateful to Jane Bennett for suggesting this point.

33. Crosbie W. Smith, "William Thomson and the Creation of Thermodynamics: 1840–1855," *Archive for History of Exact Sciences* 16, no. 3 (1977): 281.

34. Mirowski, *More Heat Than Light*, 52.

35. Grandy, *Entropy and the Time Evolution of Macroscopic Systems*, 151.

36. Ilya Prigogine and Isabelle Stengers, *Order Out of Chaos* (New York: Bantam, 1984), 106–7.

37. Mirowski, *More Heat Than Light*, 75.

38. Bernard Lovell, ed., *Royal Institution Library of Science (Being the Friday Evening Discourses in Physical Sciences Held at the Royal Institution: 1851–1939)*, vol. 1: *Astronomy* (New York: Elsevier, 1970), 294.

39. Thompson, *The Life of William Thompson*, 1125.

40. Rudolf Clausius, *The Mechanical Theory of Heat: With Its Applications to the Steam-Engine and to the Physical Properties of Bodies* (London: John Van Voorst, 1867), 357.

41. Clausius, *The Mechanical Theory of Heat*, 365.

42. Prigogine and Stengers, *Order Out of Chaos*, 120.

43. Prigogine and Stengers, *Order Out of Chaos*, 285.

44. Ilya Prigogine, *The End of Certainty* (New York: Simon and Schuster, 1997).

45. Prigogine and Stengers, *Order Out of Chaos*, 292.

46. Prigogine and Stengers, *Order Out of Chaos*, 120.

47. Mirowski, *More Heat Than Light*, 62.

48. John Theodore Merz, *A History of European Scientific Thought in the Nineteenth Century* (Gloucester, MA: Peter Smith, 1976), 96–98.

49. Mirowski, *More Heat Than Light*, 6.

50. Émile Meyerson, *Identity and Reality*, translated by Kate Loewenberg (New York: Macmillan, 1930), 92–93.

51. Meyerson, *Identity and Reality*, 215.

52. Meyerson, *Identity and Reality*, 222. Coincidentally, corporate accounting has many tricks for neglecting time to the benefit of corporations, as when oil companies include estimates of future oil supplies, yet to be pumped and often yet to be found, as part of their existing capital.

53. Grandy, *Entropy and the Time Evolution of Macroscopic Systems*, 151.

54. Clarence J. Glacken, *Traces on the Rhodian Shore: Nature and Culture in Western Thought from Ancient Times to the End of the Eighteenth Century* (Berkeley: University of California Press, 1976).

55. Prigogine and Stengers, *Order Out of Chaos*, 304.

56. Smith, *The Science of Energy*, 111.

CHAPTER 3: A GEO-THEOLOGY OF ENERGY

1. Bernard Semmel, *Imperialism and Social Reform: English Social-Imperial Thought, 1895–1914* (New York: Anchor, 1968), 7.

2. John Ruskin, *The Storm Cloud of the Nineteenth Century* (New York: John Wiley, 1884).

3. William Stanley Jevons, *The Coal Question: An Inquiry Concerning the Progress of the Nation, and the Probable Exhaustion of Our Coal-Mines* (London: Macmillan, 1865).

4. Alan Weisman, *The World without Us*, rpt. ed. (New York: Picador, 2008).

5. I would like to thank Jane Bennett for suggesting this term.

6. Crosbie Smith, *The Science of Energy: A Cultural History of Energy Physics in Victorian Britain* (London: Athlone, 1998).

7. John Theodore Merz, *A History of European Scientific Thought in the Nineteenth Century* (Gloucester, MA: Peter Smith, 1976), 203.

8. Eric Hobsbawm, *The Age of Capital: 1848–1875* (New York: Random House, 1996), 269.

9. As I will further detail in this chapter, my understanding of work and waste is drawn from M. Norton Wise and Crosbie Smith. See, for example, M. Norton Wise and Crosbie Smith, "Work and Waste: Political Economy and Natural Philosophy in Nineteenth Century Britain (I)," *History of Science* 27, no. 3 (1989); M. Norton Wise and Crosbie Smith, "Work and Waste: Political Economy and Natural Philosophy in Nineteenth Century Britain (II)," *History of Science* 27, no. 4 (1989); M. Norton Wise and Crosbie Smith, "Work and Waste: Political Economy and Natural Philosophy in Nineteenth Century Britain (III)," *History of Science* 28, no. 3 (1990).

10. Elizabeth Neswald, Bernard Lightman, and Michael S. Reidy, "Saving the World in the Age of Entropy: John Tyndall and the Second Law of Thermodynamics," in *The Age of Scientific Naturalism: Tyndall and His Contemporaries*, edited by Bernard Lightman and Michael S. Reidy (New York: Routledge, 2014).

11. The most notable exception is Philip Mirowski, *More Heat Than Light* (Cambridge: Cambridge University Press, 1989), which shows how neoclassical economics adopted the terms and ideas of the science of energy.

12. Merz, *A History of European Scientific Thought in the Nineteenth Century*, 136.

13. Jürgen Osterhammel, *The Transformation of the World: A Global History of the Nineteenth Century*, translated by Patrick Camiller (Princeton, NJ: Princeton University Press, 2014), 652.

14. Clarence J. Glacken, *Traces on the Rhodian Shore: Nature and Culture in Western Thought from Ancient Times to the End of the Eighteenth Century* (Berkeley: University of California Press, 1976).

15. Timothy Morton, "Victorian Hyperobjects," *Nineteenth-Century Contexts* 36, no. 5 (2014): 489.

16. "M. Palacio's Design for a Colossal Monument in Memory of Christopher Columbus," *Scientific American*, October 1890, 260.

17. "M. Palacio's Design for a Colossal Monument," 260.

18. Will Steffen, Paul Crutzen, and John McNeill, "The Anthropocene: Are Humans Now Overwhelming the Great Forces of Nature?," *Ambio* 36, no. 8 (2007): 614–21.

19. Dipesh Chakrabarty, "The Climate of History: Four Theses," *Critical Inquiry* 35, no. 2 (2009): 208.

20. Charles Darwin, *On the Origin of Species by Means of Natural Selection, or the Preservation of Favoured Races in the Struggle for Life*, 6th ed. (London: John Murray, 1876), 266.

21. Stephen Jay Gould, *Time's Arrow, Time's Cycle: Myth and Metaphor in the Discovery of Geological Time* (Cambridge, MA: Harvard University Press, 1987), 2.

22. Greg Myers, "Nineteenth-Century Popularizations of Thermodynamics and the Rhetoric of Social Prophecy," *Victorian Studies* 29, no. 1 (1985): 55.

23. As political theorist Kennan Ferguson points out, "practices of governmentality" depend upon "various conceptualizations of life" that are intertwined with science. He traces the importance of evolution to the formation of political science as a separate discipline in order to show how "presumptions of how life operates . . . underlay the form of politics one privileges and celebrates." Kennan Ferguson, "The Deep Biology of Politics: A Reminder," *Political Research Quarterly* 67, no. 2 (2014): 459.

24. Sigmund Freud, *Introductory Lectures on Psychoanalysis* (New York: Penguin, 1991), 326.

25. Hobsbawm, *The Age of Capital*, 260.

26. Darwin is often associated with the idea of the "survival of the fittest," but this term did not appear in *On the Origin of Species* until the fifth edition, ten years after the first edition. It was a phrase borrowed from Herbert Spencer, who had used it to describe natural selection in *Principles of Biology* in 1864.

27. Donald Worster, *Nature's Economy: A History of Ecological Ideas* (New York: Cambridge University Press, 1994), 162.

28. Hobsbawm, *The Age of Capital*, 258–59.

29. Darwin, *On the Origin of Species by Means of Natural Selection*, 57.

30. Darwin's mentions of "the Creator" throughout the text were likely in part a response to his religious critics, but they were also a reflection of his own struggle with religion. While Darwin moved away from Christianity over the course of his life, he also writes in an 1879 letter that "in my most extreme fluctuations I have never been an atheist in the sense of denying the existence of a God. I think that generally (& more and more so as I grow older) but not always, that an agnostic would be the most correct description of my state of mind." His writings leave room for at least a "theistic" account in which God sets natural laws in motion (in that same letter he affirms that theism is consistent with evolution). See Charles Darwin, "To John Fordyce," May 7, 1879, Darwin Correspondence Project, http://www.darwinproject.ac.uk/letter/entry-12041.

31. Darwin, *On the Origin of Species by Means of Natural Selection*, 52–53.

32. Charles Pence, "Nietzsche's Aesthetic Critique of Darwin," *History and Philosophy of the Life Sciences* 33 (2011): 173.

33. Robert Richards, "Darwin and Progress," *New York Review of Books*, December 15, 2005, http://www.nybooks.com/articles/archives/2005/dec/15/darwin-progress/.

34. Darwin, *On the Origin of Species by Means of Natural Selection*, 307.

35. Darwin, *On the Origin of Species by Means of Natural Selection*, 98.

36. Darwin, *On the Origin of Species by Means of Natural Selection*, 50.

37. Darwin, *On the Origin of Species by Means of Natural Selection*, 49.

38. Daniel H. Deudney, *Bounding Power: Republican Security Theory from the Polis to the Global Village* (Princeton, NJ: Princeton University Press, 2008), 202.

39. Eric Hobsbawm, *The Age of Revolution: 1789–1848* (New York: Random House, 1996), 293.

40. Darwin's *On the Descent of Man* is rife with the racist discourse of its time, often painfully so. However, Desmond and Moore argue that the fundamental drive of Darwin's work is to argue against apologists for slavery by showing that Africans and Europeans belonged to the same species and were thus biological kin. Adrian Desmond James and Moore, *Darwin's Sacred Curse: Race, Slavery, and the Quest for Human Origins* (Chicago: University of Chicago Press, 2009).

41. David Paul Crook, *Darwinism, War and History: The Debate over the Biology of War from the "Origin of Species" to the First World War* (New York: Cambridge University Press, 1994), 9.

42. Charles Darwin, *On the Descent of Man, and Selection in Relation to Sex* (London: John Murray, 1871), 159.

43. Darwin, *On the Descent of Man*, 167.

44. Michael Adas, *Machines as the Measure of Men: Science, Technology, and Ideologies of Western Dominance* (Ithaca, NY: Cornell University Press, 1990); Barry Buzan and George Lawson, *The Global Transformation: History, Modernity and the Making of International Relations* (Cambridge: Cambridge University Press, 2015), 119.

45. Adas, *Machines as the Measure of Men*, 311–13.

46. Darwin, *On the Descent of Man*, 177–78.

47. Crook, *Darwinism, War and History*, 24.

48. Darwin, *On the Descent of Man*, 178.

49. Charles Darwin, "To T. H. Huxley," December 22, 1866, Darwin Correspondence Project, http://www.darwinproject.ac.uk/entry-5315.

50. Darwin cites Haeckel in the introduction to *On the Descent of Man*, writing that Haeckel had already laid out most of the ideas Darwin was about to introduce. See Darwin, *On the Descent of Man*, 4.

51. Ernst Haeckel, Inaugural Lecture 1869, translated by W. C. Allee, quoted in Robert C. Stauffer, "Haeckel, Darwin, and Ecology," *Quarterly Review of Biology* 32, no. 2 (1957): 138.

52. Eugene Odum, *Ecology: A Bridge between Science and Society* (Sunderland, MA: Sinauer Associates, 1997).

53. Darwin, *On the Descent of Man*, 166.

54. Darwin, *On the Descent of Man*, 178.

55. This is evident, for instance, in Darwin's treatment of plants in Charles Darwin, *The Movements and Habits of Climbing Plants* (London: John Murray, 1875).

56. Stuart A. Kauffman, *Reinventing the Sacred: A New View of Science, Reason, and Religion* (New York: Basic Books, 2010); Terrence W. Deacon, *Incomplete Nature: How Mind Emerged from Matter* (New York: W. W. Norton, 2013); Lynn Margulis and Dorion Sagan, *Acquiring Genomes: A Theory of the Origin of Species* (Princeton, NJ: Basic Books, 2003); William Connolly, "Species Evolution and Cultural Freedom," *Political Research Quarterly* 67, no. 2 (2014): 441–52.

57. Allen MacDuffie, *Victorian Literature, Energy, and the Ecological Imagination* (Cambridge: Cambridge University Press, 2014), 73.

58. N. Katherine Hayles, *Chaos Bound: Orderly Disorder in Contemporary Literature and Science* (Ithaca, NY: Cornell University Press, 1990), 39.

59. William Thomson, "On the Age of the Sun's Heat," *Macmillan's Magazine* 5 (March 5, 1862): 388–93.

60. Ilya Prigogine and Isabelle Stengers, *Order Out of Chaos* (New York: Bantam, 1984), 111.

61. MacDuffie, *Victorian Literature, Energy, and the Ecological Imagination*, 50.

62. Walter Mignolo, *The Darker Side of Western Modernity: Global Futures, Decolonial Options* (Durham, NC: Duke University Press, 2011), xii.

63. Freud, *Introductory Lectures on Psychoanalysis*, 326.

64. Verses are from W. B. Yeats, "The Second Coming."

65. Wise and Smith, "Work and Waste (I)"; Wise and Smith, "Work and Waste (II)"; Wise and Smith, "Work and Waste (III)."

66. Karl Marx, "The German Ideology," in *The Marx-Engels Reader*, edited by Robert C. Tucker (New York: W. W. Norton, 1978), 172–73.

67. Jevons, *The Coal Question*, 122.

68. Thomson, "On the Age of the Sun's Heat."

69. Prigogine and Stengers, *Order Out of Chaos*, 116.

70. Crosbie Smith, *The Science of Energy: A Cultural History of Energy Physics in Victorian Britain* (London: Athlone, 1998), 16.

71. Smith, *The Science of Energy*, 20.

72. Smith, *The Science of Energy*, 6.

73. Religion was not the only possible outcome. Entropy was also an inspiration for nonlinear and nondeterministic sciences of the twentieth century that retained a role for creativity in the unfolding of natural processes. See, for example, Ilya Prigogine, *The End of Certainty* (New York: Simon and Schuster, 1997).

74. Karl Marx and Friedrich Engels, *Collected Works: 1868–1870*, vol. 43 (New York: International, 1975), 246; John Bellamy Foster and Paul Burkett, "Classical Marxism and the Second Law of Thermodynamics: Marx/Engels, the Heat Death of the Universe Hypothesis, and the Origins of Ecological Economics," *Organization and Environment* 21, no. 1 (2008): 3–37, https://doi.org/10.1177/1086026607313580.

75. Neswald, Lightman, and Reidy, "Saving the World in the Age of Entropy."

76. Isaiah 51:6, in *The Bible: Authorized King James Version* (New York: Oxford University Press, 2008), 813.

77. Crosbie W. Smith, "William Thomson and the Creation of Thermodynamics: 1840–1855," *Archive for History of Exact Sciences* 16, no. 3 (1977): 282.

78. Isaiah 51:8, in *The Bible*, 813.

79. Smith, *The Science of Energy*, 110.

80. Smith, "William Thomson and the Creation of Thermodynamics," 281.

81. Norton Wise and Smith, "Work and Waste (II)," 423.

82. Smith, *The Science of Energy*, 310.

83. Norton Wise and Smith, "Work and Waste (II)," 423.

84. Bruce Clarke, *Energy Forms: Allegory and Science in the Era of Classical Thermodynamics* (Ann Arbor: University of Michigan Press, 2001), 42.

85. Smith, *The Science of Energy*, 308–9.

86. Norton Wise and Smith, "Work and Waste (III)," 251.

87. Norton Wise and Smith, "Work and Waste (III)," 221.

88. John Tyndall, *Heat Considered as a Mode of Motion*, rev. 2nd ed. (New York: D. Appleton, 1869), 433–34.

89. Tyndall, *Heat Considered as a Mode of Motion*, 434.

90. MacDuffie, *Victorian Literature, Energy, and the Ecological Imagination*, 40.

91. MacDuffie, *Victorian Literature, Energy, and the Ecological Imagination*, 56.

92. MacDuffie, *Victorian Literature, Energy, and the Ecological Imagination*, 56.

93. MacDuffie, *Victorian Literature, Energy, and the Ecological Imagination*, 34–35.

94. MacDuffie, *Victorian Literature, Energy, and the Ecological Imagination*, 38.

95. William Gourlie, "Notice of the Fossil Plants in the Glasgow Geological Museum," in *Proceedings of the Royal Philosophical Society of Glasgow: 1841–1844*, vol. I (Glasgow: Richard Griffin, 1844), 112.

96. Anson Rabinbach, *The Human Motor: Energy, Fatigue, and the Origins of Modernity* (Berkeley: University of California Press, 1992), 70.

97. Lynn Voskuil, "Introduction: Nineteenth-Century Energies," *Nineteenth-Century Contexts* 36, no. 5 (2014): 393.

98. Balfour Stewart, *The Conservation of Energy* (New York: D. Appleton and Company, 1875), vii.

99. This is evident, for instance, in the efforts of Thomson and the Philosophical Society of Glasgow to "improve" their industrial city by appealing to the knowledge of the science of energy. See Norton Wise and Smith, "Work and Waste (III)."

100. Norton Wise and Smith, "Work and Waste (III)," 231.

101. Norton Wise and Smith, "Work and Waste (III)."

102. Jennifer Karns Alexander, *The Mantra of Efficiency from Waterwheel to Social Control* (Baltimore: Johns Hopkins University Press, 2008), 16.

103. Alexander, *The Mantra of Efficiency*, 2.

104. Alexander, *The Mantra of Efficiency*, 2–3.

105. Norton Wise and Smith, "Work and Waste (III)," 225.

106. Norton Wise and Smith, "Work and Waste (III)," 228.

107. Norton Wise and Smith, "Work and Waste (III)," 228.

108. Rabinbach, *The Human Motor*, 1.

109. Rabinbach, *The Human Motor*, 3.

110. Rabinbach, *The Human Motor*, 4.

111. Martin Geyer, "One Language for the World: The Metric System, International Coinage, Gold Standard, and the Rise of Internationalism, 1850–1900," in *The Mechanics of Internationalism*, edited by Martin Geyer and Johannes Paulmann (London: Oxford University Press, 2001).

112. Norton Wise and Smith, "Work and Waste (III)," 227.

113. Worster, *Nature's Economy*, 174.

CHAPTER 4: WORK BECOMES ENERGETIC

1. Amy E. Wendling, *The Ruling Ideas: Bourgeois Political Concepts* (Lanham, MD: Lexington, 2012).

2. Wendling, *The Ruling Ideas*, 5.

3. Wendling, *The Ruling Ideas*, 20.

4. John Locke, *Second Treatise of Government*, edited by C. B. Macpherson (Indianapolis: Hackett, 1980).

5. G. W. F. Hegel, *Phenomenology of Spirit*, translated by A. V. Miller (New York: Oxford University Press, 1977), 118.

6. Franklin is a fitting representative of the work ethic as it transitioned from a religious belief to a practical virtue. Franklin himself was more interested in how Christianity could inspire a virtuous life, rather than in its dogmatic creeds. He flirted with deism in his youth, and close to his death surmised that, while Jesus was a great moral teacher, he may not have been divine.

7. Anson Rabinbach, *The Human Motor: Energy, Fatigue, and the Origins of Modernity* (Berkeley: University of California Press, 1992), 35–36.

8. Daniel T. Rodgers, *The Work Ethic in Industrial America 1850–1920* (Chicago: University of Chicago Press, 2014), xx.

9. Amy E. Wendling, *On Alienation and Machine Production: Capitalist Embodiment in Karl Marx* (University Park: Pennsylvania State University Press, 2006), 61–62.

10. Wendling, *On Alienation and Machine Production*, 62.

11. Tamara Ketabgian, *The Lives of Machines: The Industrial Imaginary in Victorian Literature and Culture* (Ann Arbor: University of Michigan Press, 2011), 2.

12. Wendling, *On Alienation and Machine Production*, 63.

13. Iwan Rhys Morus, *When Physics Became King* (Chicago: University of Chicago Press, 2005), 126.

14. McKenzie Wark, *A Hacker Manifesto* (Cambridge, MA: Harvard University Press, 2004).

15. Rabinbach, *The Human Motor*; Rodgers, *The Work Ethic in Industrial America*.

16. E. P. Thompson, "Time, Work-Discipline, and Industrial Capitalism," *Past and Present* 38 (December 1967): 73.

17. Thompson, "Time, Work-Discipline, and Industrial Capitalism," 90.

18. Frederick Winslow Taylor, *The Principles of Scientific Management* (Mineola, NY: Dover, 1997), 30–31.

19. Taylor, *The Principles of Scientific Management*, 31.

20. Rabinbach notes that Taylorism was influential, for example, with Lenin and Antonio Gramsci. Rabinbach, *The Human Motor*, 239.

21. Rabinbach, *The Human Motor*, 36.

22. Rabinbach, *The Human Motor*, 119.

23. Rabinbach, *The Human Motor*, 116.

24. Taylor, *The Principles of Scientific Management*, 65.

25. Thompson, "Time, Work-Discipline, and Industrial Capitalism," 86; Rodgers, *The Work Ethic in Industrial America*, 12.

26. Marx, for example, refers to an accident caused by overwork in a footnote in *Capital*, vol. 1, 363.

27. Karl Marx, *Capital*, vol. 1: *A Critique of Political Economy*, translated by Ben Fowkes (New York: Penguin, 1992), 342.

28. Marx, *Capital*, vol. 1, 367.

29. Marx, *Capital*, vol. 1, 341.

30. Marx, *Capital*, vol. 1, 343.

31. J. N. Radcliffe, "West-End Milliners," in *The Social Science Review, and the Journal of the Sciences*, edited by Benjamin Richardson, vol. 2: *July to December* (London: George A. Hutchinson, 1864), 29.

32. Radcliffe, "West-End Milliners," 192.

33. Radcliffe, "West-End Milliners," 206.

34. Radcliffe, "West-End Milliners," 209.

35. Radcliffe, "West-End Milliners," 215.

36. Rodgers, *The Work Ethic in Industrial America*, 12.

37. Max Weber, *The Protestant Ethic and the Spirit of Capitalism: And Other Writings*, translated by Peter Baehr and Gordon C. Wells (New York: Penguin, 2002), 74.

38. William J. Noble, "Eight Hours as the Standard Day's Work—An Appeal in Behalf of the Same, to the Workingmen of America," vol. 2: *Testimony* (Washington, DC: U.S. Government Printing Office, 1885), 222.

39. Thomas Guthrie, *Seed-Time and Harvest of Ragged Schools, or A Third Plea, with New Editions of the First and Second Pleas* (Edinburgh: Adam and Charles Black, 1860), 29.

40. Caitlin Dewey, "GOP Lawmaker: The Bible Says 'If a Man Will Not Work, He Shall Not Eat,'" *Washington Post,* March 31, 2017, https://www.washingtonpost.com/news/wonk/wp/2017/03/31/gop-lawmaker-the-bible-says-the-unemployed-shall-not-eat/?utm_term=.e55238c7f927.

41. R. A. Leach, ed., *The Unemployed Workmen Act, 1905* (Rochdale, UK: Local Government Printing and Publishing Company, 1905), 14.

42. Guthrie, *Seed-Time and Harvest of Ragged Schools*, 20–21.

43. Guthrie, *Seed-Time and Harvest of Ragged Schools*, 110.

44. *The Remedy for Unemployment, Being Part II of The Minority Report of the Poor Law Commission* (London: Fabian Society, 1909), 66.

45. *The Remedy for Unemployment*, 10–11.

46. *The Remedy for Unemployment*, 38.

47. Guthrie, *Seed-Time and Harvest of Ragged Schools*, 20.

48. Mothers continue to arouse suspicion among welfare critics. The racialized figure of the "welfare queen" in the late twentieth century United States was an imagined figure who would have babies simply to avoid waged work.

49. *The Remedy for Unemployment*, 26.

50. *The Remedy for Unemployment*, 30.

51. For an exploration of the relationship between energy and slavery, see Andrew Nikiforuk, *The Energy of Slaves: Oil and the New Servitude* (Vancouver, BC: Greystone, 2014).

CHAPTER 5: ENERGOPOLITICS

1. Daniel H. Deudney, *Bounding Power: Republican Security Theory from the Polis to the Global Village* (Princeton, NJ: Princeton University Press, 2008), 197.

2. Deudney, *Bounding Power*; Philip Mirowski, *More Heat Than Light: Economics as Social Physics, Physics as Nature's Economics* (Cambridge: Cambridge University Press, 1989); John Bellamy Foster, *Marx's Ecology: Materialism and Nature* (New York: Monthly Review, 2000); Barry Buzan and George Lawson, *The Global Transformation: History, Modernity and the Making of International Relations* (Cambridge: Cambridge University Press, 2015); Jürgen Osterhammel, *The Transformation of the World: A Global History of the Nineteenth Century*, translated by Patrick Camiller (Princeton, NJ: Princeton University Press, 2014).

3. E. B. Worthington, *Science in Africa: A Review of the Scientific Research Relating to Tropical and Southern Africa* (London: Oxford University Press, 1938).

4. Peder Anker, *Imperial Ecology: Environmental Order in the British Empire, 1895–1945* (Cambridge, MA: Harvard University Press, 2009).

5. Anne McClintock, *Imperial Leather: Race, Gender, and Sexuality in the Colonial Contest* (New York: Routledge, 2013), 112.

6. Thanks to Robert Parks (e-mail correspondence) for pointing out to me that many ecologists intentionally did not seek to study human–nonhuman relations, but instead strove to bracket humans altogether. I am more narrowly interested here in those ecologists who were being taken up by state administrators, or who were themselves seeking to apply their science to human governance.

7. In many ways, this was a continuation of the utilitarian ethics that has haunted European conservation projects since at least the seventeenth century, as Carolyn Merchant shows. Merchant analyzes an earlier melding of organic and mechanical views of nature in favor of profit-seeking and managerial styles of land stewardship. See Merchant, *The Death of Nature: Women, Ecology, and the Scientific Revolution* (New York: HarperCollins, 1990).

8. This notion is inspired by Mitchell's analysis of the emergence of the economy as a political object in the early twentieth century and his argument that economics did not study a preexisting economic system, but rather produced the economy as a site for governance. Similarly, the energy systems into which states intervened were not simply studied but were made by thermodynamics. The implication of this is that different ways of knowing energy would produce different energy systems and governance strategies. Timothy Mitchell, "Economists and the Economy in the Twentieth Century," in *The Politics of Method in the Human Sciences: Positivism and Its Epistemological Others*, edited by George Steinmetz (Durham, NC: Duke University Press, 2005), 126–41.

9. Dominic Boyer, "Energopolitics and the Anthropology of Energy," *Anthropology News* 52, no. 5 (2011): 5–7; Dominic Boyer, *Energopower: Wind and Power in the Anthropocene* (Durham, NC: Duke University Press, 2019).

10. Achille Mbembe, "Necropolitics," *Public Culture* 15, no. 1 (2003): 11–40.

11. Ilya Prigogine and Isabelle Stengers, *Order Out of Chaos* (New York: Bantam, 1984).

12. Gilbert N. Lewis, *The Anatomy of Science* (New Haven, CT: Yale University Press, 1926), 160–61.

13. Max Planck, *The Philosophy of Physics* (New York: W. W. Norton, 1936), 111.

14. Anker, *Imperial Ecology*; Mitchell, "Economists and the Economy"; Timothy Mitchell, *Rule of Experts: Egypt, Techno-Politics, Modernity* (Berkeley: University of California Press, 2002); Alexander Anievas, Nivi Manchanda, and Robbie Shilliam, eds., *Race and Racism in International Relations: Confronting the Global Colour Line* (New York: Routledge, 2014); N. Katherine Hayles, *How We Became Posthuman: Virtual Bodies in Cybernetics, Literature, and Informatics* (Chicago: University of Chicago Press, 2008); Deudney, *Bounding Power*.

15. Mitchell, "Economists and the Economy."

16. Paul N. Edwards, *A Vast Machine: Computer Models, Climate Data, and the Politics of Global Warming* (Cambridge, MA: MIT Press, 2010).

17. Karen Barad, *Meeting the Universe Halfway: Quantum Physics and the Entanglement of Matter and Meaning* (Durham, NC: Duke University Press, 2007); N. Katherine Hayles, "Designs on the Body: Norbert Wiener, Cybernetics, and the Play of Metaphor," *History of the Human Sciences* 3, no. 2 (1990): 211–28; Hayles, *How We Became Posthuman*; William Connolly, *A World of Becoming* (Durham, NC: Duke University Press, 2011); Jane Bennett, *Vibrant Matter: A Political Ecology of Things* (Durham, NC: Duke University Press Books, 2010); Deudney, *Bounding Power*; Anker, *Imperial Ecology*.

18. Peter J. Bowler, *Reconciling Science and Religion: The Debate in Early-Twentieth-Century Britain* (Chicago: University of Chicago Press, 2014), 167.

19. J. S. Haldane, *Mechanism, Life and Personality; an Examination of the Mechanistic Theory of Life and Mind* (London: John Murray, 1913), 80.

20. Haldane, *Mechanism, Life and Personality*, 80.

21. Bowler, *Reconciling Science and Religion*, 171.

22. Haldane, *Mechanism, Life and Personality*, 28.

23. Haldane, *Mechanism, Life and Personality*, 60.

24. Franklin C. Bing, "The History of the Word 'Metabolism,'" *Journal of the History of Medicine and Allied Sciences* 26, no. 2 (1971): 158–80.

25. Lawrence Henderson, *The Fitness of the Environment; an Inquiry into the Biological Significance of the Properties of Matter* (New York: Macmillan, 1913), 24–25.

26. Cutler Cleveland, "Biophysical Economics: From Physiocracy to Ecological Economics and Industrial Ecology," in *Bioeconomics and Sustainability: Essays in Honor of Nicholas Georgescu-Roegen*, edited by John Gowdy and Kozo Mayumi (Cheltenham, UK: Edward Elgar, 1999), 125–54.

27. Wilhelm Ostwald, "The Modern Theory of Energetics," *Monist* 17, no. 4 (1907): 481.

28. Ostwald, "The Modern Theory of Energetics," 513.

29. Ostwald, "The Modern Theory of Energetics," 514.

30. Cleveland, "Biophysical Economics," 130.

31. In *Imperial Ecology*, Anker claims that, due to a lack of citation of or collaboration with the physical and natural sciences, these sciences "played little role in the ecologists' understanding of the natural world, despite their use of mechanistic and chemical terminology" (239). However, a lack of citation should not be confused with a lack of influence. Indeed, this claim is belied by the extensive role that energy plays in both schools of ecology that Anker investigates. For example, Anker says of Arthur Tansley, one of the key thinkers in his text, that "It is not always clear whether he is writing about the mind, society, or the environment, but he is certain that this world consists of channels of energy" (31).

32. Arthur Tansley, *Elements of Plant Biology* (London: George Allen and Unwin, 1922), 25.

33. Frederick Soddy, *Cartesian Economics* (London: Hendersons, 1922), 9.

34. McKinnon notes that Marx came closest by discussing the replacement of dead labor for human labor, but that he stopped short of considering the full import of energy as, for Marx, "in the last instance . . . value is produced only by human labor." See Andrew M. McKinnon, "Energy and Society: Herbert Spencer's 'Energetic Sociology' of Social Evolution and Beyond," *Journal of Classical Sociology* 10, no. 4 (2010): 440.

35. Herbert Spencer, *First Principles* (New York: Cambridge University Press, 2009), 353.

36. Herbert Spencer, "The Social Organism," *Westminster Review* 73 (1860): 91.

37. Spencer, "The Social Organism," 108.

38. Spencer, "The Social Organism," 108.

39. Alfred Lotka, *Elements of Physical Biology* (Baltimore: Waverly Press, 1925), 357–58.

40. For example, see the discussion of marginal lands and fuel in Rachel A. Nalepa and Dana Marie Bauer, "Marginal Lands: The Role of Remote Sensing in Constructing Landscapes for Agrofuel Development," *The Journal of Peasant Studies* 39, no. 2 (2012): 403–22; and Karen Rignall, "Solar Power, State Power, and the Politics of Energy Transition in Pre-Saharan Morocco," *Environment and Planning A: Economy and Space* 48, no. 3 (2016): 540–57.

41. Alfred North Whitehead, *Science and the Modern World* (New York: Free Press, 1997), 111.

42. Whitehead, *Science and the Modern World*, 111–12.

43. Whitehead, *Science and the Modern World*, 109.

44. Bentley Allan makes a similar argument about classical science discourses more broadly, showing how the adoption of scientific means affected the political ends of global institutions across modern European history. See Bentley B. Allan, "From Means to Ends: How Scientific Ideas Transformed International Politics, 1550–2010," PhD diss. (Ohio State University, 2012).

45. Ted Underwood, *The Work of the Sun: Literature, Science, and Economy, 1760–1860* (New York: Palgrave Macmillan, 2005).

46. This relationship is also examined in Anson Rabinbach, *The Human Motor: Energy, Fatigue, and the Origins of Modernity* (Berkeley: University of California Press, 1992).

47. Mary Henrietta Kingsley, *Travels in West Africa: Congo Français, Corisco and Cameroons* (New York: Macmillan, 1897), 671.

48. The notion of legibility as a driver of governance practices is drawn from James C. Scott, *Seeing like a State: How Certain Schemes to Improve the Human Condition Have Failed* (New Haven, CT: Yale University Press, 1999).

49. Joseph Needham, "Evolution and Thermodynamics (1941)," in *Time: The Refreshing River (Essays and Addresses, 1932–1942)* (London: George Allen and Unwin, 1943), 230.

50. Albert Einstein, *Ideas and Opinions* (New York: Broadway, 1995), 340.

51. Mirowski, *More Heat Than Light*.

52. Mitchell, "Economists and the Economy."

53. For instance, Anker notes that Tansley in *Imperial Ecology* was influenced by Sigmund Freud and connected ecology to the study of the human mind. Anne McClintock investigates racialized and gendered attitudes toward women's labor, social unrest, and urban crowds as they relate to Victorian and Edwardian imperial politics in *Imperial Leather*.

54. Dominic Boyer, "Energopower: An Introduction," *Anthropological Quarterly* 87, no. 2 (2014): 310.

55. Boyer, "Energopolitics and the Anthropology of Energy," 5.

56. See Michel Foucault, *"Society Must Be Defended": Lectures at the Collège de France, 1975–1976*, translated by David Macey (New York: Picador, 2003); Michel Foucault, *Security, Territory, Population: Lectures at the Collège de France 1977–1978*, translated by Graham Burchell (New York: Picador, 2009); Michel Foucault, *The Birth of Biopolitics: Lectures at the Collège de France, 1978–1979* (New York: Picador, 2010).

57. Michel Foucault, *The History of Sexuality*, vol. 1: *An Introduction*, translated by Robert Hurley (New York: Pantheon, 1978), 137.

58. Foucault, *The History of Sexuality*, vol. 1, 137.

59. Foucault, *The Birth of Biopolitics*; Foucault, *Society Must Be Defended*.

60. Foucault, *The History of Sexuality*, vol. 1, 136–37.

61. Foucault, *Society Must Be Defended*, 249.

62. Foucault, *The History of Sexuality*, vol. 1, 140–41.

63. Foucault, *Security, Territory, Population*, 49.

64. Foucault, *Security, Territory, Population*, 22fn.

65. Foucault, *Society Must Be Defended*, 257.

66. Michel Foucault, "Truth and Power," in *Power/Knowledge: Selected Interviews and Other Writings, 1972–1977*, edited by Colin Gordon, translated by Colin Gordon et al. (New York: Vintage, 1972), 125.

67. Foucault, *Security, Territory, Population*, 19.

68. Bruce Braun, "Producing Vertical Territory: Geology and Governmentality in Late Victorian Canada," ECUMENE 7, no. 1 (2000): 12–13.

69. Foucault was aware of the importance of other scientific disciplines, but explained his focus on medical sciences as stemming from his personal knowledge of them as well as their inherently close connection with social and political institutions.

In one interview, Foucault muses that studying the relationship of "theoretical physics" or "organic chemistry" to politics and society would be "an excessively complicated question" that would "set the threshold of possible explanations impossibly high." He explains that he therefore chose psychiatry to study both because of his familiarity with psychiatric hospitals but also because its more "dubious" status in science would make it easier to grasp "the interweaving effects of power and knowledge" with "greater certainty." Foucault, "Truth and Power," 109.

70. Foucault, *The History of Sexuality*, vol. 1, 138.

71. Foucault, *Society Must Be Defended*, 254.

72. St. Thomas Aquinas, *Summa Theologica*, vol. 3, part 2, sec. 2 (New York: Cosimo Classics, 2007), 1339.

73. Daniel T. Rodgers, *The Work Ethic in Industrial America 1850–1920* (Chicago: University of Chicago Press, 2014), x.

74. Foucault, *The History of Sexuality*, vol. 1, 138–39.

75. W. H. Houldsworth, "The Conditions of Industrial Prosperity," in *Industrial Remuneration Conference. The Report of the Proceedings and Papers* (London: Cassell, 1885), 232.

76. Julian Reid and Brad Evans, *Resilient Life: The Art of Living Dangerously* (Malden, MA: Polity, 2014).

CHAPTER 6: THE IMPERIAL ORGANISM AT WORK

1. Andreas Malm, *Fossil Capital: The Rise of Steam Power and the Roots of Global Warming* (Brooklyn, NY: Verso, 2016), 267.

2. See, for example, Aimé Césaire, *Discourse on Colonialism*, translated by Joan Pinkham (New York: Monthly Review, 2000); Walter D. Mignolo, *The Darker Side of Western Modernity: Global Futures, Decolonial Options* (Durham, NC: Duke University Press, 2011); Sylvia Wynter, "Unsettling the Coloniality of Being/Power/Truth/Freedom: Towards the Human, after Man, Its Overrepresentation—An Argument," *CR: The New Centennial Review* 3, no. 3 (2003): 257–337; Frantz Fanon, *The Wretched of the Earth*, translated by Richard Philcox (New York: Grove, 2005); W. E. B. Du Bois, "Worlds of Color," *Foreign Affairs* 3, no. 3 (1925): 423–44.

3. Wynter, "Unsettling the Coloniality of Being/Power/Truth/Freedom"; Irene Silverblatt, *Modern Inquisitions: Peru and the Colonial Origins of the Civilized World* (Durham, NC: Duke University Press, 2004); Walter D. Mignolo, *Local Histories/Global Designs: Coloniality, Subaltern Knowledges, and Border Thinking* (Princeton, NJ: Princeton University Press, 2000); Mignolo, *The Darker Side of Western Modernity*; Mauro Caraccioli, "The Learned Man of Good Judgment: Nature, Narrative and Wonder in Jose de Acosta's Natural Philosophy," *History of Political Thought* 38, no. 1 (2017): 44–63; Jorge Canizares-Esguerra, *How to Write the History of the New World: Histories, Epistemologies, and Identities in the Eighteenth-Century Atlantic World* (Stanford, CA: Stanford University Press, 2002).

4. Wynter, "Unsettling the Coloniality of Being/Power/Truth/Freedom," 321.

5. Wynter, "Unsettling the Coloniality of Being/Power/Truth/Freedom," 319.

6. Wynter, "Unsettling the Coloniality of Being/Power/Truth/Freedom," 321.

7. Bernard Semmel, *Imperialism and Social Reform: English Social-Imperial Thought, 1895–1914* (New York: Anchor, 1968), 18–20.

8. Victor Bérard, *British Imperialism and Commercial Supremacy*, translated by W. Foskett (New York: Longmans, Green, 1906), 279.

9. Malm, *Fossil Capital*, 19.

10. Peder Anker, *Imperial Ecology: Environmental Order in the British Empire, 1895–1945* (Cambridge, MA: Harvard University Press, 2009), 1.

11. Anker, *Imperial Ecology*.

12. Anker, *Imperial Ecology*, 239.

13. Mignolo, *The Darker Side of Western Modernity*, xii.

14. Simon J. Potter, "Empire, Cultures and Identities in Nineteenth- and Twentieth-Century Britain," *History Compass* 5, no. 1 (2007): 53–54.

15. This builds on Walter Mignolo's study of a "Western code" and its "belief that in terms of epistemology there is only one game in town." Mignolo, *The Darker Side of Western Modernity*, xii.

16. David Arnold, "Europe, Technology, and Colonialism in the 20th Century," *History and Technology* 21, no. 1 (2005): 95, https://doi.org/10.1080/07341510500037537.

17. Julian Go, *Patterns of Empire: The British and American Empires, 1688 to the Present* (Cambridge: Cambridge University Press, 2011), 4.

18. It should be noted that there is no definitional consensus for empire or imperialism. Julian Go's definition, which emphasizes power, is compelling: empire is "a sociopolitical formation wherein a central political authority (a king, a metropole, or imperial state) exercises unequal influence and power over the political (and in effect the sociopolitical) processes of a subordinate society, peoples, or space." Go, *Patterns of Empire*, 7.

19. "Lord Salisbury Was Presented on Wednesday with the Freedom of the City of Glasgow," *London Spectator*, May 23, 1891.

20. Matthew Huber, *Lifeblood: Oil, Freedom, and the Forces of Capital* (Minneapolis: University of Minnesota Press, 2013), 11.

21. Alf Hornborg, "The Fossil Interlude: Euro-American Power and the Return of the Physiocrats," in *Cultures of Energy: Power, Practices, Technologies*, edited by Sarah Strauss, Rupp Stephanie, and Lowe Thomas (Walnut Creek, CA: Left Coast, 2013).

22. Rudyard Kipling, *The Collected Poems of Rudyard Kipling* (Ware, UK: Wordsworth, 1999), 758.

23. Timothy Mitchell, *Carbon Democracy: Political Power in the Age of Oil* (London: Verso, 2013), 16.

24. Charles Sydney Goldman, ed., *The Empire and the Century: A Series of Essays on Imperial Problems and Possibilities* (London: John Murray, 1905), xviii.

25. Praising Chamberlain's tenure, Lord Alfred Milner, a vehement pro-imperialist, reflected that the turn of the twentieth century marked "the transition from the old system of *laissez-faire* and stagnation to the new policy of activity and development." Alfred Milner, "Mr. Chamberlain and Imperial Policy," in *The Life of Joseph Chamberlain* (London: Associated Newspapers, 1914), 219.

26. William Roger Louis, "Introduction," in *The Oxford History of the British Empire*, vol. 4: *The Twentieth Century*, edited by Judith Brown and William Roger Louis (New York: Oxford University Press, 1999), 4–5.

27. Thomas Richards, *The Imperial Archive: Knowledge and the Fantasy of Empire* (London: Verso, 1993), 74.

28. Helen Tilley, *Africa as a Living Laboratory: Empire, Development, and the Problem of Scientific Knowledge, 1870–1950* (Chicago: University of Chicago Press, 2011), 22.

29. Walter M. Simon, "Herbert Spencer and the 'Social Organism,'" *Journal of the History of Ideas* 21, no. 2 (1960): 294.

30. Joshua Lambier, "The Organismic State against Itself: Schelling, Hegel and the Life of Right," *European Romantic Review* 19, no. 2 (2008): 131.

31. R. B. Haldane, "Constitution of the Empire and the Development of Its Councils," in *Journal of the Society of Comparative Legislation*, vol. 4 (London: John Murray, 1902), 16.

32. James Clerk Maxwell, *Theory of Heat* (New York: Longmans, Green, 1902), 338.

33. Joseph Chamberlain, "The Changed Conditions since the Repeal of the Corn Laws—Speech Delivered 1903," in *Imperial Union and Tariff Reform: Speeches Delivered from May 15 to Nov. 4, 1903* (London: Grant Richards, 1903), 188.

34. J. L. Garvin, "The Maintenance of Empire: A Study of the Economic Basis of Political Power," in *The Empire and the Century* (London: John Murray, 1905), 140.

35. Jan Christian Smuts, *Africa and Some World Problems* (Oxford: Clarendon, 1930), 51.

36. Chamberlain, "The Changed Conditions since the Repeal of the Corn Laws," 188.

37. Charles Bruce, "The Colonial Office and the Crown Colonies," in *The Empire Review*, edited by C. Kinloch-Cooke, vol. 11 (London: Macmillan, 1906), 298.

38. Smuts, *Africa and Some World Problems*, 49.

39. David Cannadine, *Ornamentalism: How the British Saw Their Empire* (New York: Penguin, 2001), xix.

40. Du Bois, "Worlds of Color."

41. Du Bois, "Worlds of Color," 423–44.

42. E. D. Morel, *The Black Man's Burden* (Manchester: National Labour Press, 1900).

43. Kevin Grant, *A Civilised Savagery: Britain and the New Slaveries in Africa, 1884–1926* (New York: Routledge, 2004).

44. Du Bois, "Worlds of Color."

45. Marian S. Benham, *Henry Callaway: His Life-History and Work* (New York: Macmillan, 1896), 88.

46. Far from a passing concern of the moment, it was a crisis that had far-reaching ramifications for global political thought and practice. For example, Robert Vitalis argues that the larger goal of securing "white world order" in an age of empire catalyzed the field of international relations in the early twentieth century. More specifically, the lessons learned by imperial administrators in South Africa, who sought to develop "scientific methods" for unifying the empire, served as "central features" in the origins of modern international relations theory. See Vineet Thakur, Alexander E. Davis, and Peter Vale, "Imperial Mission, 'Scientific' Method: An Alternative Account of the Origins of IR," *Millennium: Journal of International Studies* 46, no. 1 (2017): 3–23; and Robert Vitalis, *White World Order, Black Power Politics: The Birth of American International Relations* (Ithaca, NY: Cornell University Press, 2017).

47. "The Empire of Man," *Nature* 113, no. 2844 (May 3, 1924): 631.

48. "The Empire of Man," 629.

49. As just one example, *Nature* emphasizes the benefits conferred on the colonies by advances in tropical medicine when describing the British Empire Exhibition. See "The Empire of Man."

50. Roy Macleod, "Passages in Imperial Science: From Empire to Commonwealth," *Journal of World History* 4, no. 1 (1993): 131.

51. "Energetic evolution" is most clearly expressed by Alfred Lotka. See Alfred Lotka, *Elements of Physical Biology* (Baltimore: Waverly, 1925); Alfred J. Lotka, "Contribution to the Energetics of Evolution," *Proceedings of the National Academy of Sciences of the United States of America* 8, no. 6 (1922): 147–51.

52. Ted Underwood, *The Work of the Sun: Literature, Science, and Economy, 1760–1860* (New York: Palgrave Macmillan, 2005), 182; Anson Rabinbach, *The Human Motor: Energy, Fatigue, and the Origins of Modernity* (Berkeley: University of California Press, 1992).

53. Tilley, *Africa as a Living Laboratory*, 17.

54. Smuts, *Africa and Some World Problems*, 46.

55. Grant, *A Civilised Savagery*, 2–3.

56. Jürgen Osterhammel, *The Transformation of the World: A Global History of the Nineteenth Century*, translated by Patrick Camiller (Princeton, NJ: Princeton University Press, 2014), 658.

57. Osterhammel, *The Transformation of the World*, 658.

58. Hortense J. Spillers, *Black, White, and in Color: Essays on American Literature and Culture* (Chicago: University of Chicago Press, 2003), 21.

59. Donald Worster, *Nature's Economy: A History of Ecological Ideas* (New York: Cambridge University Press, 1994), 172–73.

60. Spillers, *Black, White, and in Color*, 440.

61. Wynter, "Unsettling the Coloniality of Being/Power/Truth/Freedom," 266.

62. Richard Cobden, "Russia and the Eastern Question (1854)," in *Politics and Empire in Victorian Britain: A Reader*, edited by Antoinette Burton (New York: Palgrave Macmillan, 2001), 101.

63. Edward W. Said, *Orientalism* (New York: Vintage, 1979), 38.

64. Thomas Carlyle, "Occasional Discourse on the Negro Question (1849)," in *Politics and Empire in Victorian Britain: A Reader*, edited by Antoinette Burton (New York: Palgrave, 2001), 115.

65. Michael Adas, "Contested Hegemony: The Great War and the Afro-Asian Assault on the Civilizing Mission Ideology," *Journal of World History* 15, no. 1 (2004): 37.

66. Alexander Anievas, Nivi Manchanda, and Robbie Shilliam, eds., *Race and Racism in International Relations: Confronting the Global Colour Line* (New York: Routledge, 2014), 2.

67. Osterhammel, *The Transformation of the World*, 828.

68. Adas, "Contested Hegemony," 36–37.

69. Osterhammel, *The Transformation of the World*, 656.

70. Adas, "Contested Hegemony," 35–36.

71. Mary Henrietta Kingsley, *Travels in West Africa: Congo Français, Corisco and Cameroons* (New York: Macmillan, 1897), 439.

72. Césaire, *Discourse on Colonialism*, 70.

73. Césaire, *Discourse on Colonialism*, 19.

74. Césaire, *Discourse on Colonialism*, 36.

75. Césaire, *Discourse on Colonialism*, 35–36.

76. Cannadine, *Ornamentalism: How the British Saw Their Empire*, 5.

77. Cannadine, *Ornamentalism*, xix.

78. Grant, *A Civilised Savagery*; Nicholas Owen, "Critics of Empire in Britain," in *The Oxford History of the British Empire*, edited by Judith Brown and William Roger Louis, vol. 4: *The Twentieth Century* (New York: Oxford University Press, 1999), 188–211.

79. Michael Adas, *Machines as the Measure of Men: Science, Technology, and Ideologies of Western Dominance* (Ithaca, NY: Cornell University Press, 1990), 146.

80. John Harris, "Back to Slavery?," in *The Contemporary Review*, vol. 120 (London: Contemporary Review, 1921), 197.

81. Adas, *Machines as the Measure of Men*, 146–48.

82. Paul Lafargue, *The Right to Be Lazy: And Other Studies* (Chicago: C. H. Kerr, 1907), 9.

83. Adas, "Contested Hegemony," 32.

84. Mary Kingsley, *West African Studies* (London: Macmillan, 1899), 386, quoted in Adas, *Machines as the Measure of Men*, 147.

85. Anne McClintock, *Imperial Leather: Race, Gender, and Sexuality in the Colonial Contest* (New York: Routledge, 2013), 56–57.

86. McClintock, *Imperial Leather*, 57–58.

87. Herbert Spencer, "The Social Organism," *Westminster Review* 73 (1860): 108.

88. Spencer, "The Social Organism," 108.

89. Herbert Spencer, *First Principles* (New York: Cambridge University Press, 2009), 353.

90. McClintock, *Imperial Leather*, 48.

91. McClintock, *Imperial Leather*, 49.

92. Lionel Phillips, "Some Aspects of the Mining Industry in South Africa," in *The Empire and the Century* (London: John Murray, 1905), 596.

93. David Roediger, *The Wages of Whiteness: Race and the Making of the American Working Class*, rev. ed. (New York: Verso, 2007), 14.

94. Roediger, *The Wages of Whiteness*, 95.

95. McClintock, *Imperial Leather*.

96. McClintock, *Imperial Leather*, 53.

97. McClintock, *Imperial Leather*, 56.

98. McClintock, *Imperial Leather*, 252.

99. James Bryce, *Impressions of South Africa*, 3rd ed. (London: Macmillan, 1899), 212.

100. For an example, see S. F. Markham, *Climate and the Energy of Nations* (London: Oxford University Press, 1944).

101. Harris, "Back to Slavery?," 194.

102. Similarly, Morton notes that "*world* is an aesthetic construct that depends on things like underground oil and gas pipes." Timothy Morton, *Hyperobjects: Philosophy and Ecology after the End of the World* (Minneapolis: University of Minnesota Press, 2013), 106.

103. McClintock, *Imperial Leather*, 162.

104. McClintock, *Imperial Leather*, 162.

105. McClintock, *Imperial Leather*, 252–53.

106. W. E. B. Du Bois, *The Gift of Black Folk* (Boston: Stratford, 1924), 53–54.

107. McClintock, *Imperial Leather*, 211.

108. Mitchell, *Carbon Democracy*.

109. Worster, *Nature's Economy*, 179.

110. Césaire, *Discourse on Colonialism*, 42.

111. Césaire, *Discourse on Colonialism*, 42–43.

CHAPTER 7: EDUCATION FOR EMPIRE

1. Graeme J. N. Gooday, "Ayrton, William Edward (1847–1908), Electrical Engineer and Physicist," in *Oxford Dictionary of National Biography* (Oxford: Oxford University Press, 2004).

2. Henry Dyer was another early leader in setting up Japanese engineering programs. He, too, was recommended to the Japanese government by one of the luminaries of thermodynamics—his mentor, William Rankine.

3. W. H. Brock, "The Japanese Connexion: Engineering in Tokyo, London, and Glasgow at the End of the Nineteenth Century (Presidential Address, 1980)." *British Journal for the History of Science* 14, no. 3 (1981): 228.

4. Henry Dyer, *Dai Nippon, the Britain of the East: A Study in National Evolution* (London: Blackie and Son, 1904).

5. Graeme J. N. Gooday and Morris F. Low, "Technology Transfer and Cultural Exchange: Western Scientists and Engineers Encounter Late Tokugawa and Meiji Japan," *Osiris* 13 (1998): 126–27.

6. The visiting journalist from the *Japan Weekly Mail* notes that Ayrton's laboratory housed "an apparatus to test a well-known Japanese belief regarding the effect of an earthquake on a magnet." "A Visit to Professor Ayrton's Laboratory," *Japan Weekly Mail*, October 26, 1878, 1130.

7. Aimé Césaire, *Discourse on Colonialism*, translated by Joan Pinkham (New York: Monthly Review, 2000), 42.

8. Andreas Malm, *Fossil Capital: The Rise of Steam Power and the Roots of Global Warming* (Brooklyn, NY: Verso, 2016).

9. Gooday, "Ayrton, William Edward."

10. William Ayrton, "Kelvin in the Sixties," *Popular Science Monthly*, March 1908, 268.

11. Ayrton, "Kelvin in the Sixties," 260.

12. Ayrton, "Kelvin in the Sixties," 262.

13. Ayrton, "Kelvin in the Sixties," 262.

14. "A Visit to Professor Ayrton's Laboratory," 1129.

15. William Ayrton, "Report on the Course of Telegraphic Engineering, Imperial College of Engineering, Tokei, 1st October, 1877," *The Electrician*, November 2, 1878, 286.

16. "A Visit to Professor Ayrton's Laboratory," 1130.

17. Anyone who has taught children knows this instinctively to be true. The Reggio Emilia philosophy of early childhood education, for example, refers to the classroom as the third teacher. A minimalistic, organized classroom is more enticing to children, who will play more creatively and with more focus in such a space.

18. John Perry, "Prof. William Edward Ayrton, F.R.S.," *Nature* 79, no. 2038 (1908): 75.

19. "A Visit to Professor Ayrton's Laboratory," 1130.

20. Perry, "Prof. William Edward Ayrton, F.R.S.," 75.

21. William Crookes, ed., "Technical Education in England, France, and Germany," *Quarterly Journal of Science* I (1879): 790.

22. My own university, Virginia Polytechnic and State Institute, or Virginia Tech, also emerged in this period. Originally named the Virginia Agricultural and Mechanical College (1872), it adopted the more modern-sounding Polytechnic Institute in 1896.

23. Peter Meiksins and Chris Smith, eds., *Engineering Labour: Technical Workers in Comparative Perspective* (New York: Verso, 1996), 5–6.

24. Massachusetts Commission on Industrial and Technical Education, *Report of the Commission on Industrial and Technical Education* (New York: Teachers College, Columbia University, 1906). 5.

25. John Stevenson, "The Influence of Technical Schools," *Popular Science Monthly* 72 (1908): 256.

26. David F. Noble, *America by Design: Science, Technology, and the Rise of Corporate Capitalism* (Oxford: Oxford University Press, 1979), 33.

27. Noble, *America by Design*, 34.

28. Henry Towne, "Industrial Engineering," address, Purdue University, Indiana, February 24, 1905.

29. Noble, *America by Design*, 168.

30. Y. G.-M. Lulat, *United States Relations with South Africa: A Critical Overview from the Colonial Period to the Present* (New York: Peter Lang, 2008), 37.

31. Lulat, *United States Relations with South Africa*, 31–32.

32. Lulat, *United States Relations with South Africa*, 37.

33. Mark Twain, *Following the Equator: A Journey around the World* (New York: Hartford American, 1897), 687.

34. Transvaal and Orange Free State Chamber of Mines, *The Mining Industry: Evidence and Report of the Industrial Commission of Enquiry* (Johannesburg: Witwatersrand Chamber of Mines, 1897), 427.

35. Noble, *America by Design*, 168.

36. James D. Anderson, *The Education of Blacks in the South, 1860–1935* (Chapel Hill: University of North Carolina Press, 1988), 81.

37. Tiffany Willoughby-Herard, *Waste of a White Skin: The Carnegie Corporation and the Racial Logic of White Vulnerability* (Oakland: University of California Press, 2015), 142.

38. Anderson, *The Education of Blacks in the South*, 82.

39. Samuel Armstrong, *The Hampton Normal and Agricultural Institute, Opened April, 1868: Incorporated by Special Act of the General Assembly of Virginia in 1870* (Hampton, VA: Normal School Steam Press, 1879).

40. Armstrong, *The Hampton Normal and Agricultural Institute*.

41. Anderson, *The Education of Blacks in the South*, 54.

42. Armstrong, *The Hampton Normal and Agricultural Institute*.

43. "Report of the Hampton Normal and Agricultural Institute, for the Year Ending June 30, 1880," in *Annual Report of the Auditor of Public Accounts to the General Assembly of Virginia, for the Year Ending September 30, 1880* (Richmond, VA: R. F. Walker, Superintendent of Public Printing, 1881), 13.

44. Booker T. Washington, "The Atlanta Exposition Address," in *Up from Slavery* (New York: Cosimo Classics, 2007), 107.

45. W. E. B. Du Bois, *The Correspondence of W. E. B. Du Bois*, vol. 1: *Selections, 1877–1934*, edited by Herbert Aptheker (Amherst: University of Massachusetts Press, 1997), 68.

46. W. E. B. Du Bois, *The Souls of Black Folk* (New York: Oxford University Press, 2007), 38–39.

47. Anderson, *The Education of Blacks in the South*, 110.

48. Du Bois, *The Souls of Black Folk*, 27.

49. W. E. B. Du Bois, *Black Reconstruction in America, 1860–1880* (New York: Free Press, 1998), 5.

50. Du Bois, *Black Reconstruction in America*, 30.

51. Thomas T. Bryce, *Economic Crumbs, or Plain Talks for the People about Labor, Capital, Money, Tariff, Etc.* (Hampton, VA: Hampton Normal School Steam Press, 1879), 1–2.

52. Bryce, *Economic Crumbs*, 2–3.

53. Bryce, *Economic Crumbs*, 3.

54. Bryce, *Economic Crumbs*, 37.

55. Bryce, *Economic Crumbs*, 26–27.

56. Andrew Zimmerman, *Alabama in Africa: Booker T. Washington, the German Empire, and the Globalization of the New South* (Princeton, NJ: Princeton University Press, 2012), 2.

57. Zimmerman, *Alabama in Africa*, 196.

58. Zimmerman, *Alabama in Africa*, 213.

59. Zimmerman, *Alabama in Africa*, 214–15.

60. Herbert Welsh, "The Indian Question Past and Present," *New England Magazine*, October 1890, 263.

61. Harriet Beecher Stowe, "The Indians at St. Augustine," *Christian Union*, April 18, 1877.

62. *The Indian Helper*, May 27, 1887.

63. Richard Henry Pratt, "The Advantages of Mingling Indians with Whites," in *Americanizing the American Indians: Writings by the "Friends of the Indian," 1880–1900*, edited by Francis Paul Prucha (Cambridge, MA: Harvard University Press, 1973), 260.

64. Quoted in David Wallace Adams, *Education for Extinction: American Indians and the Boarding School Experience, 1875–1928*, 3rd ed. (Lawrence: University Press of Kansas, 1995), 55.

65. Armstrong, *The Hampton Normal and Agricultural Institute*, 19.

66. Merill Gates, "Address of President Gates," in *Proceedings of the Ninth Annual Meeting of the Lake Mohonk Conference of Friends of the Indian* (Lake Mohonk, NY: Lake Mohonk Conference, 1891), 9.

67. Armstrong, *The Hampton Normal and Agricultural Institute*, 17.

68. Margaret Jacobs, "Indian Boarding Schools in Comparative Perspective: The Removal of Indigenous Children in the United States and Australia, 1880–1940," in *Boarding School Blues: Revisiting American Indian Educational Experiences*, edited by Clifford Trafzer, Jean Keller, and Lorene Sisquoc (Lincoln: University of Nebraska Press, 2006), 209.

69. Jacobs, "Indian Boarding Schools in Comparative Perspective," 209.

70. "Helping the Indian to Help Himself," in *The Red Man*, vol. 2: *1909–1910* (New York: Johnson Reprint Corporation, 1971), 5.

71. "Helping the Indian to Help Himself," 6.

72. Armstrong, *The Hampton Normal and Agricultural Institute*, 19.

73. *The Indian Helper*, April 13, 1888.

74. *The Indian Helper*, December 18, 1885.

75. Quoted in Adams, *Education for Extinction*, 24–25.

76. For a contemporary example, see Bikrum Gill, "Can the River Speak? Epistemological Confrontation in the Rise and Fall of the Land Grab in Gambella, Ethiopia," *Environment and Planning A: Society and Space* 48, no. 4 (2016): 699–717.

77. Zine Magubane, *Bringing the Empire Home: Race, Class, and Gender in Britain and Colonial South Africa* (Chicago: University of Chicago Press, 2003), 162.

CONCLUSION: A POST-WORK ENERGY POLITICS

1. Paul Hawken, Amory Lovins, and L. Hunter Lovins, *Natural Capitalism: Creating the Next Industrial Revolution* (Boston: U.S. Green Building Council, 2000).

2. For example, Barry Commoner argued vociferously that environmentalists needed to challenge the systems of production as the key to sustainability. Similarly, *The Limits to Growth*, published in 1972, captured the spirit of constraint felt in the midst of the oil crisis. Barry Commoner, "The Environment," *New Yorker*, June 15, 1987; Donella H. Meadows et al., *The Limits to Growth: A Report for the Club of Rome's Project on the Predicament of Mankind*, 2nd ed. (New York: Universe, 1974).

3. Nick Srnicek and Alex Williams, *Inventing the Future: Postcapitalism and a World without Work* (New York: Verso, 2015), 109.

4. Lord notes that, alarmingly, the answer he received was that looters would be shot in the streets. Clive Lord, "Why Basic Income Can Save the Planet," *Basic Income Earth Network*, March 29, 2016, http://www.basicincome.org/news/2016/03/why-basic-income-can-save-the-planet/.

5. Timothy Morton, *Hyperobjects: Philosophy and Ecology after the End of the World* (Minneapolis: University of Minnesota Press, 2013), 1.

6. Morton, *Hyperobjects*, 49.

7. Morton, *Hyperobjects*, 108.

8. Morton, *Hyperobjects*, 17.

9. Anthony Burke et al., "Planet Politics: A Manifesto from the End of IR," *Millennium: Journal of International Studies* 44, no. 3 (2016): 3.

10. Morton, *Hyperobjects*, 19.

11. Morton, *Hyperobjects*, 21.

12. Burke et al., "Planet Politics," 12.

13. Burke et al., "Planet Politics," 16–18.

14. Burke et al., "Planet Politics," 4.

15. William Connolly, *The Fragility of Things: Self-Organizing Processes, Neoliberal Fantasies, and Democratic Activism* (Durham, NC: Duke University Press, 2013).

16. Walter D. Mignolo, *The Darker Side of Western Modernity: Global Futures, Decolonial Options* (Durham, NC: Duke University Press, 2011), xii.

17. Mark Caine et al., "Our High Energy Planet: A Climate Pragmatism Project" (Oakland, CA: Breakthrough Institute, April 2014), 18, http://thebreakthrough.org/images/pdfs/Our-High-Energy-Planet.pdf.

18. John Asafu-Adjaye et al., "An Ecomodernist Manifesto" (Oakland, CA: Breakthrough Institute, April 2015).

19. Asafu-Adjaye et al., "An Ecomodernist Manifesto."

20. Donna Haraway, "Anthropocene, Capitalocene, Plantationocene, Chthulucene: Making Kin," *Environmental Humanities* 6 (2015): 159.

21. This very conclusion also succumbed to the listicle urge.

22. Cara Daggett, "Petro-Masculinity: Fossil Fuels and Authoritarian Desire," *Millennium: Journal of International Studies* 47, no. 1 (2018): 25–44.

23. Zine Magubane, *Bringing the Empire Home: Race, Class, and Gender in Britain and Colonial South Africa* (Chicago: University of Chicago Press, 2003), 162.

24. Stephanie LeMenager, *Living Oil: Petroleum Culture in the American Century* (New York: Oxford University Press, 2016), 4.

25. Kathi Weeks, *The Problem with Work: Feminism, Marxism, Antiwork Politics, and Postwork Imaginaries* (Durham, NC: Duke University Press, 2011), 4.

26. Weeks, *The Problem with Work*, 2–3.

27. Srnicek and Williams mention the environment and energy, but only glancingly.

28. Weeks, *The Problem with Work*, 4.

29. Weeks, *The Problem with Work*, 7–8.

30. Weeks, *The Problem with Work*, 12.

31. Weeks, *The Problem with Work*, 15.

32. Srnicek and Williams, *Inventing the Future*, 116.

33. Weeks, *The Problem with Work*, 62–64.

34. Weeks, *The Problem with Work*, 8.

35. Weeks, *The Problem with Work*, 5.

36. Weeks, *The Problem with Work*, 68–69.

37. Weeks, *The Problem with Work*, 68–69.

38. Weeks, *The Problem with Work*, 196.

39. Weeks, *The Problem with Work*, 203.

40. Weeks, *The Problem with Work*, 203.

41. Weeks, *The Problem with Work*, 198.

42. Weeks, *The Problem with Work*, 219.

43. Weeks, *The Problem with Work*, 220.

44. Weeks, *The Problem with Work*, 221.

45. Weeks, *The Problem with Work*, 220.

46. Weeks, *The Problem with Work*, 229.

47. Weeks, *The Problem with Work*, 139.

48. Weeks, *The Problem with Work*, 231.

49. Weeks, *The Problem with Work*, 145.

50. Weeks, *The Problem with Work*, 146.

51. Lord, "Why Basic Income Can Save the Planet."

52. Weeks, *The Problem with Work*, 155–57.

53. Weeks, *The Problem with Work*, 162.

54. Daggett, "Petro-Masculinity."

55. Richard Hudson, "Time to Seize Energy Opportunities," House Committee on Energy and Commerce, *Idea Lab*, April 25, 2015, https://energycommerce.house.gov/news-center/idea-labs/time-seize-energy-opportunities.

56. "'Equal to Putting Every Worker in Ohio out of Work,'" House Energy and Commerce Committee, *Idea Lab*, October 1, 2015, https://energycommerce.house .gov/news-center/idea-labs/equal-putting-every-worker-ohio-out-work.

57. Daggett, "Petro-Masculinity."

58. Saskia Sassen, *Expulsions: Brutality and Complexity in the Global Economy* (Cambridge, MA: Harvard University Press, 2014).

59. Lord, "Why Basic Income Can Save the Planet."

Adams, David Wallace. *Education for Extinction: American Indians and the Boarding School Experience, 1875–1928*, 3rd ed. Lawrence: University Press of Kansas, 1995.

Adas, Michael. "Contested Hegemony: The Great War and the Afro-Asian Assault on the Civilizing Mission Ideology." *Journal of World History* 15, no. 1 (2004): 31–63.

Adas, Michael. *Machines as the Measure of Men: Science, Technology, and Ideologies of Western Dominance*. Ithaca, NY: Cornell University Press, 1990.

Alexander, Jennifer Karns. *The Mantra of Efficiency from Waterwheel to Social Control*. Baltimore: Johns Hopkins University Press, 2008.

Anderson, James D. *The Education of Blacks in the South, 1860–1935*. Chapel Hill: University of North Carolina Press, 1988.

Anievas, Alexander, Nivi Manchanda, and Robbie Shilliam, eds. *Race and Racism in International Relations: Confronting the Global Colour Line*. New York: Routledge, 2014.

Anker, Peder. *Imperial Ecology: Environmental Order in the British Empire, 1895–1945*. Cambridge, MA: Harvard University Press, 2009.

Appadurai, Arjun. *The Future as Cultural Fact: Essays on the Global Condition*. New York: Verso, 2013.

Aquinas, St. Thomas. *Summa Theologica*, vol. 3. New York: Cosimo Classics, 2007.

Arendt, Hannah. *On Violence*. New York: Harcourt, 1970.

Aristotle. *Nicomachean Ethics*. Translated by Joe Sachs. Newbury, MA: Focus, 2002.

Armstrong, Samuel. *The Hampton Normal and Agricultural Institute, Opened April, 1868: Incorporated by Special Act of the General Assembly of Virginia in 1870*. Hampton, VA: Normal School Steam Press, 1879.

Arnold, David. "Europe, Technology, and Colonialism in the 20th Century." *History and Technology* 21, no. 1 (2005): 85–106. https://doi.org/10.1080/07341510500037537.

Asafu-Adjaye, John, Linus Blomqvist, Stewart Brand, Barry Brook, Ruth Defries, Erle Ellis, Christopher Foreman, et al. "An Ecomodernist Manifesto." Oakland, CA: Breakthrough Institute, April 2015.

Ayrton, William. "Kelvin in the Sixties." *Popular Science Monthly*, March 1908.

Ayrton, William. "Report on the Course of Telegraphic Engineering, Imperial College of Engineering, Tokei, 1st October, 1877." *The Electrician*, November 2, 1878, 284–86.

Barad, Karen. *Meeting the Universe Halfway: Quantum Physics and the Entanglement of Matter and Meaning*. Durham, NC: Duke University Press, 2007.

Barker, Peter. "Stoic Contributions to Early Modern Science." In *Atoms, Pneuma and Tranquility: Epicurean and Stoic Themes in European Thought*, edited by Margaret J. Osler, 135–54. New York: Cambridge University Press, 1991.

Benham, Marian S. *Henry Callaway: His Life-History and Work*. New York: Macmillan, 1896.

Bennett, Jane. *Vibrant Matter: A Political Ecology of Things*. Durham, NC: Duke University Press, 2010.

Bérard, Victor. *British Imperialism and Commercial Supremacy*. Translated by W. Foskett. New York: Longmans, Green, 1906.

Berna, Francesco, Paul Goldberg, Liora Kolska Horwitz, James Brink, Sharon Holt, Marion Bamford, and Michael Chazan. "Microstratigraphic Evidence of In Situ Fire in the Acheulean Strata of Wonderwerk Cave, Northern Cape Province, South Africa." *Proceedings of the National Academy of Sciences* 109, no. 20 (2012): E1215–20.

The Bible: Authorized King James Version. New York: Oxford University Press, 2008.

Bing, Franklin C. "The History of the Word 'Metabolism.'" *Journal of the History of Medicine and Allied Sciences* 26, no. 2 (1971): 158–80.

Bonta, Mark, Robert Gosford, Dick Eussen, Nathan Ferguson, Erana Loveless, and Maxwell Witwer. "Intentional Fire-Spreading by 'Firehawk' Raptors in Northern Australia." *Journal of Ethnobiology* 37, no. 4 (2017): 700–718.

Bowler, Peter J. *Reconciling Science and Religion: The Debate in Early-Twentieth-Century Britain*. Chicago: University of Chicago Press, 2014.

Boyer, Dominic. "Energopolitics and the Anthropology of Energy." *Anthropology News* 52, no. 5 (2011): 5–7.

Boyer, Dominic. "Energopower: An Introduction." *Anthropological Quarterly* 87, no. 2 (2014): 309–33.

Boyer, Dominic. *Energopower: Wind and Power in the Anthropocene*. Durham, NC: Duke University Press, 2019.

Braun, Bruce. "Producing Vertical Territory: Geology and Governmentality in Late Victorian Canada." *ECUMENE* 7, no. 1 (2000): 7–46.

Bridgman. P. W. *The Nature of Thermodynamics*. Cambridge, MA: Harvard University Press, 1941. http://archive.org/details/natureofthermody031258mbp.

Brock, W. H. "The Japanese Connexion: Engineering in Tokyo, London, and Glasgow at the End of the Nineteenth Century (Presidential Address, 1980)." *British Journal for the History of Science* 14, no. 3 (1981): 227–44. https://doi.org/10.1017/S0007087400018707.

Bruce, Charles. "The Colonial Office and the Crown Colonies." In *The Empire Review*, vol. 11, edited by C. Kinloch-Cooke, 291–310. London: Macmillan, 1906.

Bryce, James. *Impressions of South Africa*, 3rd ed. London: Macmillan, 1899.

Bryce, Thomas T. *Economic Crumbs, or Plain Talks for the People about Labor, Capital, Money, Tariff, Etc.* Hampton, VA: Hampton Normal School Steam Press, 1879. https://ia801409.us.archive.org/5/items/economiccrumbsoroobryc/economiccrumbsoroobryc.pdf.

Burke, Anthony, Stefanie Fishel, Audra Mitchell, Simon Dalby, and Daniel J. Levine. "Planet Politics: A Manifesto from the End of IR." *Millennium: Journal of International Studies* 44, no. 3 (2016): 499–523.

Buzan, Barry, and George Lawson. *The Global Transformation: History, Modernity and the Making of International Relations*. Cambridge: Cambridge University Press, 2015.

Caffentzis, George. *In Letters of Blood and Fire: Work, Machines, and the Crisis of Capitalism*. Oakland, CA: PM Press, 2013.

Caine, Mark, Jason Lloyd, Max Luke, Lisa Margonelli, Todd Moss, Ted Nordhaus, Roger Pielke, et al. "Our High Energy Planet: A Climate Pragmatism Project." Oakland, CA: Breakthrough Institute, April 2014. http://thebreakthrough.org /images/pdfs/Our-High-Energy-Planet.pdf.

Canizares-Esguerra, Jorge. *How to Write the History of the New World: Histories, Epistemologies, and Identities in the Eighteenth-Century Atlantic World*. Stanford, CA: Stanford University Press, 2002.

Cannadine, David. *Ornamentalism: How the British Saw Their Empire*. New York: Penguin, 2001.

Caraccioli, Mauro. "The Learned Man of Good Judgment: Nature, Narrative and Wonder in Jose de Acosta's Natural Philosophy." *History of Political Thought* 38, no. 1 (2017): 44–63.

Cardwell, Donald S. L. *James Joule: A Biography*. New York: Manchester University Press, 1989.

Carlyle, Thomas. "Occasional Discourse on the Negro Question (1849)." In *Politics and Empire in Victorian Britain: A Reader*, edited by Antoinette Burton. New York: Palgrave, 2001.

Carnot, Sadi. *Reflections on the Motive Power of Heat*. Edited by Robert Henry Thurston. New York: John Wiley, 1897.

Ceballos, Gerardo, Paul R. Ehrlich, and Rodolfo Dirzo. "Biological Annihilation via the Ongoing Sixth Mass Extinction Signaled by Vertebrate Population Losses and Declines." *Proceedings of the National Academy of Sciences* 114, no. 30 (2017): E6089–96.

Césaire, Aimé. *Discourse on Colonialism*. Translated by Joan Pinkham. New York: Monthly Review, 2000.

Chakrabarty, Dipesh. "The Climate of History: Four Theses." *Critical Inquiry* 35, no. 2 (2009): 197–222.

Chakrabarty, Dipesh. "The Politics of Climate Change Is More Than the Politics of Capitalism." *Theory, Culture and Society* 34, no. 2–3 (2017): 25–37.

Chamberlain, Joseph. "The Changed Conditions since the Repeal of the Corn Laws—Speech Delivered 1903." In *Imperial Union and Tariff Reform: Speeches Delivered from May 15 to Nov. 4, 1903*, 176–204. London: Grant Richards, 1903.

Clarke, Bruce. *Energy Forms: Allegory and Science in the Era of Classical Thermodynamics*. Ann Arbor: University of Michigan Press, 2001.

Clausius, Rudolf. *The Mechanical Theory of Heat: With Its Applications to the Steam-Engine and to the Physical Properties of Bodies*. London: John Van Voorst, 1867.

Cleveland, Cutler. "Biophysical Economics: From Physiocracy to Ecological Economics and Industrial Ecology." In *Bioeconomics and Sustainability: Essays in Honor of Nicholas Georgescu-Roegen*, edited by John Gowdy and Kozo Mayumi, 125–54. Cheltenham, UK: Edward Elgar, 1999.

Cobden, Richard. "Russia and the Eastern Question (1854)." In *Politics and Empire in Victorian Britain: A Reader*, edited by Antoinette Burton. New York: Palgrave Macmillan, 2001.

Commoner, Barry. "The Environment." *New Yorker*, June 15, 1987.

Connolly, William. *Capitalism and Christianity, American Style*. Durham, NC: Duke University Press, 2008.

Connolly, William. *The Fragility of Things: Self-Organizing Processes, Neoliberal Fantasies, and Democratic Activism*. Durham, NC: Duke University Press, 2013.

Connolly, William. "Species Evolution and Cultural Freedom." *Political Research Quarterly* 67, no. 2 (2014): 441–52.

Connolly, William. *A World of Becoming*. Durham, NC: Duke University Press, 2011.

Crook, David Paul. *Darwinism, War and History: The Debate over the Biology of War from the "Origin of Species" to the First World War*. New York: Cambridge University Press, 1994.

Crookes, William, ed. "Technical Education in England, France, and Germany." *Quarterly Journal of Science* 1 (1879): 790–96.

Daggett, Cara. "Petro-Masculinity: Fossil Fuels and Authoritarian Desire." *Millennium: Journal of International Studies* 47, no. 1 (2018): 25–44.

Dalby, Simon. "Firepower: Geopolitical Cultures in the Anthropocene." *Geopolitics* 23, no. 3 (2018): 718–42.

Darwin, Charles. *The Movements and Habits of Climbing Plants*. London: John Murray, 1875.

Darwin, Charles. *On the Descent of Man, and Selection in Relation to Sex*. London: John Murray, 1871.

Darwin, Charles. *On the Origin of Species by Means of Natural Selection, or the Preservation of Favoured Races in the Struggle for Life*, 6th ed. London: John Murray, 1876.

Darwin, Charles. "To John Fordyce," May 7, 1879. Darwin Correspondence Project. http://www.darwinproject.ac.uk/letter/entry-12041.

Darwin, Charles. "To T. H. Huxley," December 22, 1866. Darwin Correspondence Project. http://www.darwinproject.ac.uk/entry-5315.

Deacon, Terrence W. *Incomplete Nature: How Mind Emerged from Matter*. New York: W. W. Norton, 2013.

Debeir, Jean-Claude, Jean-Paul Deléage, and Daniel Hémery. *In the Servitude of Power: Energy and Civilization through the Ages*. Translated by John Barzman. Atlantic Highlands, NJ: Zed, 1991.

Deleuze, Gilles, and Félix Guattari. *A Thousand Plateaus: Capitalism and Schizophrenia*. Translated by Brian Massumi. Minneapolis: University of Minnesota Press, 1987.

Deudney, Daniel H. *Bounding Power: Republican Security Theory from the Polis to the Global Village*. Princeton, NJ: Princeton University Press, 2008.

Dewey, Caitlin. "GOP Lawmaker: The Bible Says 'If a Man Will Not Work, He Shall Not Eat.'" *Washington Post*, March 31, 2017. https://www.washingtonpost.com /news/wonk/wp/2017/03/31/gop-lawmaker-the-bible-says-the-unemployed -shall-not-eat/?utm_term=.e55238c7f927.

Du Bois, W. E. B. *Black Reconstruction in America, 1860–1880*. New York: Free Press, 1998.

Du Bois, W. E. B. *The Correspondence of W. E. B. Du Bois*, vol. 1: *Selections, 1877–1934*. Edited by Herbert Aptheker. Amherst: University of Massachusetts Press, 1997.

Du Bois, W. E. B. *The Gift of Black Folk*. Boston: Stratford, 1924.

Du Bois, W. E. B. *The Souls of Black Folk*. New York: Oxford University Press, 2007.

Du Bois, W. E. B. "Worlds of Color." *Foreign Affairs* 3, no. 3 (1925): 423–44.

Dyer, Henry. *Dai Nippon, the Britain of the East: A Study in National Evolution*. London: Blackie and Son, 1904.

Edwards, Paul N. *A Vast Machine: Computer Models, Climate Data, and the Politics of Global Warming*. Cambridge, MA: MIT Press, 2010.

Einstein, Albert. *Ideas and Opinions*. New York: Broadway, 1995.

"The Empire of Man." *Nature* 113, no. 2844 (May 3, 1924): 629–31. https://doi.org /10.1038/113629a0.

"'Equal to Putting Every Worker in Ohio Out of Work.'" House Energy and Commerce Committee, *Idea Lab*, October 1, 2015. https://energycommerce.house .gov/news-center/idea-labs/equal-putting-every-worker-ohio-out-work.

Fanon, Frantz. *The Wretched of the Earth*. Translated by Richard Philcox. New York: Grove, 2005.

Feynman, Richard. *The Feynman Lectures on Physics*, vol. 1: *Mainly Mechanics, Radiation, and Heat*. New York: Basic Books, 2011.

Flood, Raymond, Mark McCartney, and Andrew Whitaker, eds. *Kelvin: Life, Labours and Legacy*. New York: Oxford University Press, 2008.

Foster, John Bellamy. *Marx's Ecology: Materialism and Nature*. New York: Monthly Review, 2000.

Foster, John Bellamy, and Paul Burkett. "Classical Marxism and the Second Law of Thermodynamics: Marx/Engels, the Heat Death of the Universe Hypothesis, and the Origins of Ecological Economics." *Organization and Environment* 21, no. 1 (2008): 3–37. https://doi.org/10.1177/1086026607313580.

Foucault, Michel. *The Birth of Biopolitics: Lectures at the Collège de France, 1978–1979*. New York: Picador, 2010.

Foucault, Michel. *The History of Sexuality*, vol. 1: *An Introduction*. Translated by Robert Hurley. New York: Pantheon Books, 1978.

Foucault, Michel. *Security, Territory, Population: Lectures at the Collège de France 1977–1978*. Translated by Graham Burchell. New York: Picador, 2009.

Foucault, Michel. *"Society Must Be Defended": Lectures at the Collège de France, 1975–1976*. Translated by David Macey. New York: Picador, 2003.

Foucault, Michel. "Truth and Power." In *Power/Knowledge: Selected Interviews and Other Writings, 1972–1977*. Edited by Colin Gordon. Translated by Colin Gordon, Leo Marshall, John Mepham, and Kate Soper. New York: Vintage Books, 1972.

Freud, Sigmund. *Introductory Lectures on Psychoanalysis*. New York: Penguin Books, 1991.

Garvin, J. L. "The Maintenance of Empire: A Study of the Economic Basis of Political Power." In *The Empire and the Century*. London: John Murray, 1905.

Gates, Merrill. "Address of President Gates." In *Proceedings of the Ninth Annual Meeting of the Lake Mohonk Conference of Friends of the Indian*, 7–11. Lake Mohonk, NY: Lake Mohonk Conference, 1891.

Geyer, Martin. "One Language for the World: The Metric System, International Coinage, Gold Standard, and the Rise of Internationalism, 1850–1900." In *The Mechanics of Internationalism*, edited by Martin Geyer and Johannes Paulmann. London: Oxford University Press, 2001.

Glacken, Clarence J. *Traces on the Rhodian Shore: Nature and Culture in Western Thought from Ancient Times to the End of the Eighteenth Century*. Berkeley: University of California Press, 1976.

Go, Julian. *Patterns of Empire: The British and American Empires, 1688 to the Present*. Cambridge: Cambridge University Press, 2011.

Gold, Barri J. *ThermoPoetics: Energy in Victorian Literature and Science*. Cambridge, MA: MIT Press, 2010.

Goldman, Charles Sydney, ed. *The Empire and the Century: A Series of Essays on Imperial Problems and Possibilities*. London: John Murray, 1905.

Gooday, Graeme J. N. "Ayrton, William Edward (1847–1908), Electrical Engineer and Physicist." In *Oxford Dictionary of National Biography*. Oxford: Oxford University Press, 2004. http://www.oxforddnb.com/view/10.1093/ref:odnb /9780198614128.001.0001/odnb-9780198614128-e-30509.

Gooday, Graeme J. N., and Morris F. Low. "Technology Transfer and Cultural Exchange: Western Scientists and Engineers Encounter Late Tokugawa and Meiji Japan." *Osiris* 13 (1998): 99–128.

Gould, Stephen Jay. *Time's Arrow, Time's Cycle: Myth and Metaphor in the Discovery of Geological Time*. Cambridge, MA: Harvard University Press, 1987.

Gourlie, William. "Notice of the Fossil Plants in the Glasgow Geological Museum." In *Proceedings of the Royal Philosophical Society of Glasgow: 1841–1844*, vol. 1, 109–12. Glasgow: Richard Griffin and Company, 1844.

Grandy, Walter T., Jr. *Entropy and the Time Evolution of Macroscopic Systems*. New York: Oxford University Press, 2008.

Grant, Kevin. *A Civilised Savagery: Britain and the New Slaveries in Africa, 1884–1926*. New York: Routledge, 2004.

Greenblatt, Stephen. *The Swerve: How the World Became Modern*. New York: W. W. Norton, 2011.

Guthrie, Thomas. *Seed-Time and Harvest of Ragged Schools, or A Third Plea, with New Editions of the First and Second Pleas*. Edinburgh: Adam and Charles Black, 1860.

Haldane, J. S. *Mechanism, Life and Personality; an Examination of the Mechanistic Theory of Life and Mind*. London: John Murray, 1913.

Haldane, R. B. "Constitution of the Empire and the Development of Its Councils." In *Journal of the Society of Comparative Legislation*, vol. 4, 11–18. London: John Murray, 1902.

Haraway, Donna. "Anthropocene, Capitalocene, Plantationocene, Chthulucene: Making Kin." *Environmental Humanities* 6 (2015): 159–65.

Haraway, Donna. *Modest_Witness@Second_Millennium.FemaleMan_Meets_Onco-Mouse: Feminism and Technoscience*. New York: Routledge, 1997.

Haraway, Donna. *Simians, Cyborgs, and Women: The Reinvention of Nature*. New York: Routledge, 1991.

Haraway, Donna, and Thyrza Goodeve. *How Like a Leaf: An Interview with Donna Haraway*. New York: Routledge, 1999.

Harbold, William H. "Progressive Humanity: In the Philosophy of P. J. Proudhon." *Review of Politics* 31, no. 1 (1969): 28–47.

Harding, Sandra. *Science and Social Inequality: Feminist and Postcolonial Issues*. Urbana: University of Illinois Press, 2006.

Harris, John. "Back to Slavery?" In *The Contemporary Review*, vol. 120, 190–97. London: Contemporary Review, 1921.

Hawken, Paul, Amory Lovins, and L. Hunter Lovins. *Natural Capitalism: Creating the Next Industrial Revolution*. Boston: U.S. Green Building Council, 2000.

Hayles, N. Katherine. *Chaos Bound: Orderly Disorder in Contemporary Literature and Science*. Ithaca, NY: Cornell University Press, 1990.

Hayles, N. Katherine. "Designs on the Body: Norbert Wiener, Cybernetics, and the Play of Metaphor." *History of the Human Sciences* 3, no. 2 (1990): 211–28.

Hayles, N. Katherine. *How We Became Posthuman: Virtual Bodies in Cybernetics, Literature, and Informatics*. Chicago: University of Chicago Press, 2008.

Hegel, G. W. F. *Phenomenology of Spirit*. Translated by A. V. Miller. New York: Oxford University Press, 1977.

"Helping the Indian to Help Himself." In *The Red Man*, vol. 2: 1909–1910, 5–7. New York: Johnson Reprint Corporation, 1971.

Henderson, Lawrence. *The Fitness of the Environment; an Inquiry into the Biological Significance of the Properties of Matter*. New York: Macmillan, 1913.

Heraclitus. *Heraclitus: Fragments*. Translated by T. M. Robinson. Toronto: University of Toronto Press, 1991.

Hermann, Arnold. *To Think like God: Pythagoras and Parmenides*. In *The Origins of Philosophy*. Las Vegas, NV: Parmenides, 2004.

Hobsbawm, Eric. *The Age of Capital: 1848–1875*. New York: Random House, 1996.

Hobsbawm, Eric. *The Age of Revolution: 1789–1848*. New York: Random House, 1996.

Hornborg, Alf. "The Fossil Interlude: Euro-American Power and the Return of the Physiocrats." In *Cultures of Energy: Power, Practices, Technologies*, edited by Sarah Strauss, Rupp Stephanie, and Lowe Thomas. Walnut Creek, CA: Left Coast, 2013.

Houldsworth, W. H. "The Conditions of Industrial Prosperity." In *Industrial Remuneration Conference. The Report of the Proceedings and Papers*. London: Cassell, 1885.

Huber, Matthew. *Lifeblood: Oil, Freedom, and the Forces of Capital*. Minneapolis: University of Minnesota Press, 2013.

Hudson, Richard. "Time to Seize Energy Opportunities." House Committee on Energy and Commerce, *Idea Lab*, April 25, 2015. https://energycommerce.house .gov/news-center/idea-labs/time-seize-energy-opportunities.

Iltis, Carolyn. "Leibniz and the Vis Viva Controversy." *Isis* 62, no. 1 (1971): 21–35.

Jacobs, Margaret. "Indian Boarding Schools in Comparative Perspective: The Removal of Indigenous Children in the United States and Australia, 1880–1940." In *Boarding School Blues: Revisiting American Indian Educational Experiences*, edited by Clifford Trafzer, Jean Keller, and Lorene Sisquoc, 202–31. Lincoln: University of Nebraska Press, 2006.

Jevons, William Stanley. *The Coal Question: An Inquiry Concerning the Progress of the Nation, and the Probable Exhaustion of Our Coal-Mines*. London: Macmillan, 1865.

Kauffman, Stuart A. *Reinventing the Sacred: A New View of Science, Reason, and Religion*. New York: Basic Books, 2010.

Ketabgian, Tamara. *The Lives of Machines: The Industrial Imaginary in Victorian Literature and Culture*. Ann Arbor: University of Michigan Press, 2011.

Kingsley, Mary Henrietta. *Travels in West Africa: Congo Français, Corisco and Cameroons*. New York: Macmillan, 1897.

Kingsley, Mary Henrietta. *West African Studies*. London: Macmillan, 1899.

Kipling, Rudyard. *The Collected Poems of Rudyard Kipling*. Ware, UK: Wordsworth, 1999.

Kolbert, Elizabeth. *The Sixth Extinction: An Unnatural History*. New York: Henry Holt, 2014.

Kuhn, Thomas S. *The Essential Tension: Selected Studies in Scientific Tradition and Change*. Chicago: University of Chicago Press, 1977.

Lafargue, Paul. *The Right to Be Lazy: And Other Studies*. Chicago: C. H. Kerr, 1907.

Lambier, Joshua. "The Organismic State against Itself: Schelling, Hegel and the Life of Right." *European Romantic Review* 19, no. 2 (2008): 131–37.

Latour, Bruno. *We Have Never Been Modern*. Translated by Catherine Porter. Cambridge, MA: Harvard University Press, 1993.

Leach, R. A., ed. *The Unemployed Workmen Act, 1905*. Rochdale, UK: Local Government Printing and Publishing, 1905.

LeMenager, Stephanie. *Living Oil: Petroleum Culture in the American Century*. New York: Oxford University Press, 2016.

Lewis, Gilbert N. *The Anatomy of Science*. New Haven, CT: Yale University Press, 1926.

Lewis, Simon L., and Mark A. Maslin. "Defining the Anthropocene." *Nature* 519, no. 7542 (2015): 171–80.

Locke, John. *Second Treatise of Government*. Edited by C. B. Macpherson. Indianapolis: Hackett, 1980.

Lord, Clive. "Why Basic Income Can Save the Planet." Basic Income Earth Network, March 29, 2016. http://www.basicincome.org/news/2016/03/why-basic-income -can-save-the-planet/.

"Lord Salisbury Was Presented on Wednesday with the Freedom of the City of Glasgow." *London Spectator*. May 23, 1891.

Lotka, Alfred J. "Contribution to the Energetics of Evolution." *Proceedings of the National Academy of Sciences of the United States of America* 8, no. 6 (1922): 147–51.

Lotka, Alfred J. *Elements of Physical Biology*. Baltimore: Waverly, 1925.

Louis, William Roger. "Introduction." In *The Oxford History of the British Empire*, vol. 4: *The Twentieth Century*, edited by Judith Brown and William Roger Louis, 1–46. New York: Oxford University Press, 1999.

Lovell, Bernard, ed. *Royal Institution Library of Science (Being the Friday Evening Discourses in Physical Sciences Held at the Royal Institution: 1851–1939)*, vol. 1: *Astronomy*. New York: Elsevier, 1970.

Lucretius. *Lucretius: The Way Things Are: The De Rerum Natura of Titus Lucretius Carus*. Translated by Rolfe Humphries. Bloomington: Indiana University Press, 1968.

Lulat, Y. G.-M. *United States Relations with South Africa: A Critical Overview from the Colonial Period to the Present*. New York: Peter Lang, 2008.

"M. Palacio's Design for a Colossal Monument in Memory of Christopher Columbus." *Scientific American*, October 1890.

MacDuffie, Allen. *Victorian Literature, Energy, and the Ecological Imagination*. Cambridge: Cambridge University Press, 2014.

Macleod, Roy. "Passages in Imperial Science: From Empire to Commonwealth." *Journal of World History* 4, no. 1 (1993): 117–50.

Macquorn Rankine, William John. "XVIII. On the General Law of the Transformation of Energy." *Philosophical Magazine*, Series 4, vol. 5, no. 30 (1853): 106–17.

Magubane, Zine. *Bringing the Empire Home: Race, Class, and Gender in Britain and Colonial South Africa*. Chicago: University of Chicago Press, 2003.

Malm, Andreas. *Fossil Capital: The Rise of Steam Power and the Roots of Global Warming*. Brooklyn, NY: Verso, 2016.

Malm, Andreas, and Alf Hornborg. "The Geology of Mankind? A Critique of the Anthropocene Narrative." *Anthropocene Review* 1, no. 1 (2014): 62–69.

Margulis, Lynn, and Dorion Sagan. *Acquiring Genomes: A Theory of the Origin of Species*. Princeton, NJ: Basic Books, 2003.

Markham, S. F. *Climate and the Energy of Nations*. London: Oxford University Press, 1944.

Martinez-Alier, Joan. "Ecological Economics as Human Ecology." In *Dimensions of Environmental and Ecological Economics*, edited by Nirmal Chandra Sahu and Amita Kumari Choudhury, 47–80. Hyderabad: Universities Press, 2005.

Marx, Karl. *Capital*, vol. 1: *A Critique of Political Economy*. Translated by Ben Fowkes. New York: Penguin Classics, 1992.

Marx, Karl. "The German Ideology." In *The Marx-Engels Reader*, edited by Robert C. Tucker, 146–99. New York: W. W. Norton, 1978.

Marx, Karl, and Friedrich Engels. *Collected Works: 1868–1870*, vol. 43. New York: International, 1975.

Maxwell, James Clerk. *Theory of Heat*. New York: Longmans, 1902.

Mbembe, Achille. "Necropolitics." *Public Culture* 15, no. 1 (2003): 11–40.

McClintock, Anne. *Imperial Leather: Race, Gender, and Sexuality in the Colonial Contest*. New York: Routledge, 2013.

McKinnon, Andrew M. "Energy and Society: Herbert Spencer's 'Energetic Sociology' of Social Evolution and Beyond." *Journal of Classical Sociology* 10, no. 4 (2010): 439–55.

McNeill, John Robert, and William Hardy McNeill. *The Human Web: A Bird's-Eye View of World History*. New York: W. W. Norton, 2003.

Meadows, Donella H., Jorgen Randers, Dennis L. Meadows, and William W. Behrens. *The Limits to Growth: A Report for the Club of Rome's Project on the Predicament of Mankind*, 2nd ed. New York: Universe, 1974.

Meiksins, Peter, and Chris Smith, eds. *Engineering Labour: Technical Workers in Comparative Perspective*. New York: Verso, 1996.

Merchant, Carolyn. *The Death of Nature: Women, Ecology, and the Scientific Revolution*. New York: HarperCollins, 1990.

Merz, John Theodore. *A History of European Scientific Thought in the Nineteenth Century*. Gloucester, MA: Peter Smith, 1976.

Meyerson, Émile. *Identity and Reality*. Translated by Kate Loewenberg. New York: Macmillan, 1930.

Mignolo, Walter D. *The Darker Side of Western Modernity: Global Futures, Decolonial Options*. Durham, NC: Duke University Press, 2011.

Mignolo, Walter D. *Local Histories/Global Designs: Coloniality, Subaltern Knowledges, and Border Thinking*. Princeton, NJ: Princeton University Press, 2000.

Miller, Bruce G. *Coal Energy Systems*. Burlington, MA: Academic Press, 2005.

Milner, Alfred. "Mr. Chamberlain and Imperial Policy." In *The Life of Joseph Chamberlain*, 194–232. London: Associated Newspapers, 1914.

Mirowski, Philip. *More Heat Than Light: Economics as Social Physics, Physics as Nature's Economics*. Cambridge: Cambridge University Press, 1989.

Mitchell, Timothy. *Carbon Democracy: Political Power in the Age of Oil*. London: Verso, 2013.

Mitchell, Timothy. "Economists and the Economy in the Twentieth Century." In *The Politics of Method in the Human Sciences: Positivism and Its Epistemological Others*, edited by George Steinmetz, 126–41. Durham, NC: Duke University Press, 2005.

Mitchell, Timothy. *Rule of Experts: Egypt, Techno-Politics, Modernity*. Berkeley: University of California Press, 2002.

Morel, E. D. *The Black Man's Burden*. Manchester, UK: National Labour Press, 1900.

Morton, Timothy. *Hyperobjects: Philosophy and Ecology after the End of the World*. Minneapolis: University of Minnesota Press, 2013.

Morton, Timothy. "Victorian Hyperobjects." *Nineteenth-Century Contexts* 36, no. 5 (2014): 489–500.

Morus, Iwan Rhys. *When Physics Became King*. Chicago: University of Chicago Press, 2005.

Myers, Greg. "Nineteenth-Century Popularizations of Thermodynamics and the Rhetoric of Social Prophecy." *Victorian Studies* 29, no. 1 (1985): 35–66.

Needham, Joseph. "Evolution and Thermodynamics." In *Time: The Refreshing River (Essays and Addresses, 1932–1942)*. London: George Allen and Unwin, 1943.

Needham, Joseph. *Science and Civilisation in China*, vol. 4: *Physics and Physical Technology*, part 2: *Mechanical Engineering*. Cambridge: Cambridge University Press, 1965.

Neswald, Elizabeth, Bernard Lightman, and Michael S. Reidy. "Saving the World in the Age of Entropy: John Tyndall and the Second Law of Thermodynamics." In *The Age of Scientific Naturalism: Tyndall and His Contemporaries*, edited by Bernard Lightman and Michael S. Reidy. New York: Routledge, 2014.

Nikiforuk, Andrew. *The Energy of Slaves: Oil and the New Servitude*. Vancouver, BC: Greystone, 2014.

Noble, David F. *America by Design: Science, Technology, and the Rise of Corporate Capitalism*. Oxford: Oxford University Press, 1979.

Noble, William J. *Eight Hours as the Standard Day's Work: An Appeal in Behalf of the Same, to the Workingmen of America*, vol. 2: *Testimony*, 219–22. Washington, DC: U.S. Government Printing Office, 1885.

Norton Wise, M., and Crosbie Smith. "Work and Waste: Political Economy and Natural Philosophy in Nineteenth Century Britain (I)." *History of Science* 27, no. 3 (1989): 263–301.

Norton Wise, M., and Crosbie Smith. "Work and Waste: Political Economy and Natural Philosophy in Nineteenth Century Britain (II)." *History of Science* 27, no. 4 (1989): 391–449.

Norton Wise, M., and Crosbie Smith. "Work and Waste: Political Economy and Natural Philosophy in Nineteenth Century Britain (III)." *History of Science* 28, no. 3 (1990): 221–61.

Odum, Eugene. *Ecology: A Bridge between Science and Society*. Sunderland, MA: Sinauer Associates, 1997.

Osterhammel, Jürgen. *The Transformation of the World: A Global History of the Nineteenth Century*. Translated by Patrick Camiller. Princeton, NJ: Princeton University Press, 2014.

Ostwald, Wilhelm. "The Modern Theory of Energetics." *Monist* 17, no. 4 (1907): 481–515.

Owen, Nicholas. "Critics of Empire in Britain." In *The Oxford History of the British Empire*, vol. 4: *The Twentieth Century*, edited by Judith Brown and William Roger Louis, 188–211. New York: Oxford University Press, 1999.

Pence, Charles. "Nietzsche's Aesthetic Critique of Darwin." *History and Philosophy of the Life Sciences* 33 (2011): 165–90.

Perry, John. "Prof. William Edward Ayrton, F.R.S." *Nature* 79, no. 2038 (November 19, 1908): 74–75.

Phillips, Lionel. "Some Aspects of the Mining Industry in South Africa." In *The Empire and the Century*, 586–98. London: John Murray, 1905.

Planck, Max. *The Philosophy of Physics*. London: W. W. Norton, 1936.

Plotz, John. "The Victorian Anthropocene: George Marsh and the Tangled Bank of Darwinian Environmentalism." *Australasian Journal of Ecocriticism and Cultural Ecology* 4 (2014): 52–64.

Pomeranz, Kenneth. *The Great Divergence: China, Europe, and the Making of the Modern World Economy*. Princeton, NJ: Princeton University Press, 2009.

Potter, Simon J. "Empire, Cultures and Identities in Nineteenth- and Twentieth-Century Britain." *History Compass* 5, no. 1 (2007): 51–71.

Pratt, Richard Henry. "The Advantages of Mingling Indians with Whites." In *Americanizing the American Indians: Writings by the "Friends of the Indian," 1880–1900*, edited by Francis Paul Prucha, 260–71. Cambridge, MA: Harvard University Press, 1973.

Prigogine, Ilya. *The End of Certainty*. New York: Simon and Schuster, 1997.

Prigogine, Ilya, and Isabelle Stengers. *Order Out of Chaos*. New York: Bantam, 1984.

Proudhon, Pierre-Joseph. *Philosophie du progrès*. Brussels: Alphonse Lebègue, 1853.

Pyne, Stephen. *Fire: Nature and Culture*. London: Reaktion Books, 2012.

Rabinbach, Anson. *The Human Motor: Energy, Fatigue, and the Origins of Modernity*. Berkeley: University of California Press, 1992.

Radcliffe, J. N. "West-End Milliners." In *The Social Science Review, and the Journal of the Sciences*, vol. 2: *July to December*, edited by Benjamin Richardson, 191–215. London: George A. Hutchinson, 1864.

Reid, Julian, and Brad Evans. *Resilient Life: The Art of Living Dangerously*. Malden, MA: Polity, 2014.

The Remedy for Unemployment, Being Part II of The Minority Report of the Poor Law Commission. London: Fabian Society, 1909.

Report of the Commission on Industrial and Technical Education. New York: Teachers College, Columbia University, 1906.

"Report of the Hampton Normal and Agricultural Institute, for the Year Ending June 30, 1880." In *Annual Report of the Auditor of Public Accounts to the General Assembly of Virginia, for the Year Ending September 30, 1880*. Richmond, VA: R. F. Walker, Superintendent of Public Printing, 1881.

Richards, Robert. "Darwin and Progress." *New York Review of Books*, December 15, 2005. http://www.nybooks.com/articles/archives/2005/dec/15/darwin-progress/.

Richards, Thomas. *The Imperial Archive: Knowledge and the Fantasy of Empire*. London: Verso, 1993.

Rodgers, Daniel T. *The Work Ethic in Industrial America 1850–1920*. Chicago: University of Chicago Press, 2014.

Roediger, David. *The Wages of Whiteness: Race and the Making of the American Working Class*, rev. ed. New York: Verso, 2007.

Ruskin, John. *The Storm Cloud of the Nineteenth Century*. New York: John Wiley, 1884.

Said, Edward W. *Orientalism*. New York: Vintage, 1979.

Sassen, Saskia. *Expulsions: Brutality and Complexity in the Global Economy*. Cambridge, MA: Harvard University Press, 2014.

Scott, James. *Against the Grain: A Deep History of the Earliest States*. New Haven, CT: Yale University Press, 2017.

Scott, James C. *Seeing like a State: How Certain Schemes to Improve the Human Condition Have Failed*. New Haven, CT: Yale University Press, 1999.

Semmel, Bernard. *Imperialism and Social Reform: English Social-Imperial Thought, 1895–1914*. New York: Anchor, 1968.

Serres, Michel. *Hermes: Literature, Science, Philosophy*. Baltimore: Johns Hopkins University Press, 1982.

Sieferle, Rolf Peter. *The Subterranean Forest*. Translated by Michael Osmann. Cambridge, MA: White Horse, 2010.

Silverblatt, Irene. *Modern Inquisitions: Peru and the Colonial Origins of the Civilized World*. Durham, NC: Duke University Press, 2004.

Simon, Walter M. "Herbert Spencer and the 'Social Organism.'" *Journal of the History of Ideas* 21, no. 1/4 (1960): 294.

Smil, Vaclav. *Energy and Civilization: A History*. Cambridge, MA: MIT Press, 2017.

Smil, Vaclav. *Energy in World History*. Boulder, CO: Westview Press, 1994.

Smil, Vaclav. "Science, Energy, Ethics, and Civilization." In *Visions of Discovery: New Light on Physics, Cosmology, and Consciousness*, edited by R. Y. Chiao, M. L. Cohen, A. J. Leggett, W. D. Phillips, and C. L. Harper Jr., 709–29. Cambridge: Cambridge University Press, 2010.

Smith, Crosbie. *The Science of Energy: A Cultural History of Energy Physics in Victorian Britain*. London: Athlone, 1998.

Smith, Crosbie W. "William Thomson and the Creation of Thermodynamics: 1840–1855." *Archive for History of Exact Sciences* 16, no. 3 (1977): 231–88.

Smith, George E. "The Vis Viva Dispute: A Controversy at the Dawn of Dynamics." *Physics Today*, October 2006, 32–36.

Smuts, Jan Christian. *Africa and Some World Problems*. Oxford: Clarendon, 1930.

Soddy, Frederick. *Cartesian Economics*. London: Hendersons, 1922.

Spencer, Herbert. *First Principles*. New York: Cambridge University Press, 2009.

Spencer, Herbert. "The Social Organism." *Westminster Review* 73 (1860): 90–121.

Spillers, Hortense J. *Black, White, and in Color: Essays on American Literature and Culture*. Chicago: University of Chicago Press, 2003.

Srnicek, Nick, and Alex Williams. *Inventing the Future: Postcapitalism and a World without Work*. New York: Verso, 2015.

Stauffer, Robert C. "Haeckel, Darwin, and Ecology." *Quarterly Review of Biology* 32, no. 2 (1957): 138–44.

Steffen, Will, Paul Crutzen, and John McNeill. "The Anthropocene: Are Humans Now Overwhelming the Great Forces of Nature?" *Ambio* 36, no. 8 (2007): 614–21.

Steffen, Will, Johan Rockström, Katherine Richardson, Timothy M. Lenton, Carl Folke, Diana Liverman, Colin P. Summerhayes, et al. "Trajectories of the Earth System in the Anthropocene." *Proceedings of the National Academy of Sciences* 115, no. 33 (2018): 8252–59. https://doi.org/10.1073/pnas.1810141115.

Stevenson, John. "The Influence of Technical Schools." *Popular Science Monthly* 72 (1908): 253–58.

Stewart, Balfour. *The Conservation of Energy*. New York: D. Appleton, 1875.

Stewart, Matthew. *The Courtier and the Heretic: Leibniz, Spinoza, and the Fate of God in the Modern World*. New York: W. W. Norton, 2007.

Stow, Dorrik. *Vanished Ocean: How Tethys Reshaped the World*. Oxford: Oxford University Press, 2010.

Stowe, Harriet Beecher. "The Indians at St. Augustine." *Christian Union*, April 18, 1877.

Szeman, Imre, and Dominic Boyer, eds. *Energy Humanities: An Anthology*. Baltimore: Johns Hopkins University Press, 2017.

Tansley, Arthur. *Elements of Plant Biology*. London: George Allen and Unwin, 1922.

Taylor, Frederick Winslow. *The Principles of Scientific Management*. Mineola, NY: Dover, 1997.

Thompson, E. P. "Time, Work-Discipline, and Industrial Capitalism." *Past and Present* 38 (December 1967): 56–97.

Thompson, Silvanus P. *The Life of William Thompson Baron Kelvin of Largs*. London: Macmillan, 1910.

Thomson, William. "On the Age of the Sun's Heat." *Macmillan's Magazine* 5 (March 5, 1862): 388–93.

Tilley, Helen. *Africa as a Living Laboratory: Empire, Development, and the Problem of Scientific Knowledge, 1870–1950*. Chicago: University of Chicago Press, 2011.

Towne, Henry. "Industrial Engineering." Address, Purdue University, Indiana, February 24, 1905.

Transvaal and Orange Free State Chamber of Mines. *The Mining Industry: Evidence and Report of the Industrial Commission of Enquiry*. Johannesburg: Witwatersrand Chamber of Mines, 1897.

Twain, Mark. *Following the Equator: A Journey around the World*. New York: Hartford American, 1897.

Tyndall, John. "The Constitution of the Universe." Edited by George Henry Lewes. *Fortnightly Review* 3, no. 14 (December 1, 1865): 129–44.

Tyndall, John. *Heat Considered as a Mode of Motion*, rev. 2nd ed. New York: D. Appleton, 1869.

Underwood, Ted. *The Work of the Sun: Literature, Science, and Economy, 1760–1860*. New York: Palgrave Macmillan, 2005.

"A Visit to Professor Ayrton's Laboratory." *Japan Weekly Mail*, October 26, 1878.

Vitalis, Robert. *White World Order, Black Power Politics: The Birth of American International Relations*. Ithaca, NY: Cornell University Press, 2017.

Voskuil, Lynn. "Introduction: Nineteenth-Century Energies." *Nineteenth-Century Contexts* 36, no. 5 (2014): 389–403.

Wark, McKenzie. *A Hacker Manifesto*. Cambridge, MA: Harvard University Press, 2004.

Washington, Booker T. "The Atlanta Exposition Address." In *Up from Slavery*, 105–15. New York: Cosimo Classics, 2007.

Weber, Cynthia. *Queer International Relations*. New York: Oxford University Press, 2016.

Weber, Max. *The Protestant Ethic and the Spirit of Capitalism: And Other Writings.* Translated by Peter Baehr and Gordon C. Wells. New York: Penguin Classics, 2002.

Weeks, Kathi. *The Problem with Work: Feminism, Marxism, Antiwork Politics, and Postwork Imaginaries.* Durham, NC: Duke University Press, 2011.

Weheliye, Alexander G. *Habeas Viscus: Racializing Assemblages, Biopolitics, and Black Feminist Theories of the Human.* Durham, NC: Duke University Press, 2014.

Weisman, Alan. *The World without Us,* rpt. ed. New York: Picador, 2008.

Welsh, Herbert. "The Indian Question Past and Present." *New England Magazine,* October 1890.

Wendling, Amy E. *On Alienation and Machine Production: Capitalist Embodiment in Karl Marx.* University Park: Pennsylvania State University Press, 2006.

Wendling, Amy E. *The Ruling Ideas: Bourgeois Political Concepts.* Lanham, MD: Lexington, 2012.

White, Leslie A. "Energy and the Evolution of Culture." *American Anthropologist* 45, no. 3 (1943): 335–56.

Whitehead, Alfred North. *Science and the Modern World.* New York: Free Press, 1997.

Willoughby-Herard, Tiffany. *Waste of a White Skin: The Carnegie Corporation and the Racial Logic of White Vulnerability.* Oakland: University of California Press, 2015.

Wilson, Sheena, Adam Carlson, and Imre Szeman, eds. *Petrocultures: Oil, Politics, Culture.* Montreal: McGill-Queen's University Press, 2017.

Wolf, Eric R. *Europe and the People without History.* Berkeley: University of California Press, 2010.

Worster, Donald. *Nature's Economy: A History of Ecological Ideas.* New York: Cambridge University Press, 1994.

Worthington, E. B. *Science in Africa: A Review of the Scientific Research Relating to Tropical and Southern Africa.* Oxford: Oxford University Press, 1938.

Wrangham, Richard. *Catching Fire: How Cooking Made Us Human.* New York: Basic Books, 2009.

Wynter, Sylvia. "Unsettling the Coloniality of Being/Power/Truth/Freedom: Towards the Human, after Man, Its Overrepresentation—An Argument." CR: *The New Centennial Review* 3, no. 3 (2003): 257–337.

Yergin, Daniel. *The Prize: The Epic Quest for Oil, Money and Power.* New York: Free Press, 2008.

Zhang, Dainian. *Key Concepts in Chinese Philosophy.* New Haven, CT: Yale University Press, 2002.

Zimmerman, Andrew. *Alabama in Africa: Booker T. Washington, the German Empire, and the Globalization of the New South.* Princeton, NJ: Princeton University Press, 2012.

Page numbers followed by *f* indicate pages with illustrations.

consumerism, 129–30, 197–98

"The Convergence of the Twain" (Hardy), 52

Copernicus, 60, 70

cosmologies of energy, 9–10, 16–24; change, cosmology of, 19–20; Christianity and, 50, 73–74; energy as life itself, 46–47; new, 46–50

Crook, David Paul, 64–65

Dalby, Simon, 189–90

Darwin, Charles, 55, 59–67, 122, 216n26, 216n30, 217n40; misapplication of, 134–35; tragic undertone in works of, 63–64. Works: *The Descent of Man, and Selection in Relation to Sex*, 62, 65; *On the Origin of Species*, 61, 62, 66, 216n30. *See also* evolution

death: biopower and, 125–29; genocide, 125–26, 172, 182, 184–85, 194; heat death of the universe, 48–49, 71, 73, 128, 154, 177; necropolitics, 112; racism and, 128, 177, 184; senescence theory of Earth, 21–23, 48–49, 67–68, 71

deep history, 16, 57, 70, 211n39

Deleuze, Gilles, 32

democratic ideals, 143, 160; used to justify low wages, 176–77

Dennis the Menace example, 40–42, 46, 47, 80

De Rerum Natura (Lucretius), 21–23, 48, 49, 56, 71, 210n18

Descartes, René, 23, 43

The Descent of Man, and Selection in Relation to Sex (Darwin), 62, 65

descriptive statements, 40–41

difference, 69, 134–36

Discourse on Colonialism (Césaire), 149–50

discovery narratives, 3–4, 7, 15, 18, 37, 109, 115–16

dissipation, 72–75, 80, 148; second law of thermodynamics, 42–46, 48–49, 68, 71, 79, 112, 140–41, 152

domination, logics of, 132–34, 145, 148–50, 190, 208n24

Driesch, Hans, 115, 209n3

Du Bois, W. E. B., 142–43, 158–59, 174–75, 178

Dyer, Henry, 163, 231n2

"Dynamical Theory of Heat" (Thomson), 73–74

dynamism, 100–101, 146, 157, 168; bias toward, 17–18, 20–24; of Earth, 56; education of nonwhite workers and, 175, 183–84, 186; trajectorism, 18, 20, 23, 37. *See also* productivism/productivity

Earth: dynamism of, 56; energy abundances, 31; as engine, 69; indifference of, 9, 47, 50, 53, 59; iron Earth proposal, 57, 58f; limitations of, 49, 72; pneuma and, 19–20; senescence theory of, 21–23, 48–49, 67–68, 71; as solar energy system, 25, 27, 46, 77; tragic vision of, 21–23, 49, 53

"Earth Systems Council," 189

Earth systems science, 60, 114

ecology, 2, 52, 112–21, 124; imperialism and, 109–10, 135–36; as term, 66; thermodynamics and, 109–12, 117

ecomodernism. *See* accelerationism (ecomodernism)

Economic Crumbs, or Plain Talks for the People about Labor, Capital, Money, Tariff, Etc. (Bryce), 176–78, 179, 183, 186

economics, 116–17, 122–23, 222n8; recessions, 188, 191

ecosystem, as term, 117

education, 161; cultures of, 166–67; disciplinary models, 170; docile workers as goal, 163, 169–70, 182–83; drudge work as focus of technical schools, 172–78, 182–83; dynamism and education of nonwhite workers, 175, 183–84, 186; of engineers, 164–70; French system, 166; gospel of labor, 164–66, 170; Japanese engineering, 162–64, 165, 231n2, 232n6; measurement and, 163–65; "parody of," 161, 164; second-tier technical and industrial schools, 169–70; technical, 163–64, 166; technical, and racism, 133, 170–85

precautionary principle, 194; waste-based arguments, 193–94

Environmental Protection Agency, 204–5

ergonomics, 91

ethics: of organisms, 119–21; thermodynamics and, 116–17; thermo-ethics, 121–24. *See also* work ethic

evolution, 53–55, 68, 69; adaptation, 56, 112; biblical creation narrative, 61, 73–74; Christian concerns about, 54, 61, 70, 72–74; creativity and cooperation, 120; Earth time and human time, 59, 62–63, 66–67; energy, entanglement with, 55–56; eugenic theories, 64, 122; hierarchies, 110, 116–17; human connection with animals, 62–63, 65; imperialism and, 8–9, 134–35; industrialization, application to, 64–67; natural selection, 61–63, 66–67, 110, 119; political metaphors for, 113; religious concerns about, 70; social Darwinism/racism, 64, 146–47, 160. *See also* Darwin, Charles

"Evolution and Thermodynamics" (Needham), 122

exploitation, 12, 102–3, 119–20, 122, 199–200, 206; of energy, 9, 30, 77, 144, 160; "green" commodities, 198; imperial dependence on, 102, 135, 142–43, 146, 160–61; racism of, 178, 185–86; work ethic needed to cover, 98

extension theory, 23–24

extinction, 2, 9, 25, 52, 128, 131, 182, 184–85, 201

ExxonMobil, 1, 2, 12

Factories Act of 1847 (Ten Hours Act), 92

fall, concept of, 36–37

family ethic, 200, 203

fascism, 149

fatigue, 90–94

fear, politics of, 201

feedback loops, 1, 160–61, 189–90

feminist post-work politics, 11–12, 196–99; politicizing of work, 199–206

Feynman, Richard, 40–41, 47

fire, 27, 43

Fishel, Stefanie, 189–90

flows of energy, 76, 100, 112; directional, 73–74; metabolism, 116–19; nonhuman, 126–27; planetary, 188; pneuma, 19–20

fossil fuels: coal formation, 25–27; energy as sign for, 16, 20, 32, 133; globalization of, 30–31; kerosene, 30. *See also* energy

fossil fuel systems, 4–6, 18, 38, 69, 103, 137–38; alternatives to, 192–96, 204; as assemblages, 81–82; targeting of lifeways that refuse work ethic, 185–86; temporality of, 31; waste-based critique of, 192–93; of work, 5, 8, 110, 128, 135, 156

fossils, 56, 59, 81–82

Foucault, Michel, 111, 124–31, 225n69

Franklin, Benjamin, 85, 220n6

Free Church, 72–73

freedom, 84, 89, 187–89, 194; energy freedom, 204

Freud, Sigmund, 60, 70

fuel. *See* fossil fuels

Garvin, James Louis, 141

Gates, Merrill, 182

genealogy of energy, 3, 6, 107; boundaries, 8–9; decoupling of energy and work, 11, 199; deep history, 15–16, 70, 194–95; early cosmologies of energy, 17–24; leisure as disruption, 195–96. *See also* geo-theology; thermodynamics

genocide, 125–26, 193; of Native Americans, 172, 182, 184–85

geo-theology, 7, 53–56, 107; efficiency, 78–80; of energy, 67–70; hyperobjects, 56–57, 69; pro-industrial energy logics, 67, 76–81, 85–86, 89, 149, 170; statistics and standards, 80–81; work and waste ethos, 70–76, 154, 177, 190

The German Ideology (Marx), 6–7

Germany, 73, 137, 164, 178–79

Geyer, Martin, 81

Gibbs, Josiah Willard, 80

gigajoules (GJ), 2

hunter-gatherers, 31
hyperobjects, 56–57, 69, 188

idleness, 128–29, 144, 221n48; economic
man/idle woman, 156–59; poverty,
discourse of, 96–97, 157–58; racist discourse of, 147, 157–59, 183; as resistance,
159, 186; as threat to fossil fuel regime,
185–86; as waste, 154–60, 161
Iltis, Carolyn Merchant. *See* Merchant,
Carolyn
Imperial College of Engineering (Tokyo),
162
imperialism, 5, 227n18; alternatives to,
149–50; civilizing mission, 81, 147–48,
151; Darwinism misapplied, 134–35; "discovery" of energy linked to, 3–4, 7, 109,
115–16; domination, logics of, 132–34, 145,
148–49, 208n24; ecology and, 109–10,
135–36; evolution and, 8–9, 134–35;
exploitation, dependence on, 102, 135,
142; ganglion metaphor, 140; invention
of idleness and, 154–60, 161; material
and capitalist relations of, 132–33; new
(1870s through end of World War II),
7–8, 108–14, 133, 137–45, 160, 185, 199;
organic metaphor for, 108–9, 137, 139–43,
149; as organism, 137–45, 154; politics and
categories of humankind, 134–35; science
of energy as manufactured, 37–38; social
Darwinism and, 146–47, 175; Spanish
colonization of the New World, 133–34;
steam power and, 137–38; thermodynamics linked to, 8–10, 76, 108, 133–35, 151;
trajectorism, 18, 20, 23, 37; United States,
171–85; violence and theft of land,
144–45; waste and, 137, 141–42, 144,
154–61. *See also* capitalism
Indian Helper newsletter, 183–84, 186
"Indian Question" pamphlet, 179
Indian Removal Act, 185
Indian Rights Association, 179
industrialization, 7; ambivalent effects,
51, 67; Anthropocene, role in, 9–10;

anti-industrialists, 150–51; anxieties
about, 41, 56, 61, 64, 77, 82; biopower
and, 125–31; coal as central to, 28–29;
double-ness, 159; evolution applied
to, 64–67; full employment ideal, 91;
land required, 138, 144–45, 157, 182;
naturalization of, 77, 159–60; pro-
industrial energy logics, 67, 76–81,
85–86, 89, 149, 167; Scottish Presbyterian science and, 71–73, 76, 136; stability
and, 77–78; underwork as threat to, 97.
See also capitalism; imperialism
Industrial Remuneration Conference,
130
Industrial Revolution, 3, 28–29, 32
international relations (IR), 189–90
iron Earth proposal, 57, 58*f*
irreversibility, 43–46, 48

Jackson, Andrew, 185
Japanese engineering, 162–63, 165, 231n2,
232n6
Jevons, William Stanley, 31, 52, 69, 72
Joule, James Prescott, 35, 36–37, 42, 79,
81

Ketabgian, Tamara, 86
Keystone XL pipeline, 191, 192*f*
kinetic energy, 6, 18, 23–24, 41
Kingsley, Mary Henrietta, 122, 148–49,
151–52
Kipling, Rudyard, 138
knowledge, scientific desire for, 41–42
Kuhn, Thomas, 37, 213n11

labor, as term, 83–84. *See also* work
labor movements, 92
Lafargue, Paul, 151
land theft, 144–45, 157, 182
legalistic language in science, 38–39
Leibniz, Gottfried, 23–24, 43
leisure, 84, 88–91, 186, 205–6; women of
leisure, white Victorian, 156–59, 184
LeMenager, Stephanie, 196

pneuma, 19–20

politics, 2, 4; categories of humankind, 134–35; imperial, 143–44. *See also* energy politics; post-work politics

Pomeranz, Kenneth, 29

positivism, 53

post-carbon politics, 11, 190–91, 203–4

postcolonial theorists, 133–34

post-work politics, 11–12, 151, 190–91, 197; anti-asceticism, 203–4; feminist, 196–99

poverty, 11, 34, 89, 191; idleness, discourse of, 96–97, 157–58

power, 29–30; biopower, 111, 125–31; energopower, 111–12, 124–29

pragmatism, 202

prana, 19

Pratt, Richard Henry, 179–81, 180*f*, 183

precautionary principle, 194

Presbyterian church. *See* Scottish Presbyterianism; Scottish Presbyterian scientists

present, as site of becoming, 201–2

Prigogine, Ilya, 45, 46, 50, 72

prime mover technology, 28, 30, 90

probability, 55, 80–81, 112–13

The Problem with Work (Weeks), 196–99; feminist politics in, 200–203

productivism/productivity, 80, 88, 91, 99–100, 122, 133, 144, 193; bias toward, 6, 17–19, 23–24; care regimes, 93–94, 130; critiques of, 187–88; disruption of, 195, 198–203. *See also* dynamism

profit, 28, 30, 35–38, 81, 93, 118, 149–50

progress, 18, 34, 72, 101; as linear, 47, 84, 211n39; in organisms, 63, 118

progressive views, 64, 171–72, 179–80, 185

property, 84–85

qi, 19

Rabinbach, Anson, 78, 79–80, 90–91

racism, 128–29, 217n40; bodies as racialized, 126–27, 143, 146–48, 150; death as metaphor, 128, 177, 184; energy science and, 134–35, 145–52; idleness, discourse of, 147, 157–59, 183; measurement and, 165; neo-racism, 178; organic metaphor and, 141–42; Orientalist stereotypes, 147–48; progressive, 169–70, 171–72, 179–80, 185; second-tier technical and industrial schools, 169–70; social Darwinism, 64, 146–47, 160, 175; technical education and, 133, 170–85; thermodynamics justify, 135, 175–76, 179, 185; United States, expertise in racialized labor management, 168–69; violence, technologies of, 146; wage differences justified, 155–56, 175–77; waste, concern with, 137, 141–42, 147–48, 177; Western values imposed, 148–49. *See also* slavery

Radcliffe, J. N., 93–94

Rankine, William John Macquorn, 35, 38–39, 46, 71, 231n2

raptors, use of fire, 27

Rational Self of Man, 134

Republican Party, 204

resilience, 119–22, 313

resistance: anti-work thought, 151, 197; crises of, 111; gospel of labor, preoccupation with, 135; idleness as, 159, 186; leisure as disruption, 195–96; of lower-status workers, 169–70; Nigerian Women's War of 1929, 143; post-carbon and post-work movements, 190–91; work-shyer as figure of, 98

reversibility, 43–46, 48

Richards, Robert, 63

Richards, Thomas, 139

"The Right to Be Lazy" (Lafargue), 151

Rodgers, Daniel, 86, 94, 129

Roediger, David, 155–56

Romantic thought, 52, 61, 102, 113, 139–40

Romeyn, H. C., 174

ruling logic/political rationality, 4–7, 55–56, 71, 83–84, 101–2, 107, 112, 124, 130–33, 151

Ruskin, John, 52

Sachs, Joe, 17

Salisbury, Lord, 137

Science in Africa report (1938), 109

science of energy: divinity, attributes of, 24–25, 42, 47, 53; emergence of, 15–24; energeia and entelecheia in, 17–18; heat transformations, 21, 24, 48; legalistic tones, 38–39; as manufactured, 37–38; ontological shifts in, 194–95; paradoxes, 44, 50, 112; pneuma, 19–20; post hoc adoption of earlier work, 23–24, 35, 42, 167. *See also* energy; evolution; Scottish Presbyterian scientists; thermodynamics

scientists. *See* Scottish Presbyterian scientists

Scottish Enlightenment, 72

Scottish Presbyterianism, 151; work ethic, 10–11, 50, 54, 67–70, 85–86, 94–95, 128–29, 136

Scottish Presbyterian scientists, 50, 53–54, 67–70; concern with work and waste, 70–76, 177, 190; energy politics and, 54, 71–73, 76

"Second Coming" (Yeats), 25, 70

Second Industrial Revolution, 70, 166, 171

selfhood, 134–35, 201; Blacks as "former selves" of whites, 156; slavery and self-consciousness, 85

semiosis of procedure, 146

Semmel, Bernard, 51–52

Serres, Michel, 15, 33–34, 210n18

sex, regulation of, 126–27

shipbuilding cultures, 54, 71, 78

Sieferle, Rolf Peter, 25, 28–29

slavery, 85, 142, 145, 155; abolitionists, 145, 150, 151; inorganic, 102–3. *See also* racism

Smil, Vaclav, 2, 28

Smith, Crosbie, 38, 70, 71, 73, 74, 76

Smuts, Jan Christian, 132, 141–42, 145

social Darwinism, 64, 146–47, 175

socialists, 64, 92–93, 138, 151

"The Social Organism" (Spencer), 118

social reformers, 76, 86, 89, 93–99; educational, 168, 171–72, 179, 182

social systems, 64, 117–18, 197

Soddy, Frederick, 117

solar energy, 31, 120; Earth as system of, 25, 27, 46, 77. *See also* Sun

The Souls of Black Folk (Du Bois), 174

South, Global, 11, 109, 132, 185, 318n24

South Africa, 137, 141–42, 157, 169

sovereignty, 112, 125, 130

Spanish colonization of the New World, 133–34

Spencer, Herbert, 117–18, 154, 216n26

Spillers, Hortense, 146

Srnicek, Nick, 187, 195, 197, 199

stability, 38–42, 77–78, 116

standardization, 55, 80–81, 84, 88

stasis, 17–21, 24, 79

state: biopower and, 111, 125–31; information society, 139; as machine, 96, 100; as organism, 100; work-shyer as invention of, 98, 100

statistics and standards, 55, 80–81, 129–30, 154–55

steam engines, 4, 15, 21, 24, 47; acceleration of imperialism and, 137–38; capitalist circumvention of labor's demands, 29–30, 35; pace of change and, 33–34; as prime mover technology, 28, 30, 90. *See also* coal; engines

Stevenson, John, 167

Stewart, Balfour, 78

stock market principles, 165

Stoic physics, 19, 21, 210n26

Stowe, Harriet Beecher, 180, 182

Sun: dissipation and death of, 49, 67, 68; nuclear reactions of, 25. *See also* solar energy

surveillance, 48, 79, 89, 92, 100, 144, 183

sustainability, 11, 110–11

systems thinking, 113–14, 135–36

Tait, Peter Guthrie, 35, 38, 71, 83

Tansley, Arthur, 117, 224n31, 225n53

Taylor, Frederick Winslow, 89–90, 92, 101

Taylorism, 89–90, 92, 99, 101

waged labor, 8, 88, 159–60; racism and wage differences, 155–56, 175–77; universal basic income (UBI), 202–3

wages for housework movement, 200, 202

The Wages of Whiteness (Roediger), 155–56

Wallace, Alfred Russel, 61, 65

Walmart strategy, 198

Washington, Booker T., 174

waste, 5–6; attributed to bodies, 8–9, 92, 111–12, 121, 124, 128, 154, 159; conceal-ment of, 98, 111, 121, 124, 154, 158–61, 194; efficiency and, 78; energopolitics and, 128–29; fall, concept of, 36–37; idleness as, 98, 154–60, 161; imperialism and, 137, 141–42, 144, 152; limitations to affective focus on, 193–94; as lost work, 35–36, 42–46, 74–75; measurement of, 154–55; organism and logics of, 110–12, 118–21; racial and gendered categoriza-tions, 147–48, 156, 177; resilience and, 119–20; Scottish Presbyterian concern with, 70–76, 177, 190; spiritual meaning attached to, 128–29, 160, 170; thermody-namic understanding of, 119–20, 137, 156; usefulness of, 128

water power, 29–30, 35, 43, 48

Watt, James, 38, 84, 85

Webb, Beatrice, 97–100

Webb, Sidney, 97–100

Weber, Cynthia, 6

Weber, Max, 84, 85, 94–95, 122, 178–79

Weeks, Kathi, 196–99

welfare, 96–99

Welsh, Herbert, 179

Wendling, Amy, 83, 86–87

West Africa, 178, 179

"Western code," 69–70, 136, 190, 227n15

Western values, 18, 29. *See also* geo-theology; imperialism

White, Leslie, 1

Whitehead, Alfred North, 119, 120, 121

Williams, Alex, 187–88, 195, 197, 199

Willoughby-Herard, Tiffany, 172

Wise, M. Norton, 70, 71, 74, 76

women of leisure, white Victorian, 156–59, 184

wood as fuel source, 27–28, 31

Wordsworth, William, 52

work: as alternative to life, 131; alternative visions, 102, 158–59, 170, 190–91, 198–99; care regimes, 93–94, 130; contestation of, 11–12, 16, 97–98, 111; democratization of, 86; eight-hour work-day movement, 95; end of, 102–3; energopolitics focused on, 127; energy as universal unit for, 88–90; energy's connection to, 16, 70, 83–103; as energy transformation, 5, 16, 68, 81, 83, 87, 111, 117, 177, 184–85; fossil-fueled, 5, 8, 110, 128, 135, 156; governance of, 8, 68, 81, 85–88, 101–2; governing logic of, 4–5, 11, 85–86; heat as, 20, 90; hierar-chies of, 87–88, 118, 169–70, 175–76, 183; intellectual ability of humans, 86–87; jobs, focus on, 205–6; labor as term for, 83–84; lost, 35–36, 42–46, 74–75; as "natural," 11, 80, 83, 86; overwork, 91, 92–95; as physiological problem, 90–91; piecework, 88–89; privatization of, 197, 200; reification of, 197; shift in value of, 84–86; as social convention, 11; as social system, 197; thermodynamics as central to sciences of, 89–90; time as measure-ment of, 88–90; underwork, 91, 96–102; Victorian work–life balance, 90–102. *See also* energy–work nexus; post-work politics; productivism/productivity; work ethic

work and waste ethos, 5–6, 11, 108, 148, 163; geo-theological approach, 70–76, 154, 177, 190; metabolism and, 115–18

work ethic: as capitalism's ruling idea, 83–85, 97–101; gospel of labor, 135, 142, 164–66, 170; needed to cover over exploitation, 98; predestination, 94–95; Protestant/Scottish Presbyterian, 10–11, 50, 54, 67–70, 85–86, 94–95, 128–29, 136; thermodynamics, logics of, 89–90, 111–12, 122–24, 137, 144, 167. *See also* work

working conditions, 51–52, 92–94; underpay-
    ment and forced labor, 138, 142–43, 145
work–life balance, 90–102
work-shyers, 97–100
world, concept of, 9–10, 231n102
world exhibitions, 152, 153*f*
worlds of practice, 6

Worster, Donald, 160
Wynter, Sylvia, 134, 147

Yeats, William Butler, 25, 70

Zhang, Dainian, 19
Zimmerman, Andrew, 178